Greatest Moments in Penn State Football History

Edited by
FRANCIS J. FITZGERALD

From the Sports Pages of the
Pittsburgh Post-Gazette

Published by
AdCraft
Louisville, Ky.

ACKNOWLEDGEMENTS

Research assistance: Tim Rozgonyi and the Pittsburgh Post-Gazette library; Fritz Huysman; L. Budd Thalman, Jeff Nelson, Jeff Brewer, Frank Giardina and the Penn State University Sports Information Office; The Patee Library Archives, Penn State University; Wide World Photos; Bettmann Archives; AllSport USA; College Football Hall of Fame and The Detroit News.

ISBN 1-887761-05-5

Cover and Book Design by Chris Kozlowski
Typeface: Kis-Janson

Published by:
AdCraft Sports Marketing
Kaden Tower, 10th Floor
6100 Dutchmans Lane
Louisville, KY 40205
(502) 473-1124

Royalties to the Pittsburgh Post-Gazette from the sale of this book
will be donated to the Dapper Dan Charities Youth Sports Leagues
operated by the Boys and Girls Clubs of Western Pennsylvania.

Pittsburgh Post-Gazette
DAPPER DAN
CHARITIES

CONTENTS

Contents

From Hoskins to Paterno, the Penn State Legacy Grows

By Fritz Huysman
Assistant Managing Editor/Sports
Pittsburgh Post-Gazette, June 19, 1996

Outsiders have long derided the picture postcard campus of Penn State for its rural isolation.

Like most State College residents, Ridge Riley, the late Penn State football historian extraordinare, never understood what all the fuss was about.

Writing in his 1977 book, *Road to Number One*, Riley asked how Penn State's Beaver Stadium could be described as isolated and equally inaccessible from all points when nearly 70,000 people managed to be at University Park on a half-dozen Saturdays in the fall.

If only Ridge, who passed away in 1976, could see his alma mater now.

The roads have improved but the last several miles into State College can still test the patience of the most loyal fan. Thousands of RVs and minivans continue to clog the mostly two-lane roads as motorists inch toward town from all directions over Routes 322, 220 and 26.

The sellout crowds are even bigger today. More than 93,500 now fill the enlarged Beaver Stadium, nearly tripling the local population.

Winning football remains the drawing card — a 695-293-41 all-time record and an NCAA best of 49 straight non-losing seasons from 1939-87.

Through the years, Penn State's iso-

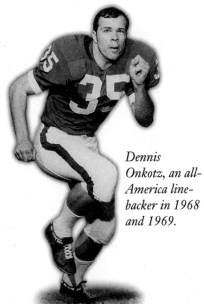

Dennis Onkotz, an all-America linebacker in 1968 and 1969.

lation provided ample space for innovative coaches like Dick Harlow, Hugo Bezdek, Bob Higgins, Joe Bedenk, Charles A. (Rip) Engle and a squeaky-voiced Brooklyn, N.Y., native, Joe Paterno.

It was under Engle (1950-65) that Penn State rose to a position of leadership in Eastern football. But it was under Paterno, his successor, that the Nittany Lions catapulted into one of the top half-dozen elite programs in the nation. And in the process, Paterno persuaded Penn State to break ranks with the Eastern establishment and join the Big Ten Conference.

By winning — at a rate of nearly 80 percent and within the rules — Paterno has a football program that is matched by few and the envy of many.

His 30-year record at Penn State is that of a living legend:

■ National championships in 1982 and 1986 while four other teams — 1968, 1969, 1973 and 1994 — were undefeated and untied.

■ Fourth all-time in career wins with 278, 45 behind the leader, Paul (Bear) Bryant.

■ Seventeen bowl victories, an NCAA record and two more than the second-place Bryant.

■ Has won 40 percent of Penn State's total victories and his teams have been ranked in the top 20 in all but six years and in the Top 10 18 times.

Greatest Moments in Penn State Football History chronicles 52 games from the 20-0 win over Pitt in 1919 to the 43-14 waxing of Auburn in the 1996 Citrus Bowl. Paterno was the head coach in 36 of these games.

Heading into his fourth Big Ten season, Paterno has developed the program to the point that Penn State pride is working for the entire team — the pride of the alumni and students and the pride the players have in themselves.

In State College they call it the "Penn

State Way." Consistency, quality and tradition are its trademarks.

Consistency is borne out in that Penn State has had only six head coaches in the past 81 years and only two — Engle and Paterno — since 1950. Six of Paterno's assistants have been at Penn State at least 15 years. Only one Big Ten head coach, Hayden Fry of Iowa, has been on the job that long.

Quality is exhibited by the players both on the field and in the classroom. Sixty-five players have been named first-team all-America a total of 75 times. Twenty-two have received first-team Academic all-America recognition.

College football programs that continue to win year after year have a tendency to develop reputations that become synonymous with their success.

Southern California is known for developing great tailbacks and Brigham Young always seems to have a great passing quarterback. Penn State under Paterno is known simply as "Linebacker U."

Over the past three decades, nine Nittany Lions linebackers have been named first-team all-America. Thirty-three have gone on to play the position in the National Football League although only Ed O'Neil in 1974 and Shane Conlan in 1987 were taken in the first round of the pro draft.

That tradition has become an effective tool in Penn State's continuing ability to recruit great linebackers. The day after spring practice ended last April, Paterno received verbal commitments from LaVar Arrington and Ron Graham, the two best junior football players in traditionally talent-rich western Pennsylvania. Both are linebackers.

Not all of Penn State's great linebackers were recruited for the position. Some were discovered after they arrived on campus.

Each spring practice Paterno tries his best athletes at linebacker, regardless of the position for which they were recruited. It's not unusual for 50 players to be trying to fill the four linebacking positions.

My personal favorite was Dennis Onkotz, an all-America in 1968 and 1969. He was so quick that in addition to playing linebacker he returned punts.

Onkotz played beside Jack Ham, the last member of his recruiting class who went on to be a unanimous all-America in 1970.

After Onkotz graduated, Ham played with Charlie Zapiec, an all-America in 1971 and John Skorupan (1972). Ham begot Jim Laslavic, Lance Mehl, O'Neil, Rich Milot, Kurt Allerman and Greg Buttle, who holds the school record for career tackles, with 343.

Chet Parlavecchio, Walker Lee Ashley, Mark D'Onofrio, Keith Goganious, Conlan, Andre Collins and Brian Gelzheiser all distinguished themselves at the position.

Paterno has actually had more all-America defensive linemen (10) than linebackers. The DL honor roll includes Mike Reid, Bruce Clark and Matt Millen.

Paterno's I formation has developed several big-time running backs: Charlie Pittman, Lydell Mitchell, Franco Harris, John Cappelletti, Matt Suhey, Curt Warner, D.J. Dozier, Blair Thomas and Ki-Jana Carter.

The bow-legged Cappelletti rushed for 1,522 yards and 17 touchdowns in 1973 to become the Lions' first and only Heisman Trophy winner.

Penn State's critics — there are legions when Penn State plays in Pitt Stadium — are quick to point out that Paterno's players have had their share of off-field problems. But, there has never been a hint of impropriety in their recruitment.

Paterno's technique is simple: He offers challenges to achievement rather than inducements.

That Penn State can win without cheating is more than some people can digest.

The critics deplore the secrecy of Paterno's program — closed practices, names of high school recruits not being released, availability of players to the news media after losses, and freshmen not listed in the media guide.

And, unlike his brethren in Pittsburgh, Ann Arbor, Mich., and Columbus, Ohio,

A Penn State football game in the early days.

Bob Higgins (left) and Rip Engle watch a game from the stands together.

Paterno has never faced a caldron of daily media scrutiny due to the school's isolation.

Those who have been through the program have found Paterno to be a many-sided personality — slightly old-fashioned, loyal, abrasive, witty, sarcastic, brilliant teacher, and possessing a world-class temper.

He has caused many a player to give serious thought of quitting.

John Gerak, a co-captain in 1992, once called life with Paterno "like playing for your dad in a bad mood."

Paterno says he doesn't care whether his players like him, but hopes they come to understand the method of his teachings after they leave football and are out in the world earning a living.

Ham, a member of both the college and professional football Hall of Fame, is one who has seen the light.

In Roy Blount Jr.'s 1973 book about the Pittsburgh Steelers, *Three Bricks Shy of a Load*, Ham said he and his Penn State teammates shared a mutual dislike for Paterno during their playing days. "It made us closer together," he said. "(Paterno) was very cold to his players, very impersonal. Though he made sure of us getting through school."

But, when it came time for his induction into the Professional Football Hall of Fame in 1988, Ham said, "it took me about five seconds to decide on Paterno to present me."

Why the turnabout?

"Joe got me going the right way," Ham said in Paterno's autobiography, *Paterno: By the Book*. "He didn't make football players larger than life … He made sure … it was your education, your family and then football."

Whenever asked about retirement, Paterno has for several years said he plans to continue coaching for another four or five years.

On occasion, Paterno, who will turn 70 in December, has suggested that he might wake up one day and decide he's had enough and retire.

Those closest to him at Penn State, however, suspect Paterno will continue to coach, health permitting, at least as long as it takes to win 46 more games. That would give him one more victory than Bryant.

One thing is certain. As long as Joe Paterno remains, Penn State opponents will find getting in and out of State College a breeze compared to the challenge they face in Beaver Stadium.

President John F. Kennedy visits with the Penn State football team after the 1961 Gator Bowl.

Mount Nittany Lions Feast on Panthers at Muddy Forbes Field

The Pittsburgh Post

Pittsburgh, Nov. 27, 1919 — For more Thanksgiving Days than they like to recall, the Mountain Lions of Penn State have advanced upon the Forbes Field salient in an effort to win a square meal and have retired, baffled and hungry, to their Mt. Nittany den to hole up for the winter … while Pitt was left in victorious possession of the field — and the turkey.

But yesterday after six disappointments, hungers and heartaches, the Mountain Lions feasted sumptuously upon Panther meat — and picked their teeth with the shinbones of a Warner eleven. Their appetite appeased by a 20-0 score, the Blue and White warriors and fans bid the Pitt fans a polite farewell — many happy returns of the day and occasion — and withdrew to their mountain fortress with Jimmy DeHart's football in their possession — the first Pitt football they've lifted since 1912.

And, what is more, the defeat was decisive. Outplayed and outgeneralled, the Panthers were overwhelmed by their opponents. And even when they got a couple of lucky breaks that gave them an opportunity to score on Penn State — and the breaks were aggravated by penalties that Penn State incurred — the Panthers' efforts to score were frustrated with an ease that

was discouraging. Only once, and that was near the end of the game, with the ball in Pitt's territory, did Pitt rip off one of its advances and make three successive first downs in their old-style form, and this advance, of which the hero was Andy Hastings, who stood head and shoulders above his mates as an all-around player, was turned back long before it became dangerous.

STATE LEADS EAST

To the writer it looks as if it will be impossible to escape rating Pennsylvania State College at the top of the heap in the East this fall. The way it smothered Pitt demonstrates conclusively that it is a team second to none — and though it has been beaten by Dartmouth — the way it overrode all other opponents, coupled with the superb power and dash of its attack and the impenetrable qualities of its defense yesterday is evidence enough to convince us and many others.

Colonel Joe Thompson, for instance. After the game we bumped into him. He was not hard to draw out. "Yes, State's the best on the gridiron this fall, and that man Higgins is the best end I ever saw. He's wonderful! — a superman of the gridiron."

And there are reasons for Colonel Joe's praise. Bob Higgins sprinted 75 yards for a touchdown after receiving a forward pass that was launched behind his own goal line, and crossed the Pitt goal line the first time with a touchdown that was enough to take the starch out of any opponent. And it was the most spectacular play we've seen

Score by Periods

Penn State	7	6	7	0	— 20
Pittsburgh	0	0	0	0	— 0

Charley (Pie) Way — "about the size of a pint of hard cider" — scored on a 53-yard run in the third quarter for Penn State's final touchdown against Pitt.

Pittsburgh's Forbes Field was a quagmire on Thanksgiving Day 1919, limiting both teams' offensive production. According to accounts, "The field was heavy, no doubt, and State went better in the mud than Pitt, but we can't see that it had any bearing."

on any gridiron.

Poor football? Yes — but superb generalship, and the result justified the long chance and the danger, for it took the ball from State's territory back of the Pitt line, removed the menace of the Blue and Gold, and was the beginning of Pitt's downfall.

It was early in the first half. On Harold Hess' first try at punting after the kickoff the ball went straight up in the air and Pitt got it on the State 23-yard line. There Pitt's attack and a penalty incurred by State took the ball to State's 6-yard line before the Panthers were stopped. Again Hess went back to punt, standing three or four yards behind his own goal line. In a case of this kind a forward pass is preposterous — unthinkable. And, simply because it was unthinkable, it was tried. A complete surprise, it worked like a dream, like a beatific miracle. Higgins started down the field, stopped on the 25-yard mark, turned, plucked the ball out of the air, and continued.

HASTINGS IS TUMBLED

The Pitt secondary defense was drawn close in. When Higgins caught the ball nobody was between him and the Pitt goal but Hastings, who was laying back about 50 yards. Enough Penn State blockers were downfield

Penn State's 1919 team finished 7-1 under Coach Hugo Bezdek (top, third from left), shutting out five opponents.

to ward off the startled Pitt backs, and two were ahead of Higgins when he set sail down into Hastings' territory. With two determined blockers bearing down on him, the startled Hastings succumbed almost without a struggle, and Higgins gamboled the last 50 yards in a sort of a dizzy, jazzy joy ramble, to the accompaniment of a mighty Penn State paean of rejoicing.

Now, we ask you, isn't that enough to take the starch out of any team?

Another Penn State touchdown was the result of a long ramble. It was the third score and came mighty soon after the second half began. Pie Way was the hero. Little Pie Way, about the size of a pint of hard cider liberally laced with bourbon — and about as strong.

It was after Hastings had punted and it was State's ball on the Pitt 47-yard line. On the very first play Way passed like a disembodied spirit through a seemingly solid Pitt line, materialized on the other side and strutted 53 yards for a score with no one to trouble him at all after his blockers had speared the Pitt secondary defense.

And there were some blockers, too, let us tell you. We've seen quite some blocking since Warner set up shop in these parts, but Hugo Bezdek is a great teacher of blocking, too, and it worked like a 21-jeweled watch yesterday, sweeping all before it, except on some occasions when the Lions essayed wide end runs. These the Panthers could stop in their tracks, but the short knife-like thrusts in close, through the line and just off tackle, penetrated deep into the Panther defense time and time again. The Pitt line was ripped apart, harpooned, knifed, lanced, gaffed and perforated until it resembled a mass of rags and tatters.

STATE'S 76-YARD DRIVE

That second touchdown, coming in the second quarter, was the culmination of a 76-yard advance which began with a 20-yard runback of a punt — the very last play of the quarter — that downed the ball on Penn State's 44 mark. Harry Robb was the hero of that return, and Robb played an important part in the dash which followed.

There was one interlude, and only one, to State's ground attack, and it came when Pitt had apparently succeeded in checking the State smashes.

Then Conover dropped back to kick a field goal from the 37-yard line — only it wasn't a field goal. Robb, who took the ball instead of Conover, shot a forward pass to Way for a 13-yard gain that took the ball to Pitt's 10-yard line. It was a pretty stratagem — well conceived and beautifully executed, and it fooled Pitt and the assembled multitudes.

Once on the 20-yard line, Penn State was not to be denied, and, in spite of Pitt's frantic resistance, lugged that ball right over and rammed it down the Panther throats by main strength.

After this touchdown Penn State again started on a scoring march beginning with Way's 40-yard kick return to past midfield before Tom Davies dragged him down. Robb, Hess and Way moved the ball in close, but State drew a 15-yard holding penalty that relieved the pressure and, after working the ball to the 6-yard line, Pitt smeared a passing attack and took the ball away, a notable achievement.

PITT HAS CHANCE

Soon after Penn State's last touchdown a heaven-sent break gave the Panthers a chance to score. Hastings had punted "way off to one side," and Robb couldn't get under it. He trotted over to the bounding ball and it sprang up and bit him on the ankle — that put it onside for Pitt and Frank Eckert, covering the punt, fell on it. It was Pitt's ball on Penn State's 16-yard line.

Hasting, Davies and Laughran tried, but couldn't gain enough yardage on the ground to worry Penn State. But State's anxiety caused an off-side play, and that gave Pitt the ball on State's five-yard mark. Here two bucks were stopped at the line of scrimmage and two passes were savagely batted down, and Pitt's last chance went glimmering.

But, though Pitt didn't score, this break evidently held the score to it final proportions, for Pitt, outputting Penn State, kept the ball in Penn State's territory, until well toward the end of the game. And when Penn State got the ball back again, as the result of many see-saws, took the ball back to State's territory, where it was when the game ended.

Some folks are saying that the heavy field helped Penn State. The field was heavy, no doubt, and State went better in the mud than Pitt, but we can't see that it had any bearing. Superior to Pitt in the mud, Penn State was undoubtedly superior to Pitt on a dry field. And had the footing been secure Penn State very probably would have scored other touchdowns, though it is probable that Pitt would have negotiated one or two, just to ease the sting of defeat.

WAS BETTER TEAM

And maybe had the Pitt faculty not become officious and DeHart had gotten in the game and James Morrow been allowed to play — maybe, we say, it would have made a difference to offset Penn State's superiority and result in a Pitt victory, even if these two had played all the way. Pitt did all it could and acquitted itself nobly. We don't say that it played as well as it has played this season, but remember that a winning team looks a thousand times better than a losing team, and Pitt looked immeasurably superior to the Pitt team that was beaten by Syracuse. Indeed, it is our humble opinion that the Pitt team of today would have done as much to the Syracuse team that beat Pitt as Syracuse would have done in return.

Higgins of Penn State was the lord of the lists, the outstanding figure, the "man on horseback." And Robb ran the team with excellent generalship and contributed a great deal to the victory. Hess, with his slashes, and Way, with his slide throughs and runs, were invincible. And Ben Cubbage, Larry Conover, Robert Osborn and the other linemen each and all contributed their noblest to the victory, ripping Pitt wide on defense and offense, making their own gains possible and tearing Pitt's abortive drives to tatters.

And when the reserves came in they stiffened the fading Panthers quite a bit.

Penn State Defeats Georgia Tech, 28-7, in Gotham Contest

The Pittsburgh Press

New York, Oct. 29, 1921 — Penn State crushed Georgia Tech by a score of 28-7 this afternoon at the Polo Grounds before a crowd of 28,000 spectators. The big event of the game was a touchdown scored by Glenn Killinger of Penn State, who received a Tech kickoff in the middle of the first quarter and ran 95 yards through the baffled and bewildered Tech defense for the touchdown, tying the score and shattering his opponents morale. For the first

few minutes the battle had every indication that Tech's slashing offensive drive coupled with the puzzling shift would drive Penn State off the field.

Securing control of the ball some 50 yards from the Penn State goal the Southern attack moved forward with a fine display of speed and power in which the belligerent D.I. Barron took the leading role. One first down followed another until Barron finally fought his way across the goal line as the 500 Georgia rooters who had traveled 1,000 miles raised enough racket to last a month. Massed in the stands

Score by Periods

Penn State	7	7	7	7	— 28
Georgia Tech	7	0	0	0	— 7

back of first base, they filled the air with a wild flutter of yellow ribbons and flowers with a vocal accompaniment that rocked the huge stadium.

But with that one big march completed, the tide swerved with a swiftness that fairly took away one's breath. Up to this point, Georgia Tech had made six first downs against none for Penn State,

but on the next kickoff the ball settled lightly into the arms of Killinger, and the red deer was on his way through the golden autumn afternoon with the entire Tech team in pursuit.

KILLINGER MAKES LONG RUN

Using a rare quality of speed and a puzzling, zig-zag shift he soon worked up his way to midfield and here, surrounded by fine blocking, he came into the open with the last tackler removed and no one swift enough to even approach his dizzy speed, he raced over

Glenn Killinger returned a kickoff 85 yards for the Nittany Lions' first touchdown.

the goal line for a play that few are lucky enough to ever see in one of the big games — a touchdown from the kickoff. Only a great back of the Killinger type is qualified to make such a play and as he bounded into the open beyond midfield the entire stands arose to pay him tribute.

He had covered 85 yards in this startling flight without being halted along the route. This was the play that turned the Southern machine upside down and settled the issue of that battle beyond any doubt. For, after this run, Penn State's powerful, well directed assault with its shifts and passes scattered Yellow Jackets up and down the field. It was easy to see that the Southern defense was far below its strong attack, for not only was its line ripped open and driven back but it was also forward passed into a state of delirium.

On play after play Killinger, Harry Wilson or Joe Lightner would lunge forward for big gains and through these advances added to the pressure. Penn State completed pass after pass with Tech helpless upon defense, floundering badly as the ball sailed from Killinger's hands down the field to the waiting receiver. On two occasions near the end of the game, Stan McCollum, surrounded by two or three Yellow Jackets, took the ball out of the air on long accurate passes (more than 30 yards) without even being annoyed by the hostile defenders around him. On one occasion, he had to leap for the ball while still upon a dead run, surrounded by many foes.

The hard, low-charging Penn State line did its part but it was Killinger who slaughtered Tech. His speed and power was too much for Georgia Tech as it vainly tried to drag him down without substantial gains. He was a wiggling, twisting, daring, flashing, line-breaking, broken-field running wonder — one of the big stars of the year. And with Wilson and Lightner at his side, the Penn State offense was too superior to Georgia Tech's poor defense to keep the issue even fairly close.

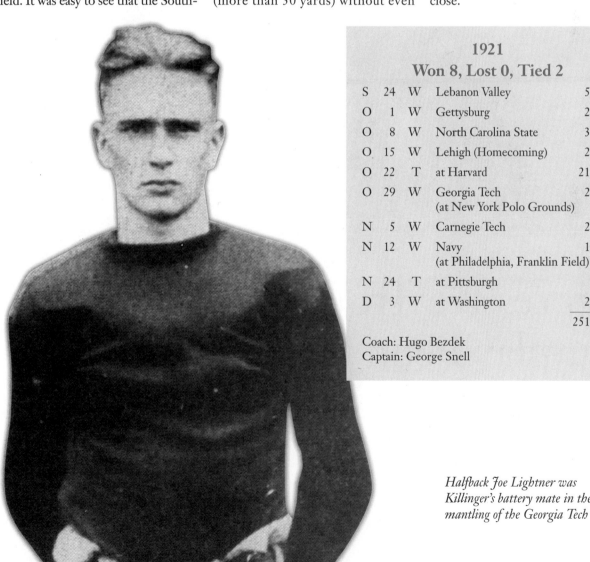

1921		
Won 8, Lost 0, Tied 2		
S 24 W	Lebanon Valley	53-0
O 1 W	Gettysburg	24-0
O 8 W	North Carolina State	35-0
O 15 W	Lehigh (Homecoming)	28-7
O 22 T	at Harvard	21-21
O 29 W	Georgia Tech (at New York Polo Grounds)	28-7
N 5 W	Carnegie Tech	28-7
N 12 W	Navy (at Philadelphia, Franklin Field)	13-7
N 24 T	at Pittsburgh	0-0
D 3 W	at Washington	21-7
		251-36

Coach: Hugo Bezdek
Captain: George Snell

Halfback Joe Lightner was Killinger's battery mate in the dismantling of the Georgia Tech defense.

Aggressive Trojans Outplay Penn State, 14-3, in Rose Bowl

BY WALTER ECKERSALL
Special to The Pittsburgh Post

Pasadena, Calif., Jan 1, 1923 — Outplayed in every department of the game, with the exception of 10 minutes of the first quarter, Penn State went down in defeat to University of Southern California, 14-3, today. It was the only defeat suffered by a Far Eastern eleven in the three intersectional games played on the West Coast dur-

A crowd of 43,000 at the Rose Bowl watched U.S.C. limit Penn State to a 20-yard drop kick by Mike Palm.

ing the holidays.

The Trojans assumed the aggressive shortly after the first 10 minutes of play, during which the Lions scored a field goal. After that, Coach Elmer Henderson's team ran the Penn State ends, drove through the line and off the tackles for consistent gains. The visitors were given 15 yards and Mike Palm and Harry (Lighthorse) Wilson advanced to the Trojans' 12-yard line. The locals held and Palm made a drop kick from the 20-yard line. In the sec-

Score by Periods

Penn State	3	0	0	—	3
U.S.C.	0	7	7	0	—	14

ond quarter Palm punted out of bounds on his 30-yard line and U.S.C. made a successful drive to the goal line with Gordon Campbell going over after a triple pass. John Hawkins kicked the extra point. In the third quarter the

Trojans again began a driving attack and Baker scored, with Hawkins adding the point-after kick.

In the final period the play was entirely in Penn State's territory and the Trojans forced the issue all the way as the game ended just as the moon was coming up.

TROJANS WELL COACHED

The Trojans, well coached in all angles of offensive and defensive football by Henderson, who learned his football at Oberlin, were masters of the situation after Palm had kicked the field goal for the visitors shortly after the opening of the game. They soon solved the Lions' compact offense by having the tackles and smashing ends drive in and smashed the plays before they were well under way.

The game started off with a most peculiar play. U.S.C. lost the toss and Penn State received on the south end of the field. Hawkins drove the ball over the goal line, but when it struck a post over the line it bounded back into the field of play. Palm of Penn State caught it on the bound and was downed on his own five-yard line.

Penn State tried two plays then Palm punted to Harold Galloway, who was stopped on his 42-yard line. The locals could gain only two yards in three attempts and then Galloway tried a forward pass. The ball hit the ground and it was the visitors' ball on their 34-yard line.

Penn State was held and Palm punted out of bounds on the Trojans' 23-yard line. The visitors held and Galloway tossed to Palm. Hayden Pythian, the Trojan end, hit Palm before he had a chance to catch the ball and Southern California was given 15 yards for interfering with a fair catch. This placed the ball on the locals' 40-yard line. Wilson, Johnny Patton and Barney Lentz advanced the ball to U.S.C.'s 12-yard line by driving through the Trojan line and off the tackles. Palm then dropped back and made a perfect drop kick from the 20-yard line.

An exchange of punts after the next kickoff left the ball in Penn State's possession on its 28-yard line on the first play. Palm fumbled and U.S.C. recovered on the visitors' 21-yard line as the quarter ended.

Panthers See State Eleven Beaten by Southern California

By Ralph S. Davis
The Pittsburgh Press

The Pitt Panthers, stopping off here on their way back home after their victory over Stanford, rooted for Hugo Bezdek and his Penn State Lions yesterday, in their game with Southern California at the Tournament of Roses Stadium.

But their rooting was in vain. "Gloomy Gus" Henderson's Trojans won rather handily, but by one less touchdown than they deserved, for a fumble within a yard of Penn State's goal robbed them of an additional tally in the final period.

Pennsylvanians would have never recognized Bezdek's Lions as the same team which met Pitt at Forbes Field last Thanksgiving Day. The trip across the continent affected them just as Pitt's did, but to a greater extent. There was absolutely no fight in them yesterday, especially in the second half. The surprising part of their game, however, was the fact that they used none of the plays they had tried against Pitt on Turkey day, but reverted to the system which Bezdek had tried prior to the Navy game, and which did not prove effective against the Middies, and was discarded afterward.

Penn State played straight football yesterday and did not bring to the front more than three different plays during the entire encounter.

Southern California knew all of Penn State's stuff, and coppered it immediately. Bill Hess, a brother of the Hess who, several years ago, starred at Penn State, is an assistant to Henderson, and he was wise to Bezdek's plans.

TOURNAMENT of ROSES
Pasadena California 1923
NEW YEAR'S NUMBER PASADENA EVENING POST

Penn State's 1923 Rose Bowl team, which finished 6-4-1, ended the season with three consecutive losses.

AND THEY FUMBLED

Roy Baker, Campbell and Howard Kincaid carried the ball to Penn State's 1-yard line and then fumbled. The visitors recovered the ball back of their goal line for a touchback. It was a tough break for the Trojans.

After an exchange of punts, Palm recovered one of Galloway's kicks on his 15-yard line. The Trojans then mounted a drive to score. Baker got around Calvin Frank and was stopped on Penn State's 10-yard line. A dandy Baker to Galloway pass — from a spread formation — placed the ball on Penn State's 1-yard line. Galloway dove for the ball and scooped it just before it touched the ground. On a triple pass formation, Campbell drove through center for a touchdown, and Hawkins converted the extra-point kick to give U.S.C. a 7-3 lead. Play for the remainder of the period was at midfield.

Baker got around Art Artelt for 30 yards and Campbell hit center for three more. Baker was then called upon three successive times and he carried the ball to Penn State's one-yard line. On the next play this great back drove off Lester Logue's block for a touchdown. Hawkins again kicked the extra point to boost U.S.C.'s lead to 14-3.

For the remainder of the quarter the play was in Penn State's territory. Coach Henderson finished the game with a number of substitutes. Most of this quarter was played in the twilight, as the game was late to start, owing to an argument between the coaches over the selection of officials. The crowd was late to arrive, and it was 3 p.m. before the teams lined up for the kick-off.

U.S.C. was easily master of the situation.

West Virginia Ties Penn State, 13-13, at Yankee Cathedral

The Pittsburgh Press

New York, Oct. 27, 1923 — A wandering Lion of Mt. Nittany and a bold Mountaineer from West Virginia fought a terrific gridiron battle in newly built, cavernous Yankee Stadium today, and when it was over they were still undecided as to superiority, for the score was 13-all.

Either team might have won by the simple twist of a kicker's toe, but fate apparently had decreed that is was to be a draw, and it was, for the extra-point kicks that might have given either side a point and victory were far wide of their marks. It was absolutely an even game from almost every angle, except that Penn State registered more first downs than West Virginia.

Both teams seemed inclined to fumble early in the game and one of these fumbles paved the way for Penn State's first touchdown five minutes after play had begun. But the same fate which had put the Lions in a position to score in this manner came to the rescue of the Mountaineers later and helped them even the count.

WILSON STARS FOR STATE

It was the son of Mrs. Wilson — the same son who beat Navy — who kept Penn State on the map again today. It was he who registered the first

Score by Periods					
Penn State	7	0	0	6	— 13
West Virginia	0	0	7	6	— 13

touchdown; he also registered the second touchdown and booted the extra point after the first time across the Mountaineer line. But it was Dick Schuster, who made the kick that would have given Penn State a triumph. And it was Guy Ekberg's toe, the toe that had already registered one true boot between the crossbars, that failed when the time came for the kick that would have sent Fat Spears' delegation back to Morgantown with the scalp of the Nittany Lions.

Harry Wilson was the same ranting, raving, running marvel today that he has always been, though he was never able to get away for one of his famous long runs to a touchdown from a kickoff, forward pass or punt.

His work today was not sensational but it was thoroughly consistent. Dashing around the ends, brushing off tackles or plunging through center, he was a grand ground-gaining maniac, good always for a fair gain, seldom stopped without some advance, but never thrown for a loss. It was he who twice plunged over the goal line and he who got away for 5, 10 and 15 yards every now and again, just when the Mountaineer defense seemed set to make a stand.

AIR ATTACK SUCCESSFUL

The aerial route was the Mountaineers' principal weapon of offense; in fact, it was forward passes that gave the West Virginians both their touchdowns. Once it was Nicholas Nardacci who got away with one for a touchdown, and then it was Pete Barnum.

The latter got his pass while running left end just before he had passed the line of scrimmage and eluded several Penn State tacklers to rush about 18 yards for the touchdown. Nardacci's run was for about the same distance.

Penn State started as if she intended to mop up — in fact, the way her backs went through and around the Mountaineers' line in the first few minutes of the game, after the recovery of a fumble, led the 30,000 or more fans to believe they had been led to a slaughter of innocents, but the Mountaineers then began to assert themselves and fought back, holding the enemy at bay for the remainder of the first half and doing their own stuff in the second.

In the latter half, the West Virginians made the Nittany outfit look just as bad as they had been made to look in the early part of the game, and before a half dozen plays had been pulled off, the Mountaineers were on

Hugo Bezdek compiled a 65-30-11 record from 1918-1929 as Penn State's head football coach.

Harry Wilson

an even basis, fighting to go ahead, which they did soon after the final quarter began.

STATE MAKES COMEBACK

At this point, Penn State started to come back. Ray Johnston, a reserve halfback, took a punt down near his own goal line, and when they had stopped him he was well into the Mountaineers' territory.

Then Wilson, alternating with Johnston on off-tackle smashes and end runs, carried the ball to a scant 12 or 15 yards from the goal line. From here, Wilson, almost singlehandedly, battered his way to a first down on the 1-yard line, then took a final plunge over center for the remaining distance to the goal line. Penn State fought the latter part of the battle without its captain, Joe Bedenk — who was injured and had to be helped off the field — but William House, who substituted, didn't offer the Mountaineers any encouragement, for he stopped everything that looked like a threat at his portion of the line.

Jules Prevost, a Penn State right tackle, proved himself a bearcat on both offense and defense. Twice he carried the ball, once from a kickoff and again from a partially blocked punt, and though he did not shine so brilliantly in either of his efforts, he made up for it by his deadly tackling and his ability to break through and stop plays in the making.

EKBERG'S PUNTING OFF-COLOR

For the Mountaineers the lion's share of the glory went to Nardacci and Ekberg, though Jack Simons, the team captain, did some great ground-gaining at various points of the game. Ekberg's punting was off-color from the start and Barnum, who replaced Armin Mahrt, finished up as the kicker. Phil Hill, who didn't get in at the start, was trotted out soon after the beginning of the second half, and though it might have been only a coincidence, it is a fact that West Virginia perked up and scored both her touchdowns after Hill was injected into the fray.

In the handling of punts, both teams seemed to lack something, but with all the fumbling, those who saw the game were convinced at the finish that they had watched two of the East's greatest teams battle to no verdict.

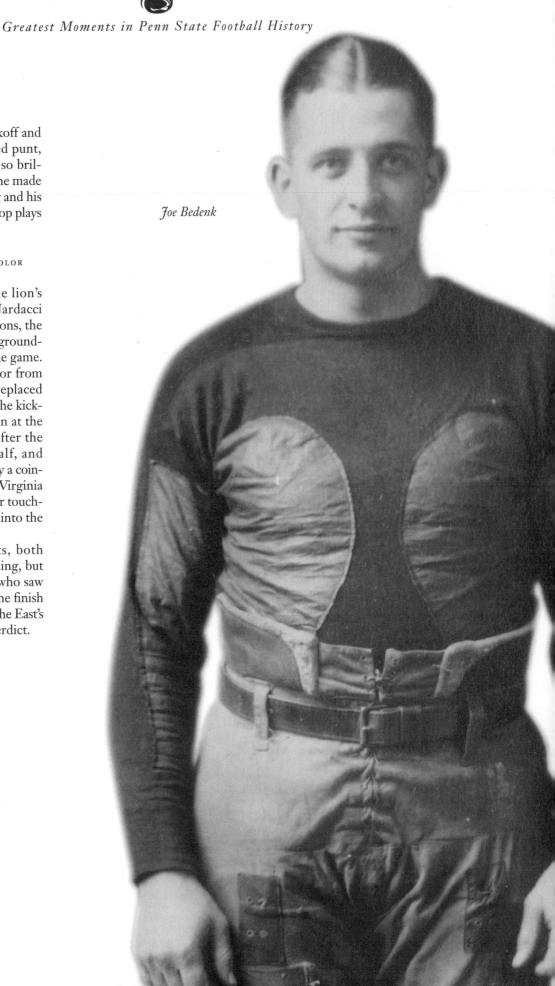

Joe Bedenk

Defense, Sloppy Field are Winners as Lions Tie Notre Dame, 0-0

By KNUTE ROCKNE
Special to The Pittsburgh Press

State College, Pa., Nov. 7, 1925 — The Nittany Lions of Penn State proved themselves to be great "mud " players here today when they tied Notre Dame, 0-0. They have a tradition here that the Lions play great ball in the mud. They proved it this afternoon.

Their defense poured in on the Notre Dame thrusts with a vengeance. They covered the Irish well on passes. Notre Dame outgained Penn State considerably, but was unable to score. Both teams had an opportunity to score a field goal, but the condition of the ball, which was heavy with mud, and the treacherousness of the footing made the two tries failures.

Notre Dame's wide sweeping runs were of no value. The Nittany Lions got to the plays before they could be formed. Both teams were fighting hard throughout, but the mud handicap proved too much of an obstacle. The Penn State offense was built close to the line and very few plays outside the tackles were tried. The most successful play Penn State used was the fake off guard. This play was responsible for at least two of Penn State's three first downs. The players slipped in the mud as if they were

Score by Periods

Notre Dame	0	0	0	0 —	0
Penn State	0	0	0	0 —	0

standing on ice and forward passing was practically impossible.

CAPTAIN GRAY SHINES

A huge Homecoming crowd gathered to watch the affair. A drizzle fell throughout the game, which added to the misery of the players. Penn State tackled hard and kept their heads up throughout the encounter. Notre Dame also played smart football. A break occurred in the third quarter when Gene Edwards punted to the Penn State 1-yard line, where John Voedisch fell on the ball.

Lions captain Bas Gray, who played superb ball throughout, was forced to punt from behind his own goal line and he booted it to his own 30. The Irish started a concentrated drive which was stopped on the 9-yard line.

Penn State, in the fourth quarter, also made a determined bid for a touchdown when August Michalske made a beautiful run of 20 yards, which placed the ball on Notre Dame's 25-yard line. The Irish held, however.

The Nittany Lion attack, aimed directly over the guards and inside of the Notre Dame tackles, was powerful, well-aimed and the choice of plays was excellent. It was simply a case of a bad day slowing up both teams. What would have happened on a dry field is a question. The marvelous Penn State defensive play and the careful way in which it covered punts would have stood in good stead on any kind of a field. The players were forced to wipe the mud from their bodies throughout the game.

It was a good game to watch and both teams should be credited with great praise because of the defensive play. Gray played one of the greatest defensive games of his career.

Michalske and Bill Pritchard are real backfield men. They would have shown far better if the field was dry and fast. Edwards of Notre Dame handled the team very nicely. Notre Dame's heads-up policy of following the ball was their real saving feature. Coach Hugo Bezdek revealed some clever backfield maneuvers and his team's line play was wonderful to watch. It was an even game throughout. Notre Dame outgained Penn State, both had opportunities to score a field goal, and the Irish completed three passes to one for Penn State, a short flip over the center of the line.

Halfback Johnny Roepke went on to captain the Nittany Lions' 1927 team, which finished 6-2-1.

George Delp, a Penn State end in 1926-28.

Scull's Accurate Toe Tells Tale of Victory for Nittany Lions

BY ROSS E. KAUFFMAN
The Pittsburgh Press

Philadelphia, Nov. 6, 1926 — Paul Scull's right foot, denied a chance at a critical time in the Illinois game a week ago, today gave Penn a 3-0 victory over Penn State on Franklin Field.

Standing on the 40-yard line in the opening period, the former Lower Marion High athlete, drop-kicked a perfect field goal as Penn's cheering section sent up a "whoop" that was heard for blocks. Before a crowd of 55,000 Scull's goal gave Penn its first victory over the Nittany Lions since 1922. Two years ago, the teams battled to a scoreless tie. There was no contest last fall.

Penn State, with a fighting team that lacked offensive drive, carried the ball within one yard of a touchdown in the second period, only to have Penn put up one of its old-time goal-line stands and take the ball over on downs.

It was a mighty close call for the Red and Blue. With the ball on the 4-yard line and first down — due to the splendid line-bucking of fullback G.R. Greene — three more yards were added on plays inside tackle.

Score by Periods

Penn	3	0	0	0	—	3
Penn State	0	0	0	0	—	0

STATE'S PASSES FAIL

Penn State tried to surprise Penn by tossing a short forward pass to the left side of the line. Johnny Roepke hurled the ball out toward the goal but George Delp, the former West Philadelphia High star, failed to get close to it and Penn was out of danger. After that Quaker quarterback Paul Murphy kicked from behind his own goal line and Penn State was throttled for the rest of the day.

Coach Hugo Bezdek's Lions were forever zipping forward passes but not with much success.

From a kick formation, Roepke hurled the ball right and left but could not make much headway, especially after the first half.

Paul Scull gave way to Paster Fields in the final period. The Main Line lad being pretty badly used up. The Red and Blue cheering section cheered him to the echo as he walked to the dressing room.

LIGHT PENN LINE HOLDS

On the last play of the game, Penn's Charley Rogers, who played a remark-able game, was injured and had to be led to the sidelines. Rogers not only handled Roepke's punts faultlessly but also made the longest run of the afternoon when he circled left end for 22 yards in the final period.

Penn's lighter line outplayed Bezdek's forwards, but the secondary defense of Penn State tightened whenever Penn advanced the ball beyond midfield.

Cy Lungreen, a Philadelphia boy, playing quarterback for Penn State, did not use very good judgment in running the plays and finally gave way to John Pincura, who was an improvement both in running the ball and diagnosing Penn's defense.

Coach Lou Young's Penn team stuck to a straight running attack most of the time, trying 10 passes but only two worked for a total of 33 yards. In first downs, Penn had 11 to State's five.

PENN OUTGAINS STATE

Penn's "hidden ball" functioned spasmodically. Whenever it looked as though the Red and Blue ballcarriers were headed for a touchdown, something always happened to slow them up.

Paul Murphy's punting gave Penn an advantage in the first half. This helped in the march that took the ball into Penn State territory and gave Scull a chance to try for a field goal. He grasped the ball like a veteran. On the first play of the second period, Scull again tried a drop kick from the 35-yard line, but it went a few yards to the right of the goal posts.

In rushing and forward passes, Penn gained 213 yards to State's 145. State tried 13 forward passes, six being successful for a gain of 78 yards. Penn tried 10 passes but only two worked for 33 yards.

Penn State Tops Pitt, 10-0; First Win Over Panthers Since 1919

By Claire M. Burcky
The Pittsburgh Press

State College, Pa., Nov. 25, 1939 — As darkness blanketed new Beaver Field and lights winked from windows of State College homes, a band of yelling, singing undergraduates proudly bore away a set of white goal posts here tonight to signify to another generation in Penn State College that the Nittany Lion once again had conquered the Pitt Panthers on the football field.

By the score of 10-0, a touchdown, an extra point, and a field goal, Penn State defeated Pitt here today, to record the first Lion triumph over the Panthers since 1919, when young Bob Higgins, now Coach Bob Higgins, captained a Nittany outfit that tied a 20-0 knot into the tail of the Panther.

And virtually every man, woman and child in the overflow crowd of 20,000 fans was ready tonight to celebrate, to tear the town wide open over an occurrence that when it comes no more often than once every 20 years, must be observed fittingly, even fightingly.

There were a few fights, flaring suddenly and ending just as abruptly, as students struggled to tear down the goal posts, but once they had uprooted them, they marched away happily, arm in arm, to make the most of the occasion.

Make 17 First Downs

"We realized we had a chance to win, and we were up for the game," Higgins said between handshakes with old grads in the Lion dressing room after the battle.

Penn State was ready, no question of that. The Lions dominated Pitt as no team has dominated the Panthers all season. They rolled up a net gain of 165 yards in 17 first downs, threatened to score one or more times in every quarter, and kept the Panthers most of the afternoon from getting away from the Pitt side of the field.

State unloosed two powerful fullbacks in Lloyd Ickes and Bill Smaltz, a pair of swift halfbacks in Chuck Peters and "Pepper" Petrella, and a savage line that revolved around Leon Gajecki, the center, who waded through the game's entire 60 minutes

to be singled out by Higgins as the one player deserving greatest praise in the victory.

Panthers Never Threaten

Pitt's rushing gains totaled 166 yards but the alert Gajecki, abetted by a pair of smashing ends, Tom Vargo and Spike Alter of Pittsburgh, never let the Panthers threaten seriously. The Penn State line smeared Pitt plays for more than 60 yards, held the Panthers passing to two completions for 16 yards, and blocked with the devastation of a tidal wave as Peters ran up and down the field for 10, 15 and sometimes 20 yards at a clip.

The Panthers played in spurts, at times shooting their ballcarriers forward for sizeable gains that appeared certain to reach the goal line. Too often, however, overeagerness in the line produced offsides that frequently provided too much of a handicap to overcome.

As a matter of fact, there were 19 penalties in the game, eight against Penn State and 11 against Pitt. Eighty-five yards were measured off against the Panthers, and this, with five fumbles, counted heavily in the final reckoning.

The Lions threatened twice in the early minutes before they finally sent Smaltz across from the 1-yard line with the opening score, moments before the first quarter ended.

Stop Lion Threat

A couple of passes by Smaltz, one by Craig White for 22 yards and another to Peters for 13, gave Penn State their first chance, and when Peters came out of a fake placekick to run for a first down, the Lions were going strong and on Pitt's 23-yard line.

Bob Higgins was 91-57-11 as Penn State's head football coach from 1930-1948.

Lions Lionize Higgins

The Pittsburgh Press

Six pallbearers, accompanied by a minister garbed in black, carried a coffin to the center of new Beaver Field today, hardly daring to hope their assignment of "Burying Pitt" actually would come true some two hours later.

But it did as Bob Higgins' best Penn State eleven in years hung a 10-0 haymaker on the Panthers, to halt a succession of 14 Pitt victories over the Nittany Lions, and to record State's first triumph over Pitt since 1919.

"We've waited 20 years for this moment, and naturally, when it has arrived, it's hard for me to express my real feelings," Higgins said in the Lion dressing rooms under the campus water tower.

"We told our kids before the game that if they outfought Pitt, man for man, we could win, and that's exactly what they did. Their spirit and determination was the deciding factor."

Higgins couldn't talk without interruptions from all sides. Old grads, some of them after his scalp in past seasons, swarmed over him, wringing his hand. Players came dripping out of the showers, jumping and yelling deliriously.

"Our ends played magnificently, too, particularly Spike Alter, our captain. And Chuck Peters, I thought, was the best back on the field. Lloyd Ickes played nearly three quarters with a broken wrist in a cast, so he deserves a lot of credit.

In handing out his praise, Higgins singled out Leon Gajecki, the center, as most deserving.

"There was no doubt about the better team," Pitt coach Charley Bowser remarked after the game. "Higgins has done a grand job with those boys, many of whom are sophomores.

"I thought Gajecki was the best man on the field, and I guess Ickes and Peters were too much for us, too."

Gajecki is a 6-foot, 190-pound senior, from Ebensburg. "He calls signals for us on defense," Higgins explained.

It was Thanksgiving Day in 1919 when Penn State, captained by Bob Higgins, not long back from the World War, beat Pitt last, 20-0. Higgins, an end, caught a pass from Harold Hess and ran almost 90 yards for the first touchdown, and the following week was Walter Camp's all-America end.

The defeat was Pitt's second in late November, the first time a Pitt eleven has been set back twice that late in the campaign for many years. It also was the fourth defeat of the year, and you'll have to look back into the records a long way to find the last time in which the Panthers have dropped four in a season.

Leon Gajecki, an all-America center in 1940.

But Pitt wasn't ready to yield a score yet. Jack Goodridge gave the Panthers the lift they needed by spilling Smaltz for a 13-yard loss on a pass attempt, and the Panthers got out of that by taking the ball at their 38.

In the next 10 seconds, Pitt came closest to a score. Dandy Dick Cassiano, with Ben Kish serving as acting captain, followed a wave of the best blocking he has been given in many games, got into the clear around left end with one blocker still leading him, and raced 33 yards downfield. Cassiano started his run down the west sideline, but at the Penn State 35, he swerved toward midfield to let another blocker get ahead of him, and then was caught from behind at the Lions 29.

Immediately, the overeager Panthers were handed two offside penalties and Gajecki spilled Bob Thurbon for a 5-yard loss on a reverse. Smaltz stopped the threat completely by intercepting Cassiano's pass to Thurbon and carting it back some 30 yards to the Pitt 40, where Ted Konetsky came up in the nick of time to crash him out of bounds.

Smaltz Scores Touchdown

This started the Lions goalward again, but Joe Connell averted a score by deflecting a Smaltz to White touchdown pass, and John Patrick's field goal attempt from the Pitt 37 was wide.

But the fates ruled that Penn State should have her score. It came in just three plays, after Cassiano fumbled and Gajecki tumbled on the ball on the Pitt 22. Peters slashed outside left tackle for 3 yards, and White took a reverse from Smaltz to the 1–yard line, where Cassiano flung him out of bounds. But the delay was only a moment, for Smaltz punched it over on the next play and Ben Pollock, a reserve tackle who had missed only three extra-point tries in two seasons, booted across the seventh point.

The Lions were back on their side of the field early in the second quarter when two roughing penalties against Pitt, one for unnecessary roughness and another for running into the kicker, gave them first down on the Panther 36.

Ickes heaved a pass good for 13 yards to Gil Radcliff, and then the Lion fullback took a spinner through the middle for first down on the Pitt 13. But Pitt rode out this threat when Mike Sekela chased Petrella back on a reverse, nearly yanked his head off with a one-handed tackle, and caused Petrella to fumble. Art Corace recovered the ball on the Pitt 21. And they sparred, gingerly, for the rest of the half.

There were long runs in the third quarter, but no serious threats. Emil Narick broke away for one of 19 yards, and White equalled it for State. George Kracum clicked off a 15-yard end run, and Narick got another for 15, but the Panthers had started from their own 11 and got only to midfield when the quarter ended.

Forced back to their own 5-yard line by Ickes' punt and an ensuing offside penalty, Kish, playing with a leg fracture in a heavy cast from ankle to knee, contributed a kick that was the punting highlight of the game. Standing deep in his end zone, he sent a low kick that traveled midfield to the State 46.

Field Goal Clinches Game

Penn State appeared to be halted by an offside penalty when Peters suddenly shook free around right end for 22 yards on a march that wound up in the final score. Ickes took over and spun down the middle for another 10. Peters bowled along for another 5, before Hal Klein and Harry Kindelberger smeared a couple of plays. And then, on fourth down with 3 yards to go, John Patrick toed a field goal squarely between the uprights from the 24, for the feat that erased virtually all Pitt hope for a tie.

Pitt hung on gamely, but futilely, for the last five minutes. Narick knocked off a 15-yard run, and Edgar Jones tossed a pass to Kish that gained 14 yards and first down on the Penn State 25.

But Vargo tossed in a monkey wrench by spilling Jones for a 13-yard loss on a pass attempt, a fumble in the backfield dropped four more, and the alert Penn State secondary thwarted aerial attempts.

Chilly Cotton Bowl Ends in Tie Between Penn State, S.M.U.

By Chester L. Smith
The Pittsburgh Press

Dallas, Jan. 1, 1948 — The man who makes the Cotton Bowl trophies went back to work today with a rush order on his hands. He had to hammer out an extra copy.

One will go to Penn State and the other to Southern Methodist to symbolize the 13-13 tie they played here before some 47,000 assorted and well-refrigerated Texans and Pennsylvanians, who carried virtually every hotel blanket in town to the stadium to fend off the chilly wind that whistled down from the north.

Most tie games leave a bad taste and provide a field day for the volunteer quarterbacks, but this one didn't. As the teams played it out, there was complete justice done all around. Anything else would have been entirely out of order.

An Eye for an Eye

Each side scored a couple of well-earned touchdowns and each bobbled one of the conversions. Larry Cooney, the reserve halfback from Langley High School of Pittsburgh, and Wally Triplett, the right half from Philadelphia, had touchdowns for the Lions. Paul Page and Doak Walker tallied for the Mustangs.

Steve Suhey, an all-America guard in 1947.

Walker was true with his first conversion, but wild on the second. The same thing happened to Ed Czekaj, Penn State's point-after-touchdown specialist.

Elwood Petchel, the tiny tyke from Easton, pitched both of Penn State's scores. To justify his glittering advance notices, Walker threw the first one for Southern Methodist and jammed over from the 2 for the second.

No Epic

This was hardly a game that will be written into football primers for future generations to copy. It was played fiercely, but the good blocking and tackling was interspersed with some that was extremely mediocre. There were fumbles that hurt both sides, plus intercepted passes and mishandling of the ball, especially in the Ponies backfield.

Even the two all-Americans finished in a dead heat for honors. Walker enjoyed a tremendous first half, while Penn State's Steve Suhey was finding the going most embarrassing. Then, in the last two periods, Suhey found himself and Walker almost dropped out of the picture.

Both Finish Unbeaten

The deadlock allowed both teams to write their seasons into the records as the year of no defeats. For Southern Methodist it was the second successive tie (19-19 with T.C.U. in the regular schedule's finale) and for Penn State it was the first time the Lions have walked off the field without being victors since the Pitt game of 1946.

The Ponies had their 13 points before the Easterners could break through. The Lions were the aggressors at first. Taking the ball on their 48 after Walker had kicked short off the side of his foot, they plowed ahead to the 17, where Earl Cook, the S.M.U. guard, barreled Bobby Williams inches short of a first down, allowing the Mustangs to take over. Francis Rogel,

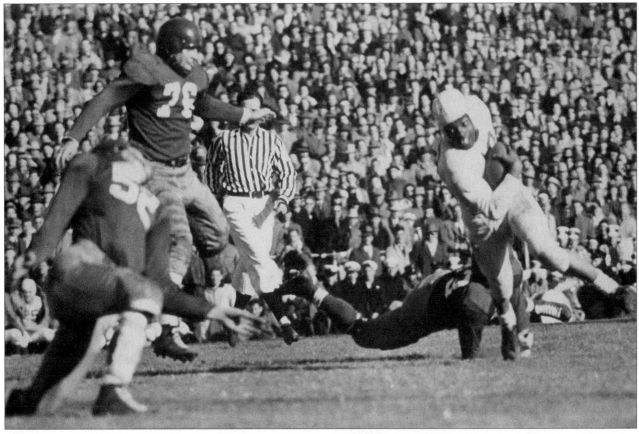

Wally Triplett, right, scored on a 6-yard pass from Elwood Petchel in the third quarter to tie the score at 13. The Nittany Lions' extra-point attempt, though, was no good, again. Neither team could score in the fourth quarter.

the sophomore fullback from North Braddock and as good a ball carrier as there was on the field, did most of the bucking and slanting in this march.

WALKER CONNECTS

But the Ponies kicked back hard. Walker ran and passed them close to their 47, then faded from his tailback position and threw high and far to Page. The latter outran Jeff Durkota, took the ball over his shoulder near the sideline and had no opposition as he sprinted goalward.

The Lions had little poise for the remainder of the first quarter.

Early in the second quarter they

Score by Periods					
S.M.U.	7	6	0	0	— 13
Penn State	0	7	6	0	— 13

forced the Ponies to punt from their 36, only to lose the advantage by being offside. It was a first down, instead, and Southern Methodist hustled all the way to Penn State's 30 before Cooney batted down a fourth-down pass to allow the Lions to take over.

PERSISTENT, THOSE PONIES

For the next 10 minutes the Blue

and White had more trouble than they could handle. Gil Johnson passed the Mustangs to the 8-yard line, where Cooney recovered a fumble by Dick McKissack. The Southwest Conference champions were back a moment later when Johnson began pitching once more.

It was McKissack, however, who put the stranglehold on Penn State. He slipped through their left guard from the 21 to the 2, leaving Walker with nothing more than a light jab at the middle for the touchdown.

It looked then like the Mustangs' game, but in the last minutes of the half Petchel pulled the Lions back into contention.

Larry Cooney, right, hauls in a pass from Elwood Petchel for a 38-yard touchdown in the second quarter to tie the score at 7-7. Earlier in the quarter, Cooney batted down a S.M.U. pass on fourth down at Penn State's 30 to stop a drive.

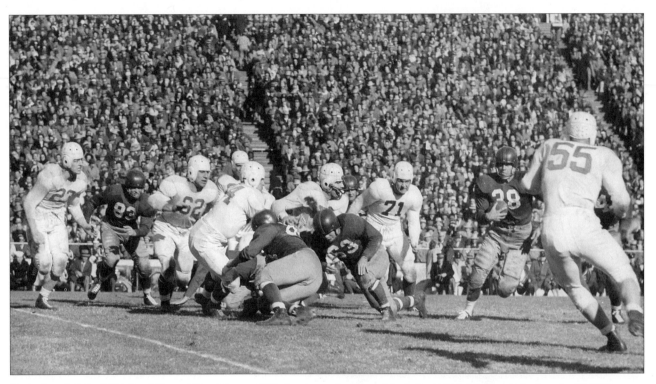

Penn State's John Wolosky (55) and Neg Norton (71) close in on Southern Methodist's Dick McKissick during the 1948 Cotton Bowl. Also pictured are the Nittany Lions' Steve Suhey (62) and Chuck Drazenovich (23).

Penn State coach Bob Higgins, second from left, shouts instructions to his team during the Cotton Bowl against S.M.U.

LIONS START ROARING

Petchel opened with a 13-yard pass to Bob Hicks from the Lions' 35, then ran for 20 yards after faking a throw. Triplett was thrown for a loss, and only seconds remained. But after he had twice missed his target, Petchel found Cooney in the end zone and connected. Czekaj converted and the Lions were roaring for the first time.

They took complete charge of the ceremonies in the second half.

S.M.U. had the ball scarcely three minutes in the third period. The Mustangs held on the 1-foot line after a 42-yard advance, but their fine work was rubbed out when Petchel brought Ed Green's punt back to the 9. Two bucks by Rogel put the ball on the 4, and Petchel connected with Triplett in the end zone on third down.

SECONDARIES ALERT

State got as far as the Ponies' 30 in the last quarter and Southern Methodist was once the same distance from the Lions' goal line.

Intercepted passes and a deal of exemplary defending by the Lion secondaries were the vital factors in preventing any scores in the fourth quarter.

The finish was hair-raising. With time for only one play, Petchell dodged four Mustang rushers and hurled the ball 45 yards into the end zone. It was aimed for Dennie Hoggard, the end. He was there, but the throw was at his knees. It trickled off his hands as the gun sounded.

'Reading Rambler' Leads Penn State Past Big Ten Champions

By Chester L. Smith
The Pittsburgh Press

Champaign, Ill., Sept. 25, 1954 — Penn State threw a numbing shock into the largest crowd that has seen an opening game in Memorial Stadium here this afternoon by turning back Illinois, the defending co-champions of the Big Ten, 14-12.

The 54,094 who sat in heat that was better suited to a dip in a cool pond than football saw more than an upset; they got an eyeful of a back who proved himself fully the equal of the Illini's magician, J.C. Caroline. This young gentleman was Lenny Moore, the "Reading Rambler," who was in the Orange and Blue's hair all afternoon.

The teams matched touchdowns — a pair apiece — but Penn State co-captain Jim Garrity of Monaca proved the difference when he kicked both extra points, while Caroline and Bob Wiman were wide and low on both their attempts to tack on the seventh point.

Jesse Arnelle and Moore were Penn State's scorers. The former gathered in a 24-yard pass from Pittsburgh's Don Bailey — who was a highly competent quarterback today — in the end zone late in the opening period. Bailey also was the key man in the second touchdown when, shortly before the intermission, he sped to his left on Illinois' 18 and lateraled to Moore, who zigged

Score by Periods					
Penn State	7	7	0	0 —	14
Illinois	6	0	6	0 —	12

and zagged past three would-be tacklers to cross the goal line not more than a yard from the sideline.

Abe Woodson, Caroline's sophomore running mate, scored twice for the Illini. He gave his side a 6-0 lead before the game was five minutes old by taking a short screen pass from Em

Lindbeck, thrown from the State 28, and out-tricking the defense to go the remaining 26 yards.

His second touchdown in the third quarter was a 17-yard cutback through State's right side.

Moore-Caroline Duel Thrills Fans

There was magnificent work today on both sides. Rosy Grier, the Lions' mammoth left tackle, wrapped himself around Illini ballcarriers time after time, while his sidekick, Arnelle, smothered at least a half-dozen plays that kept Penn State in the game. Jan Smid, the Illinois captain, was responsible more than anyone else for preventing the Lions from running wild. His performance today stamped him as one of the country's great guards.

But it was the Caroline-Moore duel that intrigued the onlookers. Caroline gained 115 yards for an average of 6.4 per try, but Lenny came away with the edge — 124 yards and an average of 7.3

An intercepted pass and a penalty that appeared harmless when it was stepped off gave Illinois its scoring opportunities.

Lindbeck picked off a throw by Bailey shortly after the kickoff on his 35 and scurried to State's 42. Caroline and Mickey Bates rushed for a first down on the 31. Woodson added three yards and then took Lindbeck's pitch to put the Illini ahead, 12-7.

Penn State took the lead before the period ended. Moore had returned a punt to Illinois' 37 and the Lions had worked their way to the 32 when they were stopped by a second interception. But Bates promptly fumbled the ball into Arnelle's hands on the 28, and three plays later Arnelle was behind the goal line with Bailey's toss in his arms.

Left, Penn State lineman Rosy Grier; Above right (clockwise), Jack Sherry, Jim Garrity, Leo Kwalik, Bob Rohland and Jesse Arnelle; Right, coaches Joe Bedenk, Rip Engle and Frank Patrick.

Lenny Moore, the Reading Rambler, scored the game-winning touchdown to defeat Illinois.

Bailey's Run Sets Up Second Touchdown

The Pittsburgh Press

Don Bailey set up the beachhead for the Lions' second touchdown when he ran 50 yards from his 26 to the Illini's 24 where Abraham Woodson overhauled him. After a short stab by Ron Younker, Bailey and Lenny Moore collaborated for what proved the winning points.

Early in the second half Illinois had possession on its 29. It was third down and 4 yards to go. When Woodson was contained for only three of them, were forced to punt.

But Penn State was offside and now the Orangemen had a first down on their 34. Lindbeck's long pass to Chuck Butler put them on Penn State's 30 and, although Lindbeck was thrown for a 6-yard loss by Jesse Arnelle, J.C. Caroline sprinted to the 14. On the second scrimmage, Woodson went what distance was left.

The Lions took control from that point to the end.

Bailey's lateral to Bill Straub for 39 yards late in the third quarter was a blow from which Illinois never fully recovered. It drove them back into their own territory. A moment before the period ended, Bailey kicked into the end zone where Caroline was

Penn State coach Rip Engle, right, diagrams a play for end Jim Garrity, left, and halfback Dick Jones. Penn State finished 7-2 in 1954.

tackled for a touchback and the Illini never got back on Penn State's side of the field.

Throughout the last 15 minutes the white-shirted Lions kept their opponents well bottled-up, and when Lenny Moore snatched a pass from

Miles Stout at midfield, Illinois' number was up.

With Moore, Bailey and Charlie Blockson on the carrying end the Lions paraded 48 yards and were within five yards of a third touchdown at the whistle.

Moore Outperforms Syracuse's Brown in Penn State Victory

By Carl Hughes
The Pittsburgh Press

University Park, Pa., Nov. 5, 1955 — There's no law against Syracuse winning a football game at Penn State, but there might as well be.

The frustrated Orange hasn't won here in 21 years, but it appeared for most of this afternoon that this time things would be different.

Bet when the points were totaled at the end, it was the same old story — although closer than usual: Penn State 21, Syracuse 20.

Certainly even the most rabid Nittany Lions fans in the sellout throng of 30,321 — let alone the Orange rooters — doubted early in the third quarter that State had a chance.

Moore Never Better

What no one had figured was that halfback Lenny Moore would suddenly throw off the cloak of despair and return to his hero pedestal. The second leading ground gainer in the nation last year, the Lions great hasn't even been in the Top 20 this campaign.

But he came up with an old-time performance just when it was needed most. In Coach Rip Engle's jubilant words, "Lenny never in his life was

Score by Periods						
Syracuse	7	6	7	0	—	20
Penn State	0	7	7	7	—	21

greater."

The senior from Reading put Penn State back in the game almost on his own and then took it away from the stunned Orange. He gained 146 yards on 22 carries — by far his biggest day of the season.

Oddly enough, he was outgained by another terrific halfback — Syracuse's Jim Brown. The Orange ace had 155 yards on 20 carries, scored all his team's touchdowns and two extra points, and threatened to turn the contest into a runaway for the New Yorkers.

Plum's Kick Vital

Moore wasn't Penn State's only hero, of course. Quarterback Milt Plum not only kicked the three vital extra points, but played 50 minutes —

about twice as much as any other signal caller for the Lions this season.

On one play, however, the biggest hero of all was Jack Farls, a substitute sophomore end from Freedom. He broke through to block one of Brown's extra-point tries to provide what eventually was the winning margin.

It didn't seem too important at the time, though. It still left Syracuse ahead, 13-0, midway in the second quarter, and the Orange seemed to be unstoppable.

Their first score came the second time they got the ball, after a Plum fumble was nabbed at the State 29. Brown stormed to the 8 on the first carry and, four plays later, he dove to a touchdown from the 2.

The second Syracuse tally was not earned as easily. It came at the end of a 68–yard drive the next time the Orange had possession.

The Lions thought momentarily that they had halted the march, but a fourth-down pass from the 6 thrown by quarterback Ed Albright was snagged by the inevitable Brown on the goal line.

Penn State, meanwhile, was making no threatening gestures and it wasn't until the half almost had run out that the Lions scored. There was just a minute to play when Albright strangely passed from his own 33.

Fullback Joe Sabol intercepted the ill-timed toss and shook off some four or five tacklers as he returned 28 yards down the sideline to the 10. Plum flipped the ball to Billy Kane on the first play and the Munhall halfback stepped the last 2 yards into the end zone.

Brown Again

That left the Orange anything but discouraged. They roared back to a

The original Beaver Stadium on the Penn State campus.

Dan Radakovich (51) receives instruction from Penn State Coach Rip Engle, left, and assistant Frank Patrick.

two-touchdown lead in just seven plays at the start of the second half.

Brown returned the kickoff 47 yards to put the march in motion. He finally burst through from the 6 to score. His extra point gave Syracuse a 20–7 lead but proved to be the visitors' last tally of the afternoon.

After that, Moore came to life and lifted the whole Penn State team up with him. The Lions moved to a touchdown following the kickoff, with a Plum pass to Kane for 19 yards, the biggest gainer. Moore took care of most of the carrying chores and finally exploded across from the 2.

Syracuse threatened to increase its margin back to two touchdowns at the start of of the final quarter. A Plum pass had been intercepted by Brown

and moments later the Syracuse halfback ripped 42 yards to the State 13. But Plum got revenge and also nipped the threat when he snagged an Albright toss in the end zone.

The Lions were given the ball on their 20, of course, and they smashed 30 yards to the winning touchdown, with Moore and fullback Bill Straub of Allison Park doing much of the smashing. The score, though, came on a 1–yard sneak by Plum.

Then he stepped back and converted the winning point.

A Syracuse fumble three plays after the kickoff was claimed by guard Sam Valentine for State at the Orange 46. That not only checked the visitors, but the Lions roared to the enemy 2 before time ran out.

Nittany Lions Dash Ohio State's Hopes for National Title

By Bob Drum
The Pittsburgh Press

Columbus, Ohio, Oct. 20, 1956 — The Penn State Lions came into this football-mad town cubs but left full-grown maneaters. And when they left, the Lions took with them Ohio State's hopes for a national championship.

While 82,584 fans sat on their hands waiting for a chance to cheer, the Penn State line manhandled its bigger opponent, and quarterback Milt Plum guided the offense to a 7-6 victory.

It was Penn State from start to finish except for two brief spurts by the Buckeyes that ran nearly the length of the field. The Bucks, seeking their ninth-straight victory and fourth of the season, were favored by as many as three touchdowns before the game.

Columbus fans figured it to be an easy Saturday for their favorites prior to five straight Big Ten contests in defense of the championship the Bucks have won two years running.

Nobody reckoned what the Penn States was thinking about.

The Lions outrushed a team that had been averaging 333 yards on the ground and made them change their mode of attack. In three previous games, Ohio State had thrown only 41 passes, but had run over the opposition with a relentless ground attack.

Score by Periods

Penn State	0	0	0	7 —	7
Ohio State	0	0	0	0 —	6

Today, the Buckeyes had to take to the air to get their only score and throw 10 passes in a desperate attempt to confuse the Lion line.

It was Plum who kicked the conversion that eventually was the difference.

It was Plum, a senior quarterback, who turned a mistake into the game-saving play. With third down and a yard to go for a touchdown, Plum juggled the ball and missed a handoff to sophomore Bruce Gilmore. Plum never lost poise, though.

He looked around and set sail through the middle of the Ohio State line to the 24-yard line and a first down.

A moment later, it was Plum who took charge again. With third down and 8 yards to go — and the Penn State bench pleading for him to get in position for a fourth-down field goal — Plum elected to pass.

He spotted Munhall's Billy Kane open on the 5-yard line and hit him right in the midsection with a pass. Kane carried right to the goal line and needed only a foot to make a score.

The quick-thinking quarterback tried two sneaks and then elected to let Gilmore go for the score with only 3:35 left to play. It was a fitting reward, for it was Gilmore who got two first downs in the key series which carried to the score.

A fantastic punt by Plum set up the winning drive early in the fourth quarter. He kicked the ball while standing behind his 20-yard line. The punt carried over the safety man's head and rolled out of bounds on the Ohio 3.

The Lions' touchdown seemed to instill new life into Ohio State. Following Plum's kickoff, the Buckeyes began to roll.

Sophomore Don Clark rushed for a first down to the 32, but the Bucks decided there wasn't enough time left to grind out the winning score, so they took to the air.

Rip Engle served as Penn State's head coach from 1950-1965. His record was 104-48-4.

Jimmy Roseboro passed to end Leo Brown for a first down on the Penn State 40. On the next play, Brown got down the right sideline unnoticed by Penn State halfback Ray Alberigi.

Roseboro tossed to him at the 15 and Brown was pushed out of bounds on a desperate lunge by Alberigi at the 4. But it was to no avail since Clark ran over right guard for a touchdown on the next play with 1:58 left to play.

Sophomore Frank Kremblas, who had missed a field goal earlier in the game from the 25, was sent in for the placement. Coach Woody Hayes of Ohio State also sent in another substitution just before Kremblas tried his kick and the Buckeyes were penalized for 12 men on the field.

Next, Kremblas had to kick from the 14. It was a long kick that went wide to the left as Penn State's bench went whooping with joy.

It was the largest crowd to watch a Penn State showing.

It was Rip Engle, the coach who was carried off the field on shoulders of the players, who made a speech before the season started.

"In Army, Syracuse, West Virginia and Pitt, Eastern football has representatives that don't have to back up to anybody," Engle said.

He forgot to mention Penn State, but the team did the talking for him today.

The middle of the Penn State line completely overshadowed Ohio State's 265 pound all-American guard, Jim Parker. Sam Valentine, Dan Radakovich and Richard DeLuca completely stopped the bread and butter of the Ohio attack — the halfback into the middle behind a hard charge by Parker.

And it was obvious that Plum was a peach today.

Milt Plum, who later starred for the Cleveland Browns and Detroit Lions in the N.F.L., completed 40 of 75 passes for 675 yards and six touchdowns in 1956.

Scrappy Lions Win Liberty Bowl, 7-0, Over Crimson Tide

By Roy McHugh
The Pittsburgh Press

Philadelphia, Dec 19, 1959 — Penn State's football team allowed precious few liberties to Alabama today in the Liberty Bowl. The Nittany Lions were unable to take many themselves, but they conned their way to finesse a touchdown as time ran out in the first half and it stood up the rest of the day for a 7-0 victory.

There were five seconds to play in the first half when Penn State hopped into a field-goal formation on the Crimson Tide's 18-yard line.

Instead of holding the ball for Sam Stellatella's placekick, however, sophomore quarterback Galen Hall threw a screen pass to sophomore halfback Roger Kochman of Wilkinsburg out on the left flank.

Alabama fell for the carpetbag trick hook, line and sinker. With an escort of four blockers, Kochman stormed down the sideline, weaving in and out as he went.

There was a shattering open-field block by Tom Mulraney and when Kochman got to the 3-yard line, where someone at last had a shot at him, he merely launched himself into the air and came down in the end zone head first. By that time the clock had run out.

Stellatella kicked the extra point

and, thereafter, nothing much happened.

The 36,211 spectators had to turn up their coat collars against a 20-mile wind from the north, but otherwise it was not a bad day for football — benevolent as anyone could hope for on this side of the Mason-Dixon line in December.

The bright blue sky would have done credit to New Orleans or Houston or Dallas and there were no reports of anyone freezing to death.

For Alabama, the wind was an ill wind. It blew no good to the Crimson Tide just before Kochman's touchdown, taking a high punt by fullback Tommy White back toward the line of scrimmage. When the ball came to rest, it had traveled four yards horizontally.

But there were 22 yards between State and the goal line and the Lions had to get there in 30 seconds. Fur-

Bob Mitinger, an all-America end in 1961.

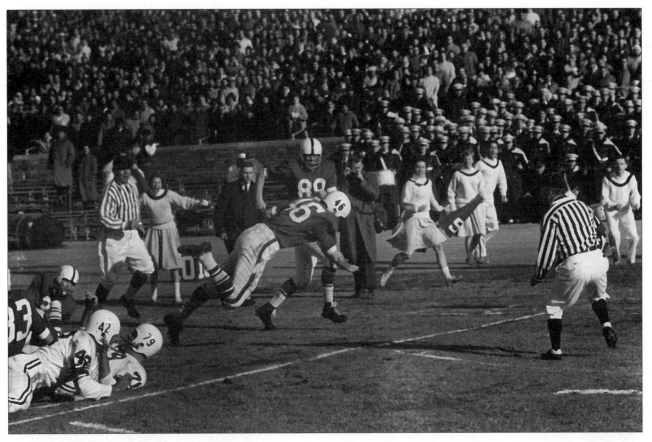

Penn State's Roger Kochman (46) lunges into the end zone for the only touchdown of the 1959 Liberty Bowl against Alabama. Kochman scored on a pass from quarterback Galen Hall after a fake field goal late in the first half.

thermore, they had to get there without Richie Lucas.

Felled by a hip injury — a bruise that practically immobilized him — Lucas had left the game after playing just a little over a quarter. In that short time he had gained more ground than anyone else was to gain all day — 54 yards running and 23 passing.

When Hall took his place, it was Penn State's ball on the Alabama 28-yard line, where Jay Huffman had recovered a fumble. Hall took the Lions inside to the 5, making two first downs himself, but there Alabama held for three plays.

On fourth down from the 1, Hall threw a rollout pass into the end zone.

Alabama's corner linebacker butted it high in the air, giving Bob Mitinger a chance to make the catch. But Mitinger dropped the ball.

It was only a reprieve for Alabama. Gary O'Steen punted into the wind and Penn State had the ball again on the Alabama 19.

The Lions got to the 5 and Stellatella actually did try a field goal, but Billy Richardson blocked it. There was 2:30 left in the half.

Alabama ran three plays and then had to punt again. White needn't have bothered. The wind-blown kick went from the 18-yard line to the 22.

Hall threw a screen pass to Pat Botula, gaining four yards and then came

the play that won the ball game.

Alabama came here billed as the toughest defensive team in the Southern Conference, and though Penn State wound up with 278 yards on the ground, the Lions hammered it out bit by bit.

There were two long drives. Lucas started one by tearing 24 yards on a keeper play after O'Steen's quick-kick with the wind at his back rolled out of bounds on the 3 — 61 yards from the line of scrimmage.

Throwing one pass — for 23 yards to John Bozick — Lucas moved Penn State to the Alabama 9, where Kochman fumbled. This was in the opening period, and the Lions never

Before the 1959 Liberty Bowl, three Penn State quarterbacks — from left, Rich Lucas, Galen Hall and Bob Ghigiarelli — knew they faced a difficult task. The 52 on the chalkboard is the total number of points Alabama allowed in the regular season.

really controlled the ball again until the fourth period.

They used up the last seven minutes going from their own 38 to the Alabama 10, every inch of the way on the ground. Satisfied with a seven-point win, they let the last 20 seconds tick off without even trying to run another play.

Penn State had one other scoring chance when Frank Korbini recovered a fumble on Alabama's 27-yard line early in the game. Nothing came of it.

Score by Periods

Penn State	0	7	0	0	—	7
Alabama	0	0	0	0	—	0

Alabama got the ball on a fumble in Penn State territory once, but fumbled right back. The exchange ended up on the Penn State 28 and that was high tide for Alabama.

The Crimson Tide's longest drive was 35 yards to the Penn State 38, where the Lions held for downs.

"Hard line play was what won it for us," Coach Rip Engle said. "We beat them at their own game."

Bearing out Engle's opinion, Chuck Janerrette was equally outstanding.

Engle, by the way, sent in the play that scored the touchdown. The Lions had never tried it before and practiced it only twice all season.

Poor weather forced the Nittany Lions to hold some very cold practice sessions. From left, Galen Hall, Tom Mulraney and Dick Hoak pose on a particularly cold afternoon with snowballs, rather than footballs.

Roger Kochman, an all-America halfback in 1962.

Penn State Shoots Down Ducks, 41-0, in Liberty Bowl

United Press International
The Pittsburgh Press

Philadelphia, Dec. 17, 1960 — Dick Hoak, a No. 2 quarterback of a No. 1 magnitude, picked up a trailing Penn State team today and led two units of the Nittany Lions to a 41-12 rout of Oregon in the ice-fringed second annual Liberty Bowl game.

Hoak, the boss-man of the Lions' second unit, dubbed the "Ready Team" by Coach Rip Engle, hit the Oregon trail after the Webfoots scored a first-period touchdown, and by overcoming goal line adversity, led Penn State to three touchdowns in the second period to put the game in the deep freeze.

Score by Periods

Penn State	0	21	0	20	—	41
Oregon	6	0	6	0	—	12

The 185-pound senior from Jeannette, Pa., not only had a hand in five of the Lions' six touchdowns, but scored two himself — one on a six-yard dash with a ballet leap into the end zone in the second period and his second on a 11-yard rollout in the fourth.

His brilliant fourth period performance saw him crowd his 11-yard touchdown sprint, an interception and a 33-yard touchdown pass to halfback Dick Pae, all in the space of four minutes.

Hoak, who won the game's Most Valuable Player Award warmed up 16,624 spectators scattered like pepper dust in the 97,000 seat Philadelphia Stadium with standout performances in all departments.

He probed the Webfoots' line with searching astuteness, ran when he had to, and passed with objectiveness which kept the one-touchdown underdog Oregon off balance.

The Webfoots, who unfortunately lost halfback Cleveland Jones on the first play from scrimmage with a kidney injury after he caught a 12-yard pass, broke into the scoring column with a first period 88-yard drive in 12 plays with quarterback Dave Grosz going over from the 1.

Then, Hoak and his No. 2 unit, which yielded the Ducks' score, took command. The Lions began a march

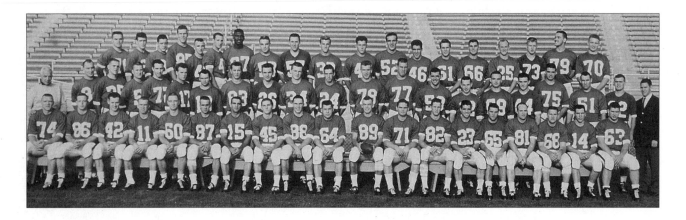

The key members of Penn State's 1960 offensive attack: Jim Kerr (41) carrying the ball with Dick Hoak (23), Bill Popp (64), Al Jacks (24) and Sam Sobczak (45) blocking.

on their 37, gambled successfully twice on fourth down running plays, and drew one break when a missed pass found a substitution delay by Oregon keeping the drive alive.

Hoak made the most of the break as the second period opened to send State to a first down on the Oregon 12 and threw a pass to Henry Oppermann, who was borrowed from the first unit, for a first down on the Oregon 1. Don Jonas, also on lend-lease from the first unit, went over from the 1 and when Oppermann, voted the most valuable lineman, converted Penn State had a 7-6 lead it never lost.

Then a 1-yard adversity struck. Penn State's first unit moved from its

20 following a punt and went as far as the Oregon 1. But Sam Sobczak fumbled into the end zone and Oregon recovered.

Jonas returned the ensuing punt 23 yards to the Oregon 37, and Hoak ran for 12 yards to the 26. Hoak followed with an 11-yard run to the 1. Penn State was offside on the next play but three 2-yard bolts sent Al Gursky over and Penn State led, 14-6.

Hoak personally took charge of the next score when he swept six yards into the end zone with 31 seconds left in the half to make it 21-6.

The Webfoots scored in the third period with Dave Grayson — voted the game's outstanding back — run-

ning 10 yards over guard.

Then the Lions, with the No. 1 unit in action, opened the fourth period chopping their way from their own five and in 15 plays Ed Caye went over from the one.

Hoak scored the next TD on his 11-yard run.

Hoak called it a day with an interception and a 15-yard return to Oregon's 33. The Lions quarterback then floated Pae into the open and hit him with a pass for the final touchdown of the game.

It was the Lions' second straight Liberty Bowl victory. They beat Alabama 7-0 in the first game last year.

Rip Engle and his 1960 team captain Hank Oppermann.

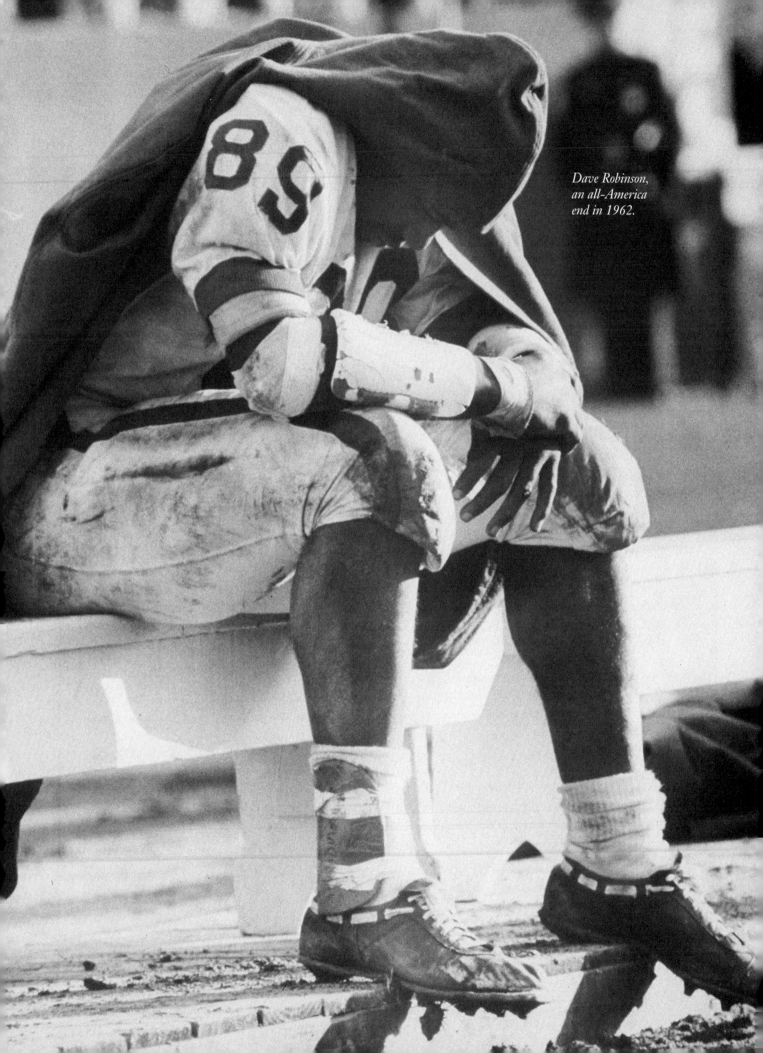

Dave Robinson,
an all-America
end in 1962.

Hall's TD Passes Lead Lions to 30-15 Gator Bowl Victory

BY CHESTER L. SMITH
The Pittsburgh Press

Jacksonville, Dec. 30, 1961 — Quarterback Galen Hall threw three touchdown passes leading Penn State to a 30-15 victory over Georgia Tech today before 50,202 fans in the Gator Bowl.

After Penn State trailed, 9-0, in the second quarter, Hall fired a pair of TD passes for a 14-9 halftime edge and added another to put the Lions in front, 20-9, after three quarters.

Tech scored a last-quarter touchdown, but State came back with a field goal by Don Jonas and another touchdown.

Score by Periods

Penn State	0	14	6	10	— 30
Georgia Tech	2	7	0	6	— 15

FIRST QUARTER

Georgia Tech won the toss and chose to receive.

Jonas' kickoff went to the Tech 24. Jake Martin took it and ran to the Tech 37. Stanley Gann went wide to the left for 11 yards.

Two more running plays earned Tech a first down at the Penn State 40, but three additional rushes netted only seven yards and Tech's Billy Lotheridge punted out of bounds at the Penn State 10.

After an offsides penalty, Roger Kochman rushed to the 9. On second down, Hall threw wild to the sidelines. Officials ruled he grounded the ball intentionally and granted Tech a safety.

On the free kick from its 20, Penn State's Pete Liske punted to William Williamson at the Tech 30 and he returned to the Tech 49. After a first down at the State 36, Tech lost two yards in three attempts and Lotheridge's punt was over the goal line.

On second down, Kochman moved to the 36 for 12 yards and a first down, but Tech had Penn State in trouble again when Hall fumbled and Frank Sexton recovered at the 33.

A Gann pass was intercepted by Pete Liske in the end zone.

Forced to punt without a first down, Penn State was again in trouble after a Lotheridge to Williamson pass covered 44 yards to a first down on the Penn State 8.

On second down, Bill Saul recovered Lotheridge's fumble at the 8 as the quarter ended.

SECOND QUARTER

Tech started a touchdown drive after a punt rolled dead on the Tech 20. Williamson got five yards and Joseph Auer picked up seven to the 32. Then Auer dashed 68 yards to the end zone. The conversion was good.

Harold Powell returned the kickoff 17 yards to the Penn State 22. Two running plays netted seven yards, then Hall passed to Kochman for nine yards and a first down at the Penn State 38 and to Dave Robinson, who caught it on the dead run up the middle for 21 yards to the Tech 38. Buddy Torris picked up 3 yards, then Hall tossed to Dick Anderson on the right sidelines for 14 yards to the 21. Al Gursky drove for eight to the 13.

Hall fired toward Gursky, who dove desperately for the ball and gathered it inches from the near-frozen ground in the end zone. Jonas converted.

With only three minutes remaining Penn State's Kochman rushed for 14 yards to the Lions 27. Hall connected with Anderson for nine yards and out of bounds stopping the clock with the ball at the Lions 36.

James Powell carried for 13 yards to the Penn State 49, then came an offside penalty against the Lions. But Hall hit Robinson on the sidelines for 10 yards and Anderson down the middle for 16 yards to the Tech 30. State called time out and there were only one minute 12 seconds remaining.

A screen pass from Hall to Anderson was good for three yards. Hall faded and looped one to Kochman for a coffin-corner catch and Penn State's

Penn State receiver Jack Curry (81) jumps high for a pass in the end zone against Georgia Tech defender Mike Page. Nittany Lions quarterback Galen Hall threw three scoring passes against Tech, leading Penn State to a 30-15 victory.

Penn State coach Rip Engle, kneeling, poses with Nittany Lions standouts (left to right) Dave Robinson, Chuck Sieminski and Roger Kochman.

second touchdown.

This was the first time in 1961 that Georgia Tech's defense had surrendered two touchdowns in a game. Jonas converted.

THIRD QUARTER

Penn State punted to Tech's 22. A Gann keeper got a first down at the 38, but Joe Blasentine recovered a Tech fumble at the Georgia 46. Nothing worthwhile materialized for the Lions and Liske punted over the goal.

Three Tech plays gained five yards, then Lotheridge punted to the Penn State 29. Rushing three times, the Lions were inches short of a first down and Liske punted to the Tech 18.

Gann moved Tech to two first downs on the ground to the Tech 43. On second down, Dave Robinson boomed through the Engineer line and not only smeared a fading Gann, but stole the ball at the Tech 35.

On the first play, that quick lineup Penn State used against Pitt and Syracuse worked again. Hall pitched to Powell, all alone down the right side and Penn State had a third touchdown. The conversion was fouled up by an offside line.

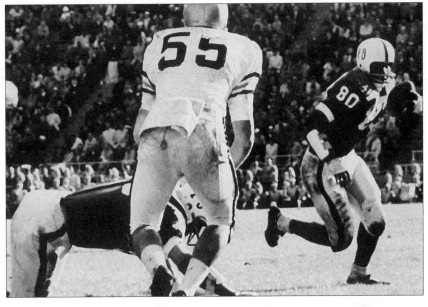

Penn State's Dave Robinson (80) picks up a block and turns the corner against Georgia Tech's Bobby Caldwell. Robinson had four receptions in the 1961 Gator Bowl.

FOURTH QUARTER

Thanks to a Lotheridge to Williamson pass play of 12 yards, Tech had a first down at the Penn State 35. But an errant pass and two futile runs netted a lost yard and conservative Tech elected to punt from the 36, the ball sailing out of the end zone.

Lacking a first down, Liske punted

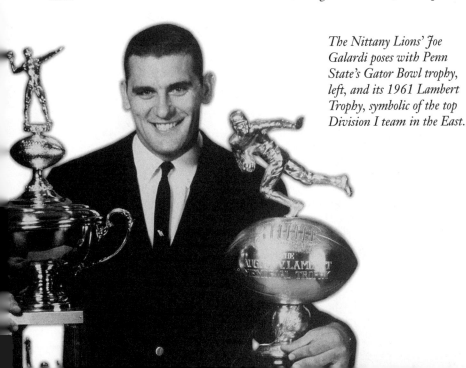

The Nittany Lions' Joe Galardi poses with Penn State's Gator Bowl trophy, left, and its 1961 Lambert Trophy, symbolic of the top Division I team in the East.

— the ball sailing low into the hands of Toner at midfield. He got four yards on the return, was gang-tackled and Penn State came out of it losing 15 yards on a penalty to its own 36.

On next play, a Lotheridge pitchout was wild, but Auer hustled back and scooped it up at the 25, then danced and skipped down the side for Tech's second TD. Gann's two-point running try was short.

With less than five minutes left, Penn State took the ball at the Tech 12 when the Engineers gambled on fourth down with a fake-punt screen pass, which fell incomplete.

Running plays put the ball square in front of the uprights on the 6-yard line and, on fourth down, Jonas kicked a field goal from the 13.

An interception by Jim Schwab put the Lions at the Tech 11 on the first play after the next kickoff. Gursky and Torris carried to the goal line and Torris plunged over. Jonas converted.

Pitt Best of Big Three After Edging Lions in 22-21 Thriller

By Chester L. Smith
The Pittsburgh Press

Pittsburgh, Dec. 7, 1963 — The Pitt Panthers treated themselves to a pre-Christmas gift yesterday at Pitt Stadium that has been a long, long time coming.

By defeating Penn State in a game that gushed with action from beginning to end, they wrapped up in a single package the district Big Three championship, a spot among the top three teams of the year nationally, the end of the Lions' three-season victory streak in the 70-year-old series and their own most artistic campaign (9-1) since 1937.

It was the first time since 1955 that the Jungle Cats had won from both Penn State and West Virginia. Old Ironsides, the hunk of steel that is symbolic of the area title, will now be a tenant in the Fitzgerald Field House for at least a year. Perhaps the Lions had a premonition of what was in store for them, for when their gear was trucked in from University Park Friday night, Old Ironsides was aboard. Now the weighty old gentleman won't have to make the return trip.

This was a game that drove the sun-drenched crowd of 51,477 — almost the bowl's capacity — close to a case of mass hysterics.

Actually the margin for the Panthers was Rick Leeson's third-period, 35-yard field, goal but they could very well

Score by Periods					
Pitt	0	12	3	7 —	22
Penn State	7	7	7	0 —	21

have been beaten in the waning moments when Ron Coates, the Lions kick specialist, missed for three points on a 37-yarder, which had ample distance but sliced off to the left.

For Pitt it was Freddie Mazurek running and passing, Leeson belting inside the tackles, a tremendous defensive effort by the alternate unit and all hands pitching in to help as the long season came to a happy end.

Touchdowns were traded at three apiece — Paul Martha, Leeson and Mazurek scoring for Pitt; and Gary Klingensmith, Jerry Sandusky and Don Caum doing the honors for State.

After their first and second touchdowns, the Panthers tried for two points, but got none. On the initial touchdown, Mazurek was run out of bounds and his second attempt — a pass — wasn't close to anyone in particular. When the third score bobbed up, it was safety first and Leeson kicked for the single point and got it.

It was Mazurek's day by a landslide. The Redstone Raider not only carried in one six-pointer personally, but set up the two that preceded it with his good right arm and his ghost-like runs when he chose to leg it instead of pitch. Those legs scurried for 142 yards and he threw for another 108. The 250 yards total gave him a season's mark of 1,595. In the Miami game last Saturday night he had broken the school's total season offense high of 1,338 yards, set by Warren Heller in 1931.

In the voting that followed, Mazurek was the unanimous winner of the James H. Coogan Award, given each year in honor of the Lions' late public relations chief, to the game's most valuable player.

Overall, the Panthers were Penn State's masters by foot, but not by air. They outrushed their old friends from

Quarterback Pete Liske threw for 173 yards against Pitt in 1963.

Penn State quarterback Pete Liske, shown firing a pass against Pitt in the teams' 1963 contest, threw for 1,117 yards and 10 touchdowns during the 1963 season, which saw the Nittany Lions finish 7-3.

the mountains by 310 yards to 128, but were outgunned overhead by Pete Liske, 173 yards to 145. The total yardage was an impressive 421 yards for Pitt, 270 for the Lions. For what must have seemed an eternity of time to their own congregation, the Jungle Cats found themselves in a jungle of their own planting. A blocked punt and two fumbles opened the door for two of the Lions' touchdowns, but on the other side of the ledger it has to be set down that they had the wherewithal to make the most of their opportunities.

The first hint that the Lions had come to Pittsburgh for something more than a weekend in the city came on the second play after the kickoff

when Liske let fly with a fling to Caum from his own 21-yard line. The play had danger written all over it from the instant the Harrisburg senior gathered it in some 10 yards away and headed downfield.

There was a massive tangle of blockers and would-be tacklers in the neighborhood of Pitt's 30, but Caum escaped the trap and was away again, not to be caught until he was high-shouldered out of bounds at the 11 by Leeson.

A personal foul on a pass by Liske that went astray set the Lions back to their 29 and when Liske was able to get back only eight yards on a flip to Dick Anderson, Coates was off the

mark on a field goal try from the 19.

But the touchdown that was denied State wasn't long in appearing ... Ed Stuckrath, the day's defensive stand-out, blocked Tom Black's fourth-down punt and Bernie Sabol covered the ball on Pitt's 17.

Short punches by Klingensmith, Chris Weber and Stuckrath pushed the Panthers to their 9. Here, Liske, feint-ed beautifully on an apparent handoff to the right, then tucked the ball into Klingensmith's midriff as the latter slanted sharply leftward. The right halfback went across untouched, and seconds later Pitt was down seven points.

The Panthers were on their way to

get six of them back before the quarter ended, but before they had been pinned down on the Lions' four after a pair of passes had miscued. This drive, for 76 yards, was highlighted by a fourth down gamble by Mazurek that had to be the most reckless of the fall.

On his own 45, Mazurak dropped back into kick formation, but instead sent Leeson straight ahead. Leeson swooped along for 34 yards to State's 21.

Staying on the ground, Mazurek, Martha and Leeson pounded away to the 4 but could go no farther.

Four plays later, Frank Hershey's punt rolled dead on his 46 and the Panthers were in gear once more.

Mazurek, Eric Crabtree and John Telesky rattled off one first down to the 32 and Mazurek went upstairs with successive passes to Bill Howley good for 12 and 16 yards. Mazurek stepped to the 2 as the period ended.

Two plays after the interruption Pitt had its touchdown. Leeson needed only inches after his lunge and Martha measured it off — by inches.

The Panthers promptly countered a stroke of good fortune with a sour note after they had kicked off. When Glenn Lehner intercepted a Liske pass, Pitt had the ball at its 37, but Mazurek's bobble, recovered by Ed Stewart gave the Lions immediate control on the 36.

They needed but seven plays to reach the end zone. Klingensmith and Weber swept to the 9 and Liske caught Sandusky behind the goal line with a high pass that called for a brilliant catch, which is what it was.

Back came the Panthers — for 80 yards and their second touchdown. Mazurek set the wheels to spinning with a 34-yard arching throw to Leeson. A holding foul cost 15 of those yards but Mazurek retrieved 16 by passing to Al Grigaliunas. Pitt then

stayed earthbound for the remaining 43 yards.

Mazurek contributed 10- and 12-yard keepers, with Martha adding seven yards, and, from the 10, Leeson jamming to the 2. Leeson then hit for 1 yard. A penalty moved the ball a foot or so closer to the goal line. Afterward, Leeson plowed in for the touchdown.

A pass interference penalty of a Mazurek pass that started on the Pitt 32 and ended with the ball on Penn State's 30 gave the Panthers a chance to try for a field goal with seconds remaining in the half. Leeson kicked from the 37 but it was short.

Old Man Fumble belted the Panthers a second time shortly after the start of the second half. Mazurek lost the ball to Anderson at the 30 and the Lions prowled to the 9, where an offensive interference call sent them back to the 25. Liske threw to Joe Vargo but for not enough, and Pitt had the ball on the 12.

The events leading up to the all-important field goal now began to unroll. Mazurek turned himself loose from his 22 and he was 42 yards away on Penn State's 36 when he was overtaken and grounded by Anderson.

When the mob was unpiled, Mazurek didn't get up and the Pitt segment of the crowd moaned when he wobbled to the bench and was replaced by Kenny Lucas.

However, the Glassport sophomore used Leeson and Bodle to reel off a first down on the 21, passed to Joe Kuzneski on the 10 and appeared to be in full command of the situation when he was stabbed for a 10-yard loss by Stuckrath.

That put Leeson in the field goal kicking role that was to mean the victory.

But it didn't seem that way when

the Lions responded to the challenge with a 74-yard stampede that didn't end until Liske had passed the last 10 yards to Caum for the third touchdown. The key plays that came before were Liske's 16-yard shot to Klingensmith, Weber's 30-yard sprint through the middle on Penn State's famed scissors, and a 14-yarder to Caum that planted the ball on the 9.

The Panthers now picked up the baton and were off and running. They opened from their 23 and were midfield, largely on a Lucas to Crabtree pass that was good for 25 yards as the third quarter closed out.

Mazurek returned for the final period and promptly risked disaster with a fourth-down toss of the dice. He got away with it, fired a pass to Bodle for 11 yards and raced seven more to Penn State's 21.

Bodle chipped in with another four, and the Redstone Raider, with an option to pitch or prance, saw an alley open to his right. Down it he scrambled for the 17 yards that were left — and the scoring for the day was over.

But not the suspense. Before the finish, the Lions took over on downs on their own 47 when Pitt misfired on a fourth-down punt attempt, and an exchange of punts left the Lions on their 42.

Pass interference on Caum swept them along to Pitt's 42. There Liske passed to Klingensmith at the 26 and to Anderson on the 22. But there was more yardage left than they cared to risk and Coates tried for his win-or-go-broke field goal. Broke was the answer.

All the Panthers needed at this point was a first down to allow them to retain the ball and as a parting gesture for the season. Mazurek did the trick with a twisting run of 27 yards. He ate the ball on the last play.

Engle Takes Nittany Lions' Defeat Hard

BY LESTER J. BIEDERMAN
The Pittsburgh Press

Rip Engle came to an outer room just off the Penn State dressing quarters, to meet the press 15 minutes after Pitt nosed out his Lions, 22-21, in a thrilling windup of the season yesterday, but his heart wasn't in his work at this time.

The veteran Lions coach was a man of mixed emotions. He had praise for the Panthers, naturally, but he had higher praise for his own players.

He also took the blame for failing to go for the two-point conversion after Penn State's third touchdown that might have given the Lions a 22-15 lead and then diplomatically blamed referee Francis Brennan for failing to signal fourth down when a field goal would have been tried.

"Pitt's good, there's no doubt about it," Engle remarked, "but if Pitt ranks itself No. 1 in the country, then we're just a point behind Pitt. They beat us by a margin of about three feet (Ron Coates missed a field goal in the last 70 seconds).

"I will say this Pitt team is the most offensive-minded I've seen and Fred Mazurek is tremendous. Really, he was the difference in the two teams. Without Mazurek, we would have won easily. He came up with the key plays and he's by far the best running quarterback we've seen."

Engle wouldn't pinpoint Pitt as the best team Penn State has met this season.

"I'd have to bracket Oregon, Ohio State, Rice and Pitt together for toughness," he added. "But we played this game without our two starting tackles (Harrison Rosdahl and Terry Monaghan) and two sub tackles (Gary Eberle and John Deibert). In fact, we used two ends as tackles. That's how hard up we were."

There were two third-quarter plays that seemed to upset Engle, since the Lions lost by one point.

"We had the ball on the Pitt 11 and then were penalized 15 yards to the 26 for offensive pass interference. I thought it was third down but the referee signaled fourth down to our quarterback and before I could get a play in, Pete Liske passed for 15 yards but short of a first down and Pitt took over on the 11.

"Had I known it was fourth down, I would have had Coates try a field goal. We were leading, 14-12, at the time and it would have made a difference."

When the Lions bolted for their third TD a few minutes later to up their margin to 20-15. Engle tried to send in a play for a two-point conversion attempt "but I wasn't alert," Engle gallantly admitted.

"We had a play off the fake kick but I didn't act in time and couldn't get my players into the game," Engle added.

Had the Lions succeeded with two points, they would have led, 22-15, and put the pressure on Pitt on the following touchdown.

Penn State had Pitt thoroughly scouted — as Pitt did Penn State — and the only play that fooled the Lions was a fake kick when the Panthers had the ball — fourth-and-three, on their own 45 — in the first quarter.

The ball went to Rick Leeson and he roared 34 yards right up the middle to the Penn State 21 when the Lions were looking for the kick. So was every one of the 51,477 fans.

Engle did reach out to praise most of his stalwarts, especially Don Caum, who ran 99 yards on four passes and brought the crowd to its feet in the first quarter on a spectacular 66-yard broken field run after taking a flat pass. He was stopped five or six times, but always broke away and zig-zagged from one side of the field to the other.

The fans were startled when referee Brennan placed the ball on end to measure for a first down on the State 11-yard line. But Brennan explained:

"The ball was 'killed' in that position by the ball carrier: That's the way he held it when stopped."

Several pro scouts were busy contacting some of the Pitt and Penn State players who have been selected in the draft. But Leeson isn't interested in the Washington offer and will attend dental school.

Lions Take to Road, Knock Off No. 2 Ohio State, 27-0

BY LESTER J. BIEDERMAN
The Pittsburgh Press

Columbus, Ohio, Nov. 7, 1964 — Penn State not only rubbed much of the gloss and glamour off previously unde-feated, second-in-the-nation Ohio State today, but made its 27-0 victory look ridiculously easy.

The Lions roared for the full 60 minutes this bright sunny after-noon and not only mystified the Buckeyes but also most of the 84,279 fans who had attended the weekly ritual at Ohio Stadium.

The performance of the Lions was unbelievably good and they, in turn, made the Bucks look unbelievably bad. Off the game today, it was difficult to visualize the Ohio State as undefeated and Penn State with a 3-4 record before the game.

The only bright spot in an other-wise exceedingly dull day for Ohio State was the defeat of Purdue by Michigan State, leaving the Buckeyes the only unbeaten team in the Big Ten.

Penn State completely dominated the game from start to finish.

The Lions scored a touchdown in every quarter, had numerous other chances, and never allowed the Buck-eyes to touch Penn State territory until the final futile minutes.

The Lions were two touchdown underdogs but they proceeded to not only pile up four TD's but to hold

Score by Periods

Penn State	7	7	6	7	—	27
Ohio State	0	0	0	0	—	0

Ohio State scoreless for the first time since 1959, when the Buckeyes and Indiana played a scoreless contest.

The Lions won everything. Their supreme effort of the season was over-whelmingly displayed in the statistics.

Penn State had 22 first downs to only five for Ohio. The Lions piled up 201 yard rushing. The Buckeyes, who specialize in ball control and rushing, had the ball only 23 times for rushes and gained but 33 yards.

The Bucks netted just two yards rushing the first quarter and wound up a minus-14 yards for the first half.

Gary Wydman, in his best day of the season, completed 12 of 22 passes for 148 yards and didn't have one inter-cepted. The Bucks' Don Unverferth completed just three in 14 and had two intercepted.

Penn State went in for the touch-down kill on four reasonably long marches. The first two covered 65 yards each, the third 41 yards and the final trip to paydirt was 63 yards long.

Wydman turned magician with an amazing display of ball handling.

On the first touchdown cruise, he hit Don Kunit with a pass in the flat that was good for 35 yards and perched the Lions on the Buckeyes' 11-yard line.

Bob Riggle wriggled through the middle for seven yards and, on third down, Tom Urbanik fled through the line for an apparent touchdown but fumbled as he tumbled into the end zone.

Fortunately, Dirk Nye was there to fall on the ball ahead of two Buckeyes and Penn State had six points. Gerry Sanker tacked on the extra point and with 8:24 gone, the Lions had a 7-0 lead that was to grow and grow and grow.

Sanker missed a field goal from the 10-yard line at the start of the second period, but the Lions came pounding back on a 65-yard march for a TD.

Wydman passed 11 yards to Bill Bowes, Urbanik charged straight ahead for 18 and before anybody realized it, Penn State was perched on the OSU 3-yard line.

Wydman went back to pass, decid-ed to run and raced around his left end for the three yards and the score. Sanker again made the kick good for a 14-0 Penn State lead.

Penn State was deep in Ohio State territory twice more before the half ended, but nothing came of it.

Penn State quarterback Gary Wydman gets off a pass over Navy's Pat Philbin in the Nittany Lions' 1964 season-opener. Navy won, 21-8; Penn State would go on to lose its first three games, and four of its first five, before finishing with five straight wins.

The Lions lost the ball on the Ohio State 15 when a fourth-down plunge failed by inches early in the third quarter, but this merely delayed them.

Dick Gingrich intercepted a pass on the Buckeyes' 41 and Wydman went to work again. He passed 12 yards to Riggle, 12 more to Bill Huber and then

Kunit and Urbanik carried the ball.

Kunit took it over with a two-yard sprint around his left and this time Sanker's kick was wide but Penn State

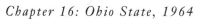

Penn State's 1964 upset of undefeated and second-ranked Ohio State made Nittany Lions players such as Glenn Ressler popular targets for autograph hunters. Penn State shocked Ohio State, 27-0, in the teams' 1964 meeting.

Penn State assistant coach George Welsh pores over some notes during a 1964 road trip.

Fullback Tom Urbanik led Penn State's 1964 team in rushing, compiling 625 yards and scoring eight touchdowns.

had a 20-0 lead.

The Buckeyes, looking worse every minute, finally chalked up a first down in the final seconds of the third quarter on two consecutive passes.

But the Lion had one mighty roar left and, with nine minutes remaining in the game, they ran and passed 63 yards in 10 plays for the final touchdown.

Urbanik ripped off 13 yards up the middle and Gary Klingensmith ran like a man on fire. Klingensmith sprinted for eight yards and kept on fighting for extra yardage.

Then Kunit and Dave McNaughton took over. Kunit turned his left end for 12 yards, McNaughton added seven over the middle and Kunit tore around his left end for the last five yards.

Sanker's kick was true and the Penn State lead rose to 27-0 and the Buckeye diehards began to leave the stadium.

Penn State Blows Past Hurricanes, Just Missing a Shutout

By Roy McHugh
The Pittsburgh Press

Miami, Sept. 29, 1967 — Charlie Tate, Miami's head football coach, put it all together last night after losing to Penn State in the Orange Bowl, 17-8.

"Their defense was stronger than I expected," he said.

It was stronger than anybody expected.

Non-existent against Navy a week ago, Penn state's defense had Miami shut out with 47 seconds to play. This made it very difficult for Miami to substantiate the betting odds that made the Hurricanes an 11-point favorite.

The first quarter, which was scoreless, decided the game. Miami made a first down on the 9-yard line and could get no farther. Then a fumble gave Miami the ball on the 35 and again nothing happened except a second missed field–goal attempt by Ray Harris.

Joe Paterno's young Lions — six sophomores were playing on the defensive unit, three of them 18-year-olds — now perceived that they were not going to be run out of the stadium.

After that, with each minute that went by, Penn State's defense became harder to move and Miami's offense became easier to stop.

Score by Periods

Penn State	0	6	8	3	— 17
Miami	0	0	0	8	— 8

And the initiative switched to the Lions. After missing two field-goal attempts, from slightly beyond Don Abbey's range, they missed a first down on Miami's 1-yard line and then put an end to the stuttering.

Late in the second quarter, Bob Campbell zig-zagged through Miami for a 50-yard run. On the next play, from Miami's 15, quarterback Tom Sherman threw a touchdown pass to Ted Kwalick, alone in the end zone.

The Lions thus completed a 90-yard drive and, though Abbey missed the extra point, their troubles were over.

They put on another drive in the

Ted Kwalick (82) scored the Lions' first touchdown with a 15-yard reception, alone in the end zone.

Penn State's Warren Hartenstine hammers a Maryland player in the teams' 1967 game.

third quarter, this time going 59 yards with Sherman passing to Abbey from the 7 for the touchdown.

A two-point conversion on a pass to Jack Curry and Abbey's fourth-quarter field goal from 24 yards put the Lions so far ahead that Miami's fair-weather friends in the crowd of 39,516 started heading for home.

As time ran out, Miami got down to the Penn State 3, but Neal Smith, a non-scholarship sophomore in the Lions' defensive backfield, broke up two passes in the end zone.

Miami wasn't going to score, it appeared. Then, on fourth down at the Penn State 17, Campbell, back to punt, saw he was not being rushed, decided to run, changed his mind about a yard from the line of scrim-mage and tried to kick on the move. The ball squirted off his foot and Mi-ami had it.

Bill Miller at once threw a 24-yard touchdown pass to Jimmy Cox.

Earlier, both Miller and Miami's other quarterback, Dave Olivo, had been missing their receivers and Mia-mi's running attack got the Hurricanes nowhere.

Vince Opalsky, the sophomore from McKeesport who ran for close to 100 yards against Northwestern last week, gained 9 yards and no one else was much better.

After Campbell's long run, a scis-sors play on which he changed direc-tions when his blockers weren't where he thought they'd be, the Lions found it easy to run on Miami. Sherman completed 15 of 24 passes and mixed up his plays well.

When Penn State lost to Navy and with Miami and U.C.L.A. coming up, it seemed that the Lions would be off to an 0-3 start. Now they are 1-1 and everybody is wondering how Miami,

Tom Sherman threw 2 touchdown passes against Miami.

Florida State Rallies in Fourth Quarter, Ties Lions, 17-17

By Roy McHugh
The Pittsburgh Press

Jacksonville, Fla., Dec. 30, 1967 — Penn State gambled and tied in the Gator Bowl yesterday. On their own 15-yard line, 17 points ahead in the third quarter, the Lions tried a fourth-down quarterback sneak. Within the next minute, Florida State had two touchdowns — not one touchdown, but two — and when Grant Guthrie kicked a 26-yard field goal 15 seconds before the end of the game, it all came out even, 17-17.

"I blew it," said Joe Paterno, Penn State's coach, "I've been around football long enough to know better."

But the night before, Paterno had said the Lions were going to have some fun. This they did.

Paterno changed his lineup around to stymie Florida State's passing game and to get a little more mileage out of Ted Kwalick, the all–American tight end.

He used offensive and defensive formations the Lions never had tried before. And for two quarters, he looked like a genius.

Kwalick, acclaimed as the best tight end in the country, played wingback. "We had to get the ball to Kwalick to win," Paterno said, but one of those times a touchdown resulted.

From some crazy formations, including one that resembled a "Y," tailback Charlie Pittman ran for 128

yards. And on defense, the Lions had three men playing new positions and Tim Montgomery "roaming the outfield," all in the interest of greater quickness.

Kim Hammond, Florida State's quarterback, set Gator Bowl records for passes completed (37) and passing yardage (362) and Ron Sellers, the split end, caught 14 of Hammond's passes for still another Gator Bowl record, but Penn State prevented them from executing their trademark play, the long bomb.

And at halftime, the Lions led by two touchdowns and a field goal. The record Gator Bowl crowd of 68,019 had nothing left to enjoy but the bright, balmy weather.

Then the third quarter started and so did Florida State. Presently, the Seminoles had a first down on the

Ted Kwalick, an all-America end in 1967 and 1968.

Penn State quarterback Tom Sherman (25) loses the ball after a hard hit from Florida State's Floyd Ratliff during the 1967 Gator Bowl.

3-yard line. But Penn State held as Jim Kates, the new middle guard, stopped a quarterback sneak from inside the 1 and Jim Litterelle chopped Hammond down on the 5 as he attempted a roll-out.

The Lions got out to the 15, with one foot to go on fourth down — and it happened.

Tom Sherman bucked straight ahead and the Florida State line hardly budged.

"The kids wanted to try it," said Paterno "and I didn't think anybody could stop a sneak on us."

According to Sherman, nobody did.

"I went up Lenkaitis' back," he said (Bill Lenkaitis is the Penn State center), "and I was over the 15-yard line. Then someone grabbed me by the seat of the pants and pulled me back."

Paterno said: "It was a very debatable call until I see the movies."

Anyway, it was now Florida State's ball, and two plays later Hammond passed 15 yards to Sellers for a touchdown, Sellers taking the ball on the 5 and dodging across the goal line.

Guthrie converted, Florida State kicked off and immediately afterward the Seminoles had the ball again. The kickoff went to Pittman, Mike Blatt jarred him into a fumble and Chuck Elliott recovered for Florida State on the Penn State 22.

A screen pass — Hammond to Bill Mooreman — put the Seminoles inside the 1, and this time Hammond's sneak made the end zone.

Penn State's offense, in the second half, produced only one first down and it came with three minutes left in the fourth quarter. Dan Lucyk gained two yards off tackle, enabling Penn State to keep the ball for another minute and a half. But when a third-and-five sweep by Pittman gained one yard less than the Lions needed, they had to punt, and Hammond passed Florida State right down the field.

First, though, he burst through the middle for 21 yards.

Fighting the clock, the Seminoles were lining up without a huddle. Hammond passed 13 yards to Lane Fenner, 12 to Moreman for a first down on the 13 and five more to Fenner, who fell out of bounds on the 8.

Then Hammond overthrew Moreman and Penn State's Bob Capretto saved a touchdown by knocking the ball out of Sellers' hands in the end zone.

So Guthrie came in and kicked a field goal.

Florida State coach Bill Peterson explained why he went for a tie.

"If we were the ones who were 17 points ahead, I'd have gone for the win," he said. "But the way we came back, I felt I couldn't throw it away."

Sherman had opened the scoring for Penn State with a field goal from the 27 in the first quarter. In the second quarter, he missed one from the 31, but Florida State was offside and Sherman got a touchdown out of it by passing to Jack Curry in the corner of the end zone on a play good for nine yards.

Then in the last two minutes of the half, Penn State drove 82 yards for a touchdown. Pittman ran 36 on a draw play, but it was Sherman himself who kept the Lions going. Blitzed on fourth down at the Florida State 27, he got away from four tacklers and scrambled down to the 12.

On the next play, after faking to Lucyk, he passed to Kwalick alone in the end zone.

Thus, two of the seven passes Sherman completed went for touchdowns. Hammond threw 53 times, still another Gator Bowl record, for his 37 completions.

Nittany Lions running back Bob Campbell looks for running room.

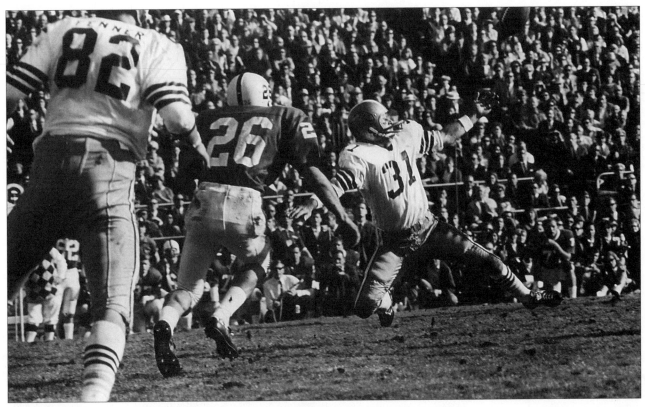

Penn State defender Neal Smith (26) looks to break up a second-quarter pass intended for Florida State's Bill Gunter (31). After taking a 17-0 lead in the first half, Smith and his teammates saw the Seminoles score 17 points in the second half.

Penn State had four interceptions and got to Hammond several times behind the line of scrimmage, with Frank Spaziani, Neal Smith and Steve Smear leading the rush.

"I said if we could get four interceptions and throw Hammond for four losses, we'd win," Paterno reflected. "Obviously, I wasn't right."

Don Abbey, the Lions' injured sophomore fullback, did not get into the game, even for a field goal attempt, but Bob Campbell was in uniform for the first time since a knee operation in October. He did the punting for Penn State.

One of his punts went 68 yards over the safety man's head and gave the Lions

Score by Periods

Penn State	3	14	0	0	— 17
Florida State	0	0	14	3	— 17

a breathing spell in the fourth quarter.

Paterno, who had held secret practices for 10 days before the game, said "the changes we made were great. They really helped us, but Florida did a great job of adjusting at halftime.

"I was pleased with the way we took the bomb away from them, though they had one and didn't hang onto it."

Sellers, in the clear once, dropped a pass when Capretto came up from behind. Later, Hammond overthrew

Sellers when Sellers was free for a touchdown catch.

"This is a funny ball club," Paterno said. "I don't know how to put my finger on it, but we get ahead and get tight. We get a little bit cautious."

The Lions won most of their games this season — they had an 8-2 record — by jumping off to an early lead and then surviving.

Someone asked Paterno about the rumor that the New York Jets want him to be their new coach.

"After the fourth-and-one call," he said, "I may not be coaching anywhere next year."

It was only an exit line, and not a bad one.

12th Man Boosts 'Dead' Lions in Orange Bowl Victory

By Roy McHugh
The Pittsburgh Press

Miami, Jan. 1, 1969 — Two minutes to play on a moon-less Miami night in the Orange Bowl. Kansas had the ball. Kansas had a first down. Kansas had a seven–point lead. There was no way Penn State could win.

Over the public-address system in the press box came the announcement that seemed to make it final: "Most Valuable play-er — Donnie Shanklin of Kansas."

There was no way Penn State would win, but Penn State won.

Penn State won, 15-14, on Chuck Burkhart's touchdown run in the clos-ing seconds and Bob Campbell's run for a two-point conversion after Kansas had given the Lions a second chance.

The last two minutes were pure, unadulterated insanity

It really started with Mike Reid, the toughest piano player in Altoona, bounding through the Kansas defense and dropping Jayhawk quarterback Bobby Douglass for a six-yard loss on second down. Situation still hopeless. But Penn State called a time out, stop-ping the clock.

Then here was Reid again, after Douglass and spilling him for a seven-yard loss. Another time out and now Kansas was punting from its 25-yard line.

In rushed Neal Smith from his safe-ty position to get a hand on the ball as it left the kicker's foot. The punt slant-ed off to the left and bounced to the Penn State 49-yard line.

Penn State had a minute 16 seconds and it obviously wouldn't be enough, for Kansas had been stopping the Lions cold.

Only this time the play was "One Go." On "One Go," Burkhart goes back with the ball and Campbell goes straight down the field. As Burkhart went back, the Kansas pass rush came — but not before Burkhart threw.

The ball came down between two defensive backs and right into Camp-bell's arms on the Kansas 20. Camp-bell stumbled forward. The Kansas backs stumbled after him, and he fell on the 3.

Penn State's last time out stopped the clock with 66 seconds left. Then it was Tom Cherry into the line for no gain and Cherry again into the line for no gain. Without a huddle, the Lions got over the ball.

Burkhart, taking the snap, faked to Don Abbey, then he faked to Charlie Pittman. Finally, all by himself, Burkhart rolled to his left and into the end zone untouched.

With fifteen seconds left, 14-13, there was no doubt what Penn State would do — go for two points, play to win. Burkhart rolled out and passed, but too high for Ted Kwalick's des-perate leap.

One Too Many

The Kansas band was on the field, Kansas rooters in the crowd of 77,000 were pouring down from the stands. And the officials were gesturing wild-ly, holding up their hands and point-ing to a flag on the goal line.

Kansas had stopped the conversion try with 12 men, which no matter how

Penn State's Charlie Pittman finished with 58 yards rushing and two receptions.

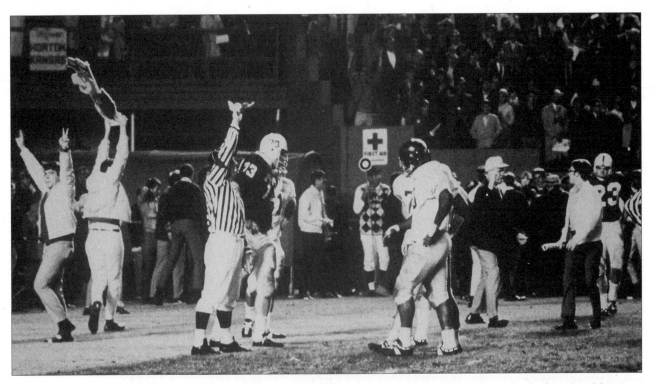

Kansas fans celebrate after the Jayhawks stopped Penn State's potential game-winning two-point conversion, but the celebration turned out to be premature. An official holds up a penalty flag, signalling that Kansas has 12 men on the field for the play.

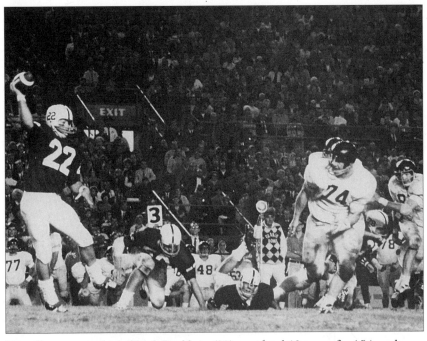

Penn State quarterback Chuck Burkhart (22) completed 12 passes for 154 yards.

you count it, is one too many. Suddenly, pandemonium sets in.

The penalty moved the ball from the 3 to inside the 2. And this time it was no pass, it was Campbell sweeping to his left, hurling himself over the goal line as Cherry took out the cornerback and Charlie Zapiec took out the all-American Kansas end, John Zook.

On the clock, it said 15 seconds.

When the clock was down to zero, on the first play after Penn State's kickoff, Steve Smear had a death grip on the 6-foot-4 Douglass and the Lions had topped off an undefeated season, making 19 games since the last time anyone beat them.

"To be honest," said Reid in the locker room, "I don't know how we won this one."

In the first quarter, Penn State had

It's official — State's Ted Kwalick, left, and Dennis Onkotz were 1968 all-Americans.

given the ball to Kansas three times — on two interceptions and a fumble — and, after the second interception, Kansas running the ball nine times, drove 45 yards to a touchdown, with Mike Reeves scoring from the 2.

AHEAD BUT TIED

Before the half was over, Penn State tied at 7-7 in much the same way, going 47 yards in six plays, all on the ground. The touchdown came on a 13-yard trap, Pittman up the middle undeterred.

Penn State finished the half outgaining Kansas by a 2-1 margin, Campbell alone running for 93 yards, but the score was still 7-7.

Quarterback Burkhart Invented the Play

BY ROY McHUGH
The Pittsburgh Press

Chuck Burkhart invented the play. He invented it as he took the ball from center.

It was third down on the Kansas 3-yard line with Penn State behind, 14-7, and 22 seconds left in the Orange Bowl game.

Only moments before, on the sideline, Coach Joe Paterno had given his quarterback a sequence of three plays to run without a huddle, for Penn State had exhausted its supply of timeouts.

The first two were straight off-tackle plays and they had gained exactly nothing. Now Chuck Burkhart was to use the Penn State scissor play, faking to Don Abbey, the fullback, and handing off to Charlie Pittman, the halfback, when Pittman criss-crossed.

But as he looked out over the line and into the eyes behind the cages on the red Kansas helmets, Burkhart decided to do something else.

"I don't know why," he was saying in the Penn State locker room, which had a placid, sweetly reasonable air last night, as if nobody thought it unusual at all to win an Orange Bowl game impossibly.

"Sometimes you have things in the back of your mind," Burkhart said. "I was going to hand off, but you can sense things happening. I made a fake and out of the corner of my eye I couldn't see anyone off to the left."

ONE FOR THE MONEY

So Burkhart pivoted and ran. The Kansas defense tackled Abbey, it tackled the empty-handed Pittman. But Burkhart was running off by himself around end and over the goal line.

Said a faintly bemused Bob Campbell, "We don't even have that play. But it worked, so we should put it in the book."

Penn State does have the play, a sweep to the left, on which Campbell scored the two-point conversion that won the game.

And Penn State has the play on which Burkhart passed 48 yards to Campbell, setting up the play he originated on the spot.

"It's call 'One Go,' I think," Campbell said, "Either 'One Go' or

Score by Periods

Penn State	0	7	0	8	— 15
Kansas	7	0	0	7	— 14

Once when Douglass passed from his 9-yard line with Smear wrapped around his ankles, Dennis Onkotz deflected the ball and Mike Smith intercepted it, making a 23-yard runback to the 11. At the 6, however, Cherry fumbled and then, on the last play of the half, Rusty Garthwaite missed a 31-yard field goal attempt.

The third quarter started with Burkhart completing three straight third-down passes and moving Penn State to the Kansas 5. There the underrated Kansas line yielded only four and a half yards to Cherry in three carries. Then Emory Hicks, a linebacker, shot through to nail Pittman on the 2 and the ball belonged to Kansas.

Douglass, running and passing, got field position for Kansas early in the fourth quarter. Penn State had to punt from its 14 and Shanklin, winning his premature MVP spurs, returned the ball 46 yards to the 7.

Two plays later, John Riggins bolted across from the 1.

As time passed, and Penn State did nothing, it looked like the end. But it wasn't.

The 1969 Orange Bowl program.

'One Up.' No, it's 'One Go.' "

It sure was.

Burkhart, smiling — Burkhart always is smiling — said, "I really didn't get everything I wanted on the ball," but his coach was in no mood to quibble.

"I wish," Paterno sighed, "that somebody would say something nice about Burkhart. The maligned Burkhart. The lousy passer.

"Chuckie's had bad passes all year. He had a couple of bad passes tonight, but I've said a thousand times when he comes back to the bench, he's never licked. He has character and he's got that innate quality that makes him a big-leaguer, a winner."

You could look it up. As a starting quarterback, both in high school and college, Burkhart has yet to play in a losing game.

The same thing is true of Charlie Pittman. Then there's Campbell.

"He's been our money player all year," said Steve Smear.

Someone asked Campbell if he knew that Donnie Shanklin of Kansas, in an election that took place before the game was over, had won the MVP award.

"Who's Shanklin?," he asked, honestly puzzled. Then it came to him. "Is he the one who ran back the punt?"

FORGET A TIE

"Well, that figures," he said. "How many people went home?"

When the crowd did go home, Paterno was going to see to it that no one had wasted his time.

He never considered — even briefly — going for a one-point conversion and a tie.

"You go to a bowl to win," Paterno said.

Kansas coach Pepper Rodgers might have won it with a fourth-quarter field goal when Kansas was still leading. But on fourth and one at Penn State's 5-yard line, he called a running play and the Lions stopped it.

"I considered a field goal," drawled Rodgers, "but not until after I called the running play."

Kansas might have won it, too, if there had not been an extra man on the field when Penn State's first try for the two-point conversion turned into an incomplete pass.

"We goofed up," Pepper said. "Oh, it was awful."

He glanced at Jim Ryan, the newspaper photographer from Topeka who won all his races last year except the big one, the one in the Olympics.

"When you win all the time, losing is twice as bad," Rodgers said. "Isn't it, Jim?"

Inspired Lions Bounce Back to Defeat Syracuse

By Phil Musick
The Pittsburgh Press

Syracuse, N.Y., Oct. 18, 1969 — A great football team beat a good football team on a bad day, and everyone agreed — as a character builder — Joe Paterno has few peers.

After giving a classic performance yesterday of the old, old football exercise — "sucking in your guts" — the Nittany Lions to a man pointed to pride as the raison d'etre for Syracuse's sudden and unexpected demise before a record Homecoming crowd of 42,291 that really didn't believe what it saw.

When it was over and Penn State had jammed 15 points into a hectic 3:17 of the fourth quarter to whip the inspired Orangemen, 15-14, the fans stood and gave Coach Ben Schwartzwalder's dead-game troops a standing ovation.

Paterno would have stood and applauded too had he not been in the Lions' dressing room and drinking deeply of the sweet, sweet essence of victory.

"I wish someone would say how great our football team really is," he said of his Lions, who made Syracuse their 16th consecutive victim and protected the nation's longest non-losing streak, 24 games.

Score by Periods

Penn State	0	0	0	15	— 15
Syracuse	7	7	0	0	— 14

Legendary Lions: Lydell Mitchell (23), Lenny Moore and Charlie Pittman (24).

"When you beat a good football team on a bad day you're great. They were awful strong ... awful strong."

Craggy old Archbold Stadium — a concrete inner-city bowl that leaves you expecting the Christians vs. the Lions at any moment — hummed from beginning to end.

Punt returns of 61, 46 and 46 yards by a sophomore back who Schwartzwalder says "always runs out of gas," Greg Allen, allowed the Orange to completely dominate the first half.

But the Lions' character came to the fore in the final two quarters, along with a defensive effort that finally turned off Syracuse's electrifying attack.

"I told our kids at halftime that I didn't care if we won or lost, but that they would find out something about themselves as men in the second half," Paterno said. Knute Rockne, himself, couldn't have said it better.

Inspired, the Lions took it to Syracuse in the fourth quarter after being totally stymied in the first three periods and being down, 14-0, going into the last 15 minutes.

"I was really worried if we could ever move the ball on them," Paterno admitted after Penn State had won its third straight Homecoming encounter and handed Syracuse its second loss in five games. "We practiced all week on the big play."

That practice paid a dividend in the fourth quarter when sophomore fullback Franco Harris roared through a block by guard Charlie Zapiec and outran a Syracuse defender 36 yards for the touchdown that tied the game, 14-14. Mike Reitz's extra point untied it and Penn State's hopes for its second straight undefeated season received a shot in the arm.

"A run like that's instinctive," said Harris, who went all the way at full-

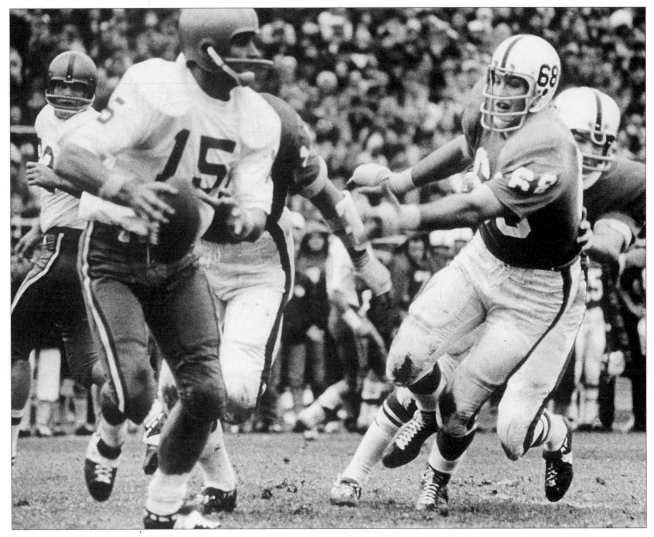

Above, Penn State's Mike Reid puts on a heavy rush in the Nittany Lions' 15-14 victory over Syracuse in 1969. Below, Reid, right, and Charlie Pittman were named all-America by the American Football Coaches Association.

back because of an injury that benched veteran Don Abbey. "We never lost confidence, we knew what we could do in the clutch."

What Penn State could do in the clutch became apparent with 10:18 remaining to play when a Lions defense that had been embarrassed all afternoon came alive with a vengeance as linebacker Jack Ham recovered an Al Newton fumble at the Orange 32.

Seven plays later, a pass interference

penalty against Syracuse safety Don Dorr gave the Lions the ball at the Orange 4-yard line. On the next play Lydell Mitchell rammed over for the touchdown that gave Lions fans some hope. It even gave Paterno hope.

"It was in my mind that we had to get the big play," Paterno said. "We had to get momentum and I knew we couldn't ram one down their throats."

The imperturbable Penn State defense was willing to try, however, and

Lydell Mitchell, left, led Penn State in rushing in both the 1970 and 1971 seasons, and finished with 2,934 career yards. Franco Harris, right, had five 100-yard rushing games during his career.

stiffened Syracuse on three straight plays in the series following the Lions' first touchdown.

Syracuse punted, Harris hit for a yard to the Orange 36 and then made a bit of philosophy by Zapiec stand up when he burst away for the touchdown that tied it with 7:01 left to play.

"If we couldn't have won this kind of a game, we couldn't have had a great season," said Zapiec. "We'll remember this one for a long time."

Harris will, indeed, remember it for a long time. His two-point run for the conversion after the Penn State touchdown was pivotal and came after he failed on a previous attempt, getting a second chance due to a Syracuse penalty.

Among other things, it gave rise to a feeling, not shared by Paterno, that it's all downhill from Syracuse for the Lions, who face lightweights such as Ohio U., Boston College and Pitt in their final five games.

The first of Syracuse's three interceptions set up the Orangemen's first touchdown, as Gary Bletch returned a Chuck Burkhart pass 32 yards to the Lions 24. Tailback Ron Trask got 13 yards to the 8-yard line and Newton punched over from a yard out.

Again, Allen streaked away on a punt, this time taking one 46 yards as Syracuse set up shop on the Lions 6-yard line with only :45 gone in the second quarter. Quarterback Randy Zur

then rolled wide to his right and cut back for six yards and Syracuse's second touchdown.

But the Orange blew a third scoring opportunity when Allen carried his third punt reception 46 yards to the Penn State 29. A minute later, on a fourth-and-one play from the Lions 3, Allen fell down on a sweep.

"That was the key play," said Paterno. "It kept us in the game. It would have been very rough getting 21 points back with them fired up like that."

Above, Charlie Pittman, who led Penn State with 706 yards rushing in 1969, turns the corner; Left, Penn State's 1969 starting offensive unit poses for a group shot.

Burkhart Has Last Laugh on Missouri in Orange Bowl Win

By Phil Musick
The Pittsburgh Press

Miami, Jan. 1, 1970 — Exit Chuck Burkhart ... laughing. He stood there in front of his locker, sticking out a hairless chest defiantly, and his catfish grin told it all: "Yeah, you boobs," it snickered, "you don't believe it, do you."

Chuck Burkhart, Penn State's "poor soul," the kid who could "only" win, was the 36th Orange Bowl's most valuable back. Uneasy reporters, who had mocked his talents, were Burkhart's delight.

Forcing nine turnovers — seven on pass interceptions — Penn State made powderkeg Missouri victim No. 30, 10-3, but the most brilliant defensive effort in the school's history was saved by a Burkhart offensive effort.

For probably the first time in his life, Burkhart was cocky. He completed 11 of 26 passes for 187 yards and the only touchdown in a game that saw Penn State's defense simply overpower and out-talent Missouri's quicksilver offense.

"A couple of more games and we'll get the Big Eight title," crowed Burkhart to the unbelievers, who finally had to believe.

The Lions' 22nd straight win, third this year over a Big Eight foe, was heady stuff. "Yeah, I'd like to try the pro's," Burkhart laughed. Not a writer

Score by Periods

Penn State	10	0	0	0	— 10
Missouri	0	3	0	0	— 3

blinked; no one sneered. Best of all, the pros like a winner.

The explanations for Penn State's triumph over a team that had averaged 36 points a game fell like the rain that drenched a record crowd of 78,282 during the second half.

But perhaps the most pertinent one came earlier in the week when Lions assistant coach Frank Patrick said of Missouri quarterback Terry McMillan, "he throws long and he throws high. I like the high part."

McMillan, manhandled by Penn

State defensive tackles Steve Smear and Mike Reid, the game's most valuable lineman, threw more interceptions (five) than completions (four).

The seven pass thefts set an Orange Bowl record and scotched the five Missouri drives that had reached Penn State territory.

"That's the best secondary ever put together," said Lions defensive boss Jim O'Hora, after backs George Landis and Neal Smith and linebacker Denny Onkotz had each picked off two Tigers passes. The other Penn State interception was made by end Gary Hull.

"How could any team in the country be better than Penn State?" asked Missouri coach Dan Devine, who had no excuses and few explanations.

"Terry wouldn't want any excuses and I don't either," Devine said. "We couldn't block Smear and Reid. They got in there and got the job done. I did a poor job preparing my team in so many ways, I couldn't be specific."

Devine wouldn't elaborate and McMillan, shaken up in the second quarter by Reid, sat over in a corner crying.

His replacement, junior Chuck Roper, knew how he felt. Roper threw two interceptions himself and the last one, by Landis with 53 seconds to play, proved that the Penn State defense wasn't too whipped to do it — as a school official cried — "one more time."

Missouri, held to a 35-yard field goal by Henry Brown with 1:56 to go in the second quarter, gasped out one final drive in the final two minutes on a pair of Roper-to-end-John Henley passes for 10 and 33 yards, but Landis, hobbled by a knee injury, was equal to the test.

The red-haired junior, who blanked one of Missouri's most potent weapons,

Penn State's defense gave up 306 total yards in the 1970 Orange Bowl, but allowed only three points and forced nine Missouri turnovers, including seven pass interceptions.

end Mel Gray, stole a pass for Henley at the Lions 3 and returned it to the Tigers' 42.

Smoke bombs burst on the field and thousands of youngsters roared on to the soggy Orange Bowl turf. They knew it was over, but Burkhart had to kill a minute with four sneaks to prove it to the officials.

Missouri's best weapons in the first half were punt returns of 47 and 48 yards by Jon Staggers, and the Tigers got to the Lions' 26, 47, 7, 18 and 8 only to have Reid put them back in the bag.

Missouri tried to contain the all-America tackle with another all-American, offensive tackle Mike Carroll, but Carroll wasn't quite ready for Reid, who forced three Tiger turnovers in the first half and another in the third quarter.

The game began in 75-degree temperatures and Missouri immediately picked up momentum behind Staggers' power sweeps.

But Brown missed a 47-yard field goal try on the Tigers' first series. On the following series, the Lions' Mike Reitz drilled home a 29-yard field goal to put Penn State on the board with 3:42 remaining in the opening quarter.

On Missouri's first play from scrimmage following the Lions kickoff, Reid racked Tigers fullback Joe Moore and linebacker Mike Smith recovered the first of Missouri's four fumbles at the losers' 28.

Burkhart, who had lost a contact lens on the prior series, rolled out and threw to halfback Lydell Mitchell for the game's only touchdown. "I probably throw better without it," grinned Burkhart.

Mitchell's score, set up by tight end Pete Johnson's crackback block, made it 10-0, with 3:23 to play in the period.

Staggers returned a Penn State punt 64 yards in the final minute of the second quarter, but Reid blew in on McMillan and his wobbly pass was snatched by Hull.

Burkhart, who was dropped for 76 yards in losses, faltered briefly in the second quarter, throwing an interception, but Missouri couldn't capitalize on it.

"I always thought Burkhart was a great passer, but we never gave him an opportunity like we did tonight," said Penn State coach Joe Paterno, who told a few reporters yesterday morning that Penn State would pass "at least 20 times," and "couldn't run outside."

Landis intercepted at the Missouri 34 midway in the quarter, but Penn State was forced to punt. McMillan then ran 30 yards to set the Tigers up at the Penn State 9. But, on a reverse, Lions end John Ebersole stripped Gray of the ball and recovered it at the 22 to end that threat.

Staggers' second sprint with a punt later put Missouri in possession at the

Penn State's Lydell Mitchell (23) scores the only touchdown of the 1970 Orange Bowl, a 28-yard pass from Chuck Burkhart that got past Missouri's Lorenzo Brinkley.

Penn State 18, but Reid shook off Carroll to rip McMillan, and Onkotz swiped a pass at the 4.

Late in the first half, Missouri parlayed a 40-yard pass from McMillan to Moore and some shifty inside running by Staggers to move 85 yards to the Penn State 8-yard line.

Landis' Miracle Allows Him to Seal Lions' Win

The Pittsburgh Press

Fate, thought George Landis, was in his corner when he intercepted a pass last night to nail down Penn State's 10-3 Orange Bowl triumph over Missouri.

"It was a miracle," Landis said of his recovery from a knee injury he received three days ago when he stepped into a hole during practice. "I jumped maybe a foot or so in the air and came down in the hole, and my leg collapsed"

"I prayed so hard … so hard. I couldn't even walk on it when I got up Wednesday and I put ice on it all night."

Landis intercepted two passes and played Missouri's sprint-champion pass receiver Mel Gray closely, shutting out the slick split end for the first time this season.

His interception on the Penn State 3 with 56 seconds remaining wiped out the last of an endless series of Missouri drives.

"Gray had run right by me the series before," Landis explained his critical interception. "On that last play I stood here, and that ran through my mind."

Gray couldn't run through Landis' zone in the Penn State secondary, however. "Yeah, I adjusted for him," Landis grinned. "I played away from him. I was running so deep I could barely make out the quarterback."

The quarterback of whom Landis was speaking wasn't Terry McMillan, who sat out much of the second half

Linebacker Dennis Onkotz (35) intercepted two passes against Missouri — as did Penn State teammates George Landis and Neal Smith.

But Reid and Smear dumped McMillan back on the 17 and Missouri settled for Brown's field goal to make it 10-3.

That was it, Neal Smith picked off his 11th and 12th interceptions in the second half and Onkotz and Landis each got a second steal.

Missouri tried a 52-yard field goal that missed early in the final quarter, after Penn State blew one from the 18 with just 2:50 into the period.

Burkhart set it up with a throw to Pete Johnson for 56 yards, but two straight offensive penalties checked the drive. When Charlie Pittman was stopped at the 1-yard line, Paterno elected to try the field goal.

"A field goal wins it," said Paterno. "I didn't want to do the same thing we did last year down here." Penn State beat Kansas, 15-14, in the 1969 classic on a last-second touchdown scamper by … uh … Burkhart.

Would Penn State be No. 1 nationally when the final tally is made?

"I'm up to my ears in polls — I'm tired of the controversy," said Paterno.

"People said I was sour grapes, that I shot off my mouth. But I was willing to go out on a limb for my kids. Maybe we're not the best, but how could anyone be better?"

Don't worry about it, Joe. Everybody said Burkhart couldn't pass, too.

after stopping Mike Reid's right shoulder with his rib cage.

"My back has been bothering me," McMillan told a St. Louis writer, "but I don't want an excuse."

Missouri officials successfully shielded McMillan from the impudent Eastern press, as they had all week.

"Get out of here, he doesn't want his picture taken," growled a Missouri assistant coach, one of a cordon of people who protected McMillan much more successfully than the Tiger offensive line.

Coach Joe Paterno wanted no part of any No. 1 talk. He just told it like it was.

"It was our great second half defense,' he said. "George kept yelling to throw more, but I wanted to sit on the 10-3 lead. I didn't want to take any chances."

Taking chances is a part of the Paterno makeup, but backfield coach George Welsh's advice was rejected.

Paterno had done his gambling early this week when he moved Penn State out of its normal man-to-man pass defense and shifted to a zone. "I felt we could play a zone on them but they tried to run the ball and they simply couldn't handle Reid and Smear."

Paterno wasn't worried that his defense, which had the finest of its many fine hours, would finally surrender its stamina and let a chance at being No. 1 be lost to Missouri's explosive offensive.

"I told them at halftime that 'you can't run out of gas … you worked too hard to get here,' " said Paterno. "We told them that you just don't get tired in a game like this."

Landis, warned by Paterno at halftime, "not to lose Gray in the zone," wasn't even winded. "What do you mean, tired?" he asked.

Penn State Explodes in 2nd Half, Rips Longhorns, 30-6

BY PHIL MUSICK
The Pittsburgh Press

Dallas, Jan. 1, 1972 — Penn State, trailing by 6-3 at halftime, broke loose for 17 points in the third quarter and went on to butcher Texas in the Cotton Bowl yesterday.

Lydell Mitchell and John Hufnagel

Texas quarterback Eddie Phillips loses most of his jersey as he is dropped for a 6-yard loss by Jim Laslavic (47) of Penn State.

led the Lions' second-half charge as the Penn State defense stopped the Longhorns in their tracks.

Penn State survived the vaunted Texas wishbone on the Longhorns' first offensive series. Texas drove to the Penn State 30, but quarterback Eddie Phillips was trapped for losses on two straight plays and the Longhorns punted, downing the ball at the Lions 2-yard line.

Penn State couldn't move the ball and a 28-yard punt by Bob Parsons gave Texas excellent field position at the Lions 35 and it was worth three points.

The Longhorns moved to the 19, but Phillips lost a yard and threw an incomplete pass and, with 1:14 to play in the first quarter, Steve Valek kicked a 29-yard field goal to give Texas a 3-0 lead.

The wishbone snapped the next time Texas had the ball. Fullback Dennis Ladd was racked up by linebackers John Skorupan and Tom Hull at the Longhorn's 20 and fumbled the ball into the hands of defensive halfback Chuck Mesko.

Penn State, with Mitchell getting

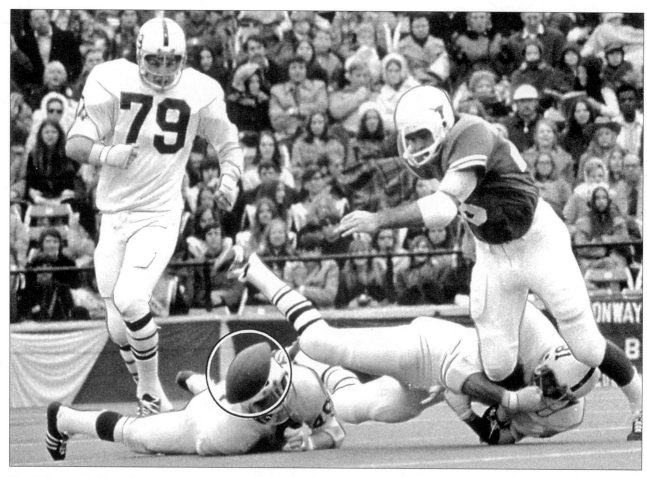

Texas' Dennis Ladd, right, lost control of the ball after a hard hit by Penn State's John Skorupan (81) in the second quarter. Texas went into halftime with a 6-3 advantage, but the second half turned ugly for the Longhorns, who yielded 27 points.

yardage off tackle, drove to the Texas 5, but a third-down reverse cost the Lions a yard and Alberto Vitiello kicked a 21-yard field goal with 10:38 left in the first half.

The stalemate survived until the final play of the second quarter when Valek kicked a 40-yard field goad to give the Longhorns a 6-3 lead.

Texas struck suddenly to go ahead. Penn State had moved to the Longhorn 40, but with 19 seconds remaining in the half Texas linebacker Glenn Gaspard made a one-handed interception of a Hufnagel pass and returned it 23 yards to the 40.

Score by Periods

Penn State	0	3	17	10 —	30
Texas	3	3	0	0 —	6

Two Phillips' passes to split end Pat Kelley set up Valek's second field goal. Coming into the game, he had missed five of six attempts.

Forcing Penn State to scramble after the ground-control attack of the wishbone offense, Texas controlled the ball for 16:59 of the first half, but twice lost scoring opportunities because of fumbles and ran for only 199 yards.

Defensive end Jim Laslavic, keying on Phillips much of the time, made 10 tackles in the first half.

Texas' third fumble proved costly. On the opening series of the second half, Phillips fumbled a handoff. Laslavic accidentally kicked in 10 yards downfield and Lions linebacker Charlie Zapiec outran Don Burrisk for the ball, covering it on the Longhorn 41.

It took Penn State just five plays to earn a 10-6 lead, only four minutes into the third quarter. Mitchell, who had 48 yards rushing on 11 carries in the first half, hit the middle for 20 and, a play later, Hufnagel drilled a pass to

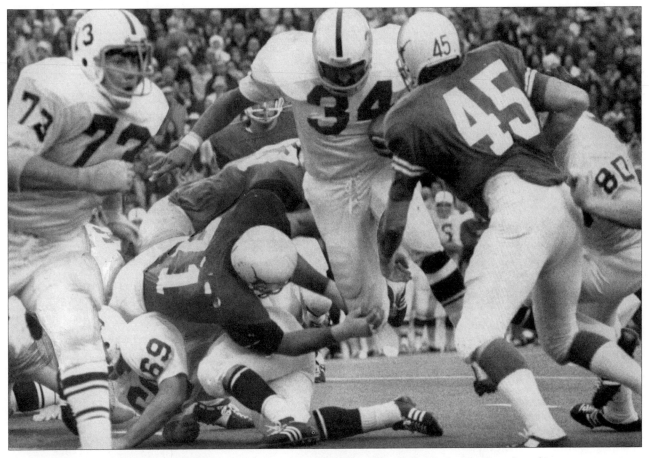

Franco Harris (34) bulls through the Texas line during the third quarter. Harris finished with 47 yards rushing.

tight end Bob Parsons at the Texas 1. Mitchell bucked over for the touchdown and Vitiello converted.

Less than three minutes later, Penn State struck again. On the second play after a Texas punt, Hufnagel rolled to his right at the State 35 and threw a strike to split end Scott Sharzynski, who had gotten 15 yards behind Texas safetyman Mike Bayer. The 65-yard pass play gave Penn State a 17-6 lead with 8:44 to play in the third quarter.

Coach Joe Paterno, left, leads the Nittany Lions in a victory cheer following Penn State's thrashing of Texas in the 1972 Cotton Bowl.

Paterno Proclaims 1973 Lions: 'Best Team I Ever Had'

By BILL HEUFELDER
The Pittsburgh Press

Miami, Jan. 1, 1974 — If Penn State is not the best college football team in the land, it is No. 1 among the eight clubs Joe Paterno has coached at the school. Who says so? Joe Paterno.

"This is the best team I've ever had," he said after the fifth–ranked Lions beat stubborn L.S.U., 16-9, last night in the Orange Bowl on a surface that, if it were used as a bath mat, would cause more fatalities than automobiles.

Paterno conducted his own poll among the players in the dressing room. "The vote was unanimous," he grinned. "We're No. 1.

"Seriously, I don't know if we're No. 1, but we have as much right as anyone to be there. We're 12-0. I'm not going to say we're better than anyone else. That's silly. But we're as good as anyone else until someone beats us."

Well, L.S.U., twice-beaten during the regular season, had the best chance of any Penn State opponent this year. What the Tigers couldn't overcome was the Penn State defense and sturdy pass blocking that enabled Tom Shuman to combine with Chuck Herd on a spectacular 72-yard scoring play.

Neither club could conquer the treacherous Poly-Turf, soaked by a pre-game shower.

Score by Periods

Penn State	3	13	0	0	— 16
L.S.U.	7	0	2	0	— 9

"L.S.U. was the quickest, toughest opponent against us for the longest stretch," Paterno complimented.

The officials perhaps buoyed L.S.U.'s persevering spirit with a couple of calls which, as the unerring television instant replay attested, proved they used bad judgment.

On Penn State's first series of the second quarter, Herd snapped up a long Shuman pass in full stride near the end line. An official ruled Herd had stepped out of the end zone before catching the ball. The camera showed otherwise.

The Lions surrendered the ball on Brian Masella's punt, but held the Tigers inside the 20, forcing them to kick.

Gary Hayman, who led the nation in punt-return average, was well on his way to a touchdown runback when the play was called dead. An official signaled Hayman had touched a knee to the ground as he slipped on the Poly-Turf at the start of the run. Again, the replay proved the official wrong.

"I asked the referee on the next series and he said my knee touched and that was the only way I could have been ruled down," said Hayman, who had outraced the L.S.U. defense at the 25 when an official motioned for him to stop.

"I didn't argue with him," Hayman said, "but I know my knee didn't touch."

The series ended successfully, however, when Herd came back to snatch Shuman's long pass with one hand and carry it into the end zone with two defenders in futile pursuit for a 72-yard scoring play.

Chris Bahr, who gave another zany kicking performance — hitting a 44-yard field goal yet missing an extra point — converted and sent the Lions ahead, 10-3. The soccer all-American connected on only 32 of 42 conversions during the regular season.

With 2:19 left in the half, John Cappelletti completed a 74-yard drive by hurtling over the stacked L.S.U. defense from the 2.

A Heisman Trophy winner who had twice rushed for more than 1,000 yards in a season, the big tailback ran out of running room against the Tigers. Despite the absence of two regular linebackers, they held him to 50 yards in 26 carries, a meager 1.6 average.

Penn State's Chuck Herd (25) is off and running — and behind the L.S.U. secondary — on a 72-yard touchdown pass from Tom Shuman in the first half of the Nittany Lions' 16-9 Orange Bowl victory.

"The holes weren't there," admitted his favorite blocker, guard Mark Markovich. "We just had trouble blocking their defenses."

Cappelletti, who suffered a slightly sprained ankle last Friday, refused to use the injury as an excuse. "No, it didn't bother me," he said. "Their defense just played well. Their linebackers were plugging the holes. I don't feel badly. I just tried to do the best I could."

Cappelletti was bothered by the Poly-Turf, calling it "the worst surface I ever played on."

Paterno said he thought "Cappy played a good game," despite netting

only 50 yards. "The trouble was we weren't making the holes."

With 1:30 left in the half, L.S.U. was in trouble with a fourth-and-one situation on its 19, so Penn State called a time out, hoping to conserve enough time to increase its 16-7 lead.

Instead, a Lions penalty on the L.S.U. punt and the clever maneuvering of quarterback Mike Miley soon put the ball on the Penn State 9 with 11 seconds left.

Miley then hit Joe Fakier on a four-yard gain that demoralized L.S.U. coach Charlie McClendon. "We thought he was gonna score,"

McClendon said, "but Fakier got stuck." Defensive back Jim Bradley rushed up to flatten the receiver.

"We didn't anticipate that," McClendon said. "That man (Bradley) was not supposed to be anywhere near Fakier, but he ignored our wide man."

Without any more time outs, the Tigers, trailing 16-7, could not make use of the final two seconds. Miley elected to throw the ball away in an unsuccessful effort to kill the clock.

Early in the fourth quarter, it was Randy Crowder, Penn State's all-American defensive tackle, who confused the line and picked off Miley's pass over

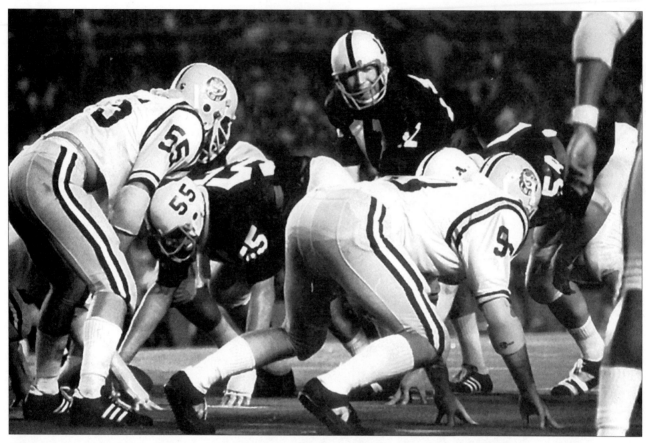

Penn State quarterback Tom Shuman (12) was only 6-for-17, but his TD pass to Chuck Herd was the game's key play.

the middle at the L.S.U. 39.

"He started to go inside me," explained another all-American, stumpy guard Tyler Lafauci, "then he went outside and back inside again. Then he just stood there with his hands up in the air.

"I didn't know what to think."

The Tigers moved into a position to at least gain a tie when Masella fell on a high snap from center in the end zone for a safety.

So the Lions turned once more to their strength — the defense — to preserve the third Orange Bowl triumph of the Paterno era.

Making what proved to be their last

Heisman Trophy winner John Cappelletti (22) was held to 50 yards, but scored once.

L.S.U. coach Charlie McClendon, left, and Penn State coach Joe Paterno shake hands after the Nittany Lions' victory.

Chuck Herd is congratulated by Penn State assistant Booker Brooks after catching a Tom Shuman pass and racing 72 yards for the Nittany Lions' first touchdown.

serious threat, the Tigers, on fourth-and-three at the Penn State 27, called on their leading runner, Brad Davis. He took a pitchout, but quickly was upset by linebacker Doug Allen and went down at the 31, a four-yard loss.

"I called a switch at the line before the snap," Allen said, "so I took the 'pitch' man and the end in front of me covered the quarterback. The way they lined up dictated it."

Only once did the Tigers dominate the Penn State defensive unit and that was on the opening drive when they scored within four minutes.

"We weren't taking off," Crowder said. "Instead of making things happen, we were letting them make things happen. After that, we started taking off."

Linebacker Ed O'Neil took off on the subject of the polls and Notre Dame's 24-23 win over Alabama in the Sugar Bowl, which was billed as the national championship.

"I think we're the number one team in the country," he protested.

"I heard a lot of talk on TV last night about Notre Dame saying it's the champion. I don't think they won the championship because they haven't played us."

BY STEVE HALVONIK
Pittsburgh Post-Gazette

John Cappelletti hadn't planned on talking about his 11-year-old brother Joey, who was stricken with leukemia, when he stood to deliver his 1973 Heisman Trophy acceptance speech.

"Most of the things I had put on paper were the mundane things — people to thank, football memories," Cappelletti said. "I had been thinking about Joseph, some things had been going through my head. When I saw my family sitting down front, something just clicked."

Cappelletti, who was seated next to Vice President Gerald Ford at the dais, opened his speech with the usual tributes to teammates, parents, and other acquaintances. But his voice began to quake as he focused on Joey and his brother's losing fight with cancer.

Most of the guests at The Waldorf-Astoria were unaware of Joey's illness. Many began to weep after John recalled the day that Penn State coach Joe Paterno had visited his house on a recruiting trip and found Joey on the couch, ill.

"A lot of people think I go through a lot on Saturdays, getting bumps and bruises," John Cappelletti said, holding back tears. "But for me, it's only on Saturdays and only in the fall. For Joey, it's all year round and it's a never-ending battle.

"The Heisman Trophy is more his

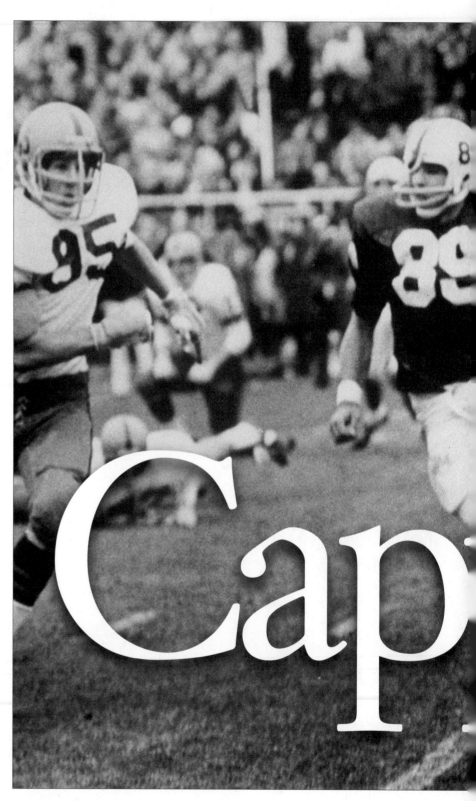

Cap

John Cappellitti brushes a tear from his eye as he returns to his seat following an emotion-filled speech in which he dedicated his Heisman Trophy to his younger brother, Jospeh, who was battling cancer.

In a scene from the CBS-TV movie, "Something for Joey," John Cappellitti (Mark Singer) listens to advice from his coach, Joe Paterno (Paul Piscerni).

Prior to the Heisman Dinner, Cappellitti poses for a photo being taken by his younger brother, Joseph.

than mine because he's been a great inspiration to me … if I can dedicate this trophy to him tonight and give him a couple of days of happiness, it would mean everything."

By now, "everybody in the room was fighting runaway emotion," Paterno said in his autobiography, *Paterno: By the Book*. "The vice president sat there all flushed. His eyes, I thought, glistened."

Even Bishop Fulton J. Sheen, a polished speaker who had to deliver the benediction, found Cappel-

letti a tough act to follow.

"Maybe for the first time in your lives you have heard a speech from the heart and not from the lips," Sheen told the audience. "Part of John's triumph was made by Joseph's sorrow. You don't need a blessing. God has already blessed you in John Cappelletti."

Cappelletti's powerful speech resonated across the nation, striking a deep emotional chord in football and non-football fans alike. It inspired a made-for-TV movie, called *Something*

In this series of photos, Cappelletti shows the great talent that earned him both the Heisman and Maxwell trophies in 1973.

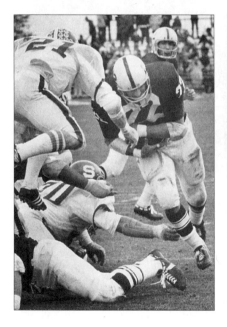

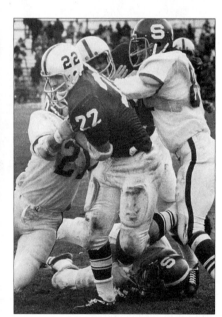

For Joey. And it has become part of Heisman history.

"John's acceptance speech is considered the most moving ever given at these ceremonies," the Downtown Athletic Club, the Heisman's sponsor, says in its annual awards program.

Joseph Cappelletti lost his fight with leukemia, passing away in 1976. But his memory still shines brightly in John's home in Laguna Niguel, Calif.

The Heisman Trophy that he dedicated to his brother sits on a mantel in the family room. Pictures of Joseph, clutching the Heisman, are on display in the children's playroom.

Cappellitti says he still thinks about his brother, whom he always calls "Joseph," whenever he looks at the Heisman.

"I still have vivid memories of the awards dinner and my family," he says.

And of his unprecedented career at Penn State.

Cappelletti is the only Nittany Lion to win a Heisman Trophy, and it came at the end of what still ranks as the second-best rushing season in school history. Cappelletti plowed for 1,522 yards and 17 touchdowns and led Penn State to its third undefeated season in six years.

Only Lydell Mitchell has ever gained more yards in a season, picking up 1,567 in 1971.

Cappelletti's 286 rushing attempts and three 200-yard rushing games still stand as school records.

Although he started at tailback for only two seasons, Cappelletti still ranks sixth in career rushing, with 2,639 yards.

The converted defensive back rushed for 100 or more yards 13 times in his storybook career with the Lions,

averaging 5.1 yards a carry.

Cappelletti rushed for 1,117 yards as a junior, but wasn't mentioned as a leading Heisman contender before his senior season. He sat out Penn State's 14-0 loss to Oklahoma at the end of his junior year, denying him valuable exposure in the national media.

Cappelletti picked up 735 yards

during Penn State's 7-0 start in 1973, but remained little more than a dark-horse because of the media bias against Eastern football.

Cappelletti forced everyone to take a second look at himself and at Penn State with an incredible closing kick — 787 rushing yards in the final four games.

Cappelletti still recalls how it all started, with a private pep talk from Paterno just before Game 8, against Maryland.

Paterno told Cappelletti not worry about Heisman speculation. Focus instead on what you can can control — your performance on the field, Paterno counseled. The rest will fall into place.

Cappelletti went out and carried the ball a school-record 37 times, for 202 yards, against the Terrapins.

"That was the game that started the boom for Cappelletti as a Heisman candidate," Paterno recalled.

Cappelletti followed that with 41 carries for 220 yards in a 35-29 victory over North Carolina State.

"I think I probably got as much, or more, satisfaction out of that game than from any other at Penn State," he says.

Cappelletti continued his roll by bulling for 204 yards against Ohio University, giving him an NCAA-record three straight games of 200 or more yards rushing.

By the season finale, Cappelletti was in the thick of the Heisman race. He clinched the trophy with his 161-yard effort in a 35-13 win over the Pitt Panthers, sealing Penn State's unde-

In his senior season, Cappellitti rushed for 1,522 yards and 17 touchdowns.

feated (11-0) regular season.

Penn State's Orange Bowl matchup against L.S.U. was anti-climactic.

In spite of their undefeated record, the Lions were a non-factor in the championship picture. The glamour game was Notre Dame and Alabama in the Sugar Bowl.

Penn State beat L.S.U., 16-9, but finished fifth in the final Associated Press and UPI polls.

Notre Dame, which upset Alabama, 24-23, was crowned No. 1 by The Associated Press.

Paterno was livid that his Lions had been snubbed yet again. So he con-

ducted his own poll in the Penn State locker room. He came out and proclaimed Penn State No. 1, and ordered championship rings for players and coaches.

Paterno's gesture notwithstanding, the Orange Bowl remained a letdown for players, Cappelletti admits.

"I think the bowl game was kind of overshadowed because we couldn't win the national championship," says Cappy, who gained just 50 yards on 26 carries against L.S.U.

Cappelletti spent 10 years in the National Football League, but never reached the heights he attained at Penn

State.

The Los Angeles Rams took him on the first round of the 1974 draft, but he languished on the bench for two season before moving into the starting lineup.

He gained 2,246 yards in six seasons with the Rams, including 688 in 1976.

He sat out 1979 on injured reserve and the Rams dealt him the following year to the San Diego Chargers. He played there four years and retired after the 1983 season.

He was elected to the National Football Foundation and College Hall of Fame in 1993.

*Cappelletti rambles through the Pitt
secondary for big yardage in 1973.*

Lions Turn Cinderella Bears into Pumpkins in Cotton Bowl

By Bill Heufelder
The Pittsburgh Press

Dallas, Jan. 1, 1975 — Penn State bloodied Cinderella's nose yesterday with its 41-20 victory over Baylor in the 39th annual Cotton Bowl.

The Bears, who rebounded dramatically from a 2-9 season to break Texas' six-year domination of the Southwest Conference, held together through the first half and emerged with a 7-3 lead.

They fell behind on the opening Penn State series of the third quarter when fullback Tom Donchez powered into the end zone from the 2, ending an 80-yard drive.

When Tom Shuman ignored Dennis DeLoach's fierce rush and lofted a perfectly thrown 49-yard scoring pass to freshman Jimmy Cefalo, Baylor turned into a pumpkin.

Shuman, who had passed erratically in the first half and once overlooked a receiver wide open at the Baylor 5, finished with 226 yards passing and the game's most valuable offensive player award.

The sixth-ranked Lions scored five successive times, beginning with Shuman's throw that pushed them ahead, 17-14, as they recovered from a bewildering retreat on the previous possession.

They incurred a double penalty on a play in which Donchez carried a swing pass 64 yards into the Baylor end zone. Teammate Jim Eaise was called for offensive pass interference and Shuman was slapped with a non-contact personal foul for flipping the official's flag.

"I apologized to the official," Shuman explained. "He told me, 'You're a pain in the —.' He was kind of sour all day."

Instead of a touchdown, the Lions were stuck on their own 12, from where Brian Masella punted.

"That wasn't a penalty," Coach Joe Paterno said. "That was a forfeit."

The controversial play proved to be more costly to the Bears, who lost

Steve Beaird hurdles through an opening in the Lions defense.

Penn State's Jimmy Cefalo (44) eludes the Baylor defense for a fourth-quarter touchdown. The Nittany Lions scored 24 points in the final period to turn a close game into a 41-20 rout.

safety Ken Queensberry when a down-field block crumpled his right knee. Queensberry, although unable to return, received the game's defensive award for his 12 tackles and two fumble recoveries.

His absence seemed to allow more light into the Baylor pass defense, which already was relying on a pair of freshman cornerbacks.

"The passes and reverses," Baylor linebacker Derrel Luce said, "really started hurting us. We were always one play behind. On defense, you've got to control the tempo."

Yeah, like the Penn State defense. It stumbled into three offside penalties on the Bears' scoring drive in the first quarter, but owned the Bears in the second half.

Stubby Steve Beaird, a 1,000-yard rusher during the year, was held to 12 yards after gaining 72 in the opening half, as the Lions poured through Baylor to disrupt Neal Jeffrey's passing game.

"They did a super job of adjusting," said Jeffrey after managing seven of 19 completions and a tipped 35-yard touchdown pass that fell conveniently into the hands of Ricky Thompson in the third quarter.

"We should have given Neal more

Score by Periods

Penn State	0	3	14	24	—	41
Baylor	7	0	7	6	—	20

time on those passes," his center, Aubrey Schulz, said. "A bunch of times, Penn State stunted and that messed up our timing."

The tacklers arrived in bunches to bring down the 5-foot-6½, 196-pound Beaird. "It wasn't the first hit that bother me," he said. "It was the second, third and fourth guys coming in."

After Cefalo's scoring catch, the Lions reverted to the power-I, with Donchez, who led all rushers with 116 yards, blocking for Neil Hutton, a darting, elusive sophomore.

Picking up 79 yards in 12 carriers, Hutton spurred Penn State to a touchdown, which came on Cefalo's three-yard run, and a 33-yard field goal by Chris Bahr midway through the final quarter that put Penn State in front, 27-14.

Baylor coach Grant Teaff, a Baptist deacon, said he was keeping the faith until safety Mike Johnson picked off Jeffrey's pass on first down and returned it to the Bears' 18. Five plays later, Shuman scored from the 2.

In the waning seconds, Joe Jackson, a reserve linebacker, offset a Baylor touchdown by returning an onside kick 50 yards for the final touchdown.

If Beaird was overwhelmed by the Penn State defense, he was short on his opinion of the Lions as a team.

"If Penn State played in the Southwest Conference," he said, "it would be hard for them to win it. They'd probably be in the top three, though."

It was an assessment that sounded like a fairy tale.

Penn State tight end Randy Sidler latches onto a pass.

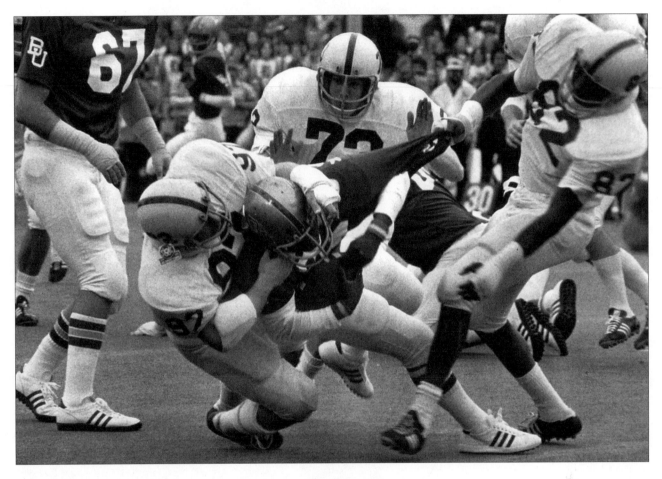

Above, Baylor fullback Pat McNeil is wrestled by Penn State's Greg Murphy (82) and Rich Kriston (92);
Below, Nittany Lions' quarterback Tom Shuman looks downfield for a receiver.

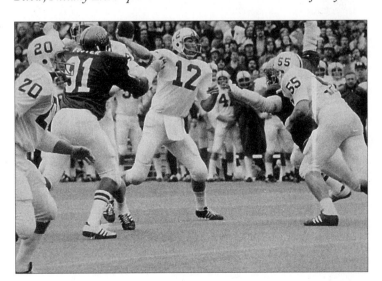

Penn State Wins 'Kicking Game' Against Pitt, 7-6

BY RUSS FRANKE
The Pittsburgh Press

Pittsburgh, Nov. 22, 1975 — For Carson Long, in his own tearful words, it was a "horrible thing" for him and the Pitt football team. For Penn State it was a beautiful thing. A 7-6 win in the clutch.

Penn State survived its toughest battle with Pitt in 10 years yesterday, and a near-capacity crowd at Three Rivers Stadium and a national television audience saw a thriller that wound up as one of the most heartbreaking losses in Pitt history.

This was the year, Pitt people felt, to break Penn State's Eastern superiority, and the Panthers almost pulled it off with a brilliant defensive effort, only to miss their opportunities in a frenzied ending.

Long went into the game as one of the most accurate placement-kickers in the country as well as one of the proudest fathers — his wife, Peggy, had given birth to a baby girl only hours before — but the highly-keyed junior came out the most disappointed man in the world, missing field goals from the 13- and 35-yard lines in the final minute-and-a-half, plus a 51-yarder earlier in the fourth quarter.

Pitt had scored first on Elliott Walker's 37-yard blast up the middle in the

Score by Periods

Penn State	0	0	0	7	— 7
Pitt	0	6	0	0	— 6

second period, but Tom Odell blocked Long's extra-point try, and it turned out to be the difference on the scoreboard.

The Nittany Lions got that one back on another big run, a naked 28-yard slash off left tackle in the middle of the final quarter. Chris Bahr's placement made it 7-6 and it was the third straight year Penn State was forced to come from behind late to beat the Panthers.

The win gave Penn State a 9-2 record to take into the Sugar Bowl against Alabama and the loss left Pitt at 7-4, the same record as last year, with a Dec. 26 date against Kansas in the Sun Bowl.

"Offensively, we got whipped up

front," said Pitt's Johnny Majors, "But I've never seen a line play as well defensively as ours did. And I've never seen two teams hit that hard, especially on defense. My hat's off to Penn State for the way they played us."

Big hits by Al Romano, Don Parrish, Randy Cozens, Randy Holloway, Arnie Weatherington and Tom Perko, in particular, drew repeated roars from the Pitt fans in the chilled crowd of 46,846 (there were roughly 5,000 no-shows), as Pitt gained the edge defensively.

The Panthers knocked five fumbles loose and recovered three of them. They also picked an interception off Chuck Fusina, the freshman quarterback who relieved John Andress in the third period.

Joe Paterno had said beforehand there was no way his defense could stop Tony Dorsett, and Dorsett bolstered his bid for another all-American year by ripping off 125 yards on 28 carries, ending the regular season with 1,544 yards and a three-year total of 4,234.

"Overall, I thought we beat them in everything but the game," said Dorsett. "Football is funny — you play so good and you still wind up on the wrong end. I know how Carson Long feels. Remember, I fumbled on the 1-yard line at Notre Dame last year and we lost the game.

"Penn State did a good job on our option plays. They strung it out almost as good as West Virginia did. But that wasn't the reason we lost."

The Panthers indicated what kind of a tense struggle it would be when they gambled on their first series and won, with Matt Cavanaugh diving off the right corner for three yards and a first down at his 45. Apparently, they mustered their nerve to do it after Dorsett had breezed for 30 yards on his first carry of the game.

Chris Bahr's fourth-quarter extra point proved to be the difference in Penn State's victory.

From then until the Panthers scored, however, it was purely a defensive struggle spiced by some mistakes on both sides, as State continued to play the option well and the Pitt defense kept the middle stopped against the running of Woody Petchel, Duane Taylor and Jimmy Cefalo, who played at tailback instead of wingback in a surprise switch by Paterno.

A couple of penalties for clipping and holding plus an interception by linebacker Ron Hostetler stopped the Panthers in the second period, and then it was Pitt's turn to create a turnover. Andress passed 20 yards to Mickey Shuler but Dennis Moorehead banged Shuler immediately to knock the ball away and recover on the State 48.

Dorsett hit a hole for 11 yards and then Walker broke into the middle, got some room with a fake and broke Gary Petercuskie's tackle on the way to a touchdown.

The Lions got a break when Larry Swider went back to punt at his 26 and Ron Coder blitzed in cleanly to tackle him, but Pitt got the ball back when Randy Cozens belted Petchel and the ball squirted away, Randy Holloway recovering.

Late in the third period, Fusina threw deep for Tom Donovan and Bob Jury made an easy interception at his 11.

Fusina, thrilled to be home for the first time in three months — he is the latest in a long line of quarterbacks from McKees Rocks — said he was aware that other receivers were open but that "I was going for all the marbles. I guess I messed up."

The Lions forced another punt to the State 29, and this time the Lions finally got their offense together to march back all the way.

A pass interference call put the ball

Coaches' Kicking Prediction Comes True

BY PAT LIVINGSTON
The Pittsburgh Press

It was a game, the coaches agreed last week, that could be decided by the kickers.

And Penn State's dogged 7-6 victory over Pitt at Three Rivers Stadium yesterday was exactly that. Of all things, Chris Bahr's fourth-quarter extra point decided it.

Both coaches, Joe Paterno of Penn State and Johnny Majors of Pitt, blessed with two of the country's top placement kickers mentioned that, in a close game, a field goal might be the difference between winning and losing.

It never quite came to that.

Pitt's kicker, Carson Long, had three shots at turning the game around in the last five minutes, but the Panther junior, who in the second quarter had seen his streak of 60 straight extra points broken, missed each of those shots. Two of them were long ones, but the other was a heartbreaker.

Long missed it, wide to the right, from the 13-yard line.

It was a bonus attempt, at that. The hearts of the Panthers fans sank moments earlier when Long's 51-yard shot fell short of the goal post, wide to the left, with four minutes left in the game.

But miraculously, Chuck Fusina, the Lions' quarterback, fumbled on second down when hit by Dennis Moorhead and Bob Jury, a standout on defense for the Panthers all evening, snatched the ball to his chest before it rolled out of bounds at the State 29.

A 24-yard pass to Gordon Jones gave Pitt a golden opportunity, but Jones, dueling a Penn State defender, cut outside and stumbled out of bounds at the Lions 5. Had he cut inside, it would have been a touchdown.

Still, no one in the crowd of 46,846 really expected Jones' wrong turn to have any effect on the outcome. There was still Long's chance to redeem himself.

But on fourth down, on a chip shot, Long inexplicably missed again.

Nobody gets three shots, but, once again, the Panthers were back in Penn State territory, the result of a pass interference call at the 35, with 18 seconds on the clock. And again Long missed.

The missed field goal detracted from what otherwise might have been a brilliant game between two evenly matched teams. For those who like wide-open, high-scoring football, the game might have left them unfulfilled, for there were only the touchdown runs, 37 yards by Elliott Walker and 28 by Steve Geise, to bring them to their feet.

But there was plenty of defensive football on the Tartanturf — hard-hitting, two-fisted football in which the lines didn't break or bend. Even the touchdowns came on plays which caught the defense out of position, not weakened.

The first half, largely a parry-and-thrust session in which each team tried to establish dominion over the field, was largely Pitt's not only because Walker had burned the Lions with his touchdown run, but because the Lions never satisfactorily came up with a solution to Tony Dorsett, who had ripped them for 77 yards in 13 carries.

Dorsett's presence was felt even on Walker's score, an explosive burst through the middle and a move on the safety man that left the Panthers back with a clear route to the end zone.

The hole was there because Greg Buttle, Penn State's all-American candidate at linebacker, was off like Admiral Halsey's fleet in the battle of the Philippines cruising after a decoy, Dorsett in this case.

Geise's touchdown, which caught the Panthers off-stride, came on a third-and-one situation, as Pitt massed its five-man front to stop what it construed to be an attack inside.

But Geise, cutting to daylight, sprinted left, got beyond the end, and, unharried by pursuing linebackers, raced untouched into the end zone.

Bahr's kick, although no one was quite prepared to concede it at the time, wrapped up the bruising battle for the Sugar Bowl-bound Lions.

Above, Pitt kicker Carson Long, right, missed three fourth-quarter field goals in the Panthers' 7-6 loss. Below, Johnny Majors visits prior to the game.

on the 42 and Cefalo, Fusina and Steve Geise took turns carrying to the Pitt 28. Geise was supposed to hit inside, looking for a first down against a short yardage defense, but the hole wasn't there and he veered left, catching the Pitt cornerback inside, and scored untouched.

Here the going got even stickier. The Panthers gang-tackled Fusina at the side-line, and when he fumbled, Jury came up with it on the State 29 with 3:49 to play and Pitt appeared headed for a sure win. Cavanaugh ducked a fierce rush and threw a 28-yarder to Gordon Jones who made a spectacular catch on the 6.

Mike Johnson made a great touchdown-saving tackle on the sideline.

Pitt was in business, but so was the State defense. Walker was stopped at the 1 and Dorsett lost to the 9. Walker got 3 yards in moving the ball toward the center of the field for Long, but his try for a 23-yarder sailed wide right and it appeared Pitt was done.

But the Pitt defense came up with another giant effort and forced Bahr to punt to the Pitt 40. There were 37 seconds left, and the Panthers got yet another chance when Cavanaugh found Rodney Clark open and threw. The Lions were called for interference at their 35 and then Cavanaugh passed to Karl Farmer on the 25, Farmer hopping out of bounds to stop the clock with nine seconds left.

Long's field goal try of 45 yards dropped in front of the goal post and Penn State had its 10th straight win over Pitt.

Long, comforted in the arms of his sidekick and placement-holder Swider, was choked with disappointment as he left Three Rivers. Did the blocked extra-point affect his concentration on his field goal attempts?

"What a horrible thing," he said. "I had everything lined up. The snaps were good and the holds were good. There was no excuse for it."

After Fiesta Win, Penn State On Road To National Crown

BY BILL HEUFELDER
The Pittsburgh Press

Tempe, Ariz., Dec. 25, 1977 — For Arizona State, the eleventh annual Fiesta Bowl was a test of its preparedness for joining the enlarged Pac-8 next year. Pummeled in the second half, the Sun Devils came up short, 42-30, against Penn State.

As far as the seventh-ranked Lions are concerned, the bowl on Christmas Day hopefully was the start of something big. The returnees will be chasing a prize that has eluded all Penn State teams before them: a national championship.

"As soon as that last second ticked off, I was thinking about next year," said Matt Millen, the ebullient sophomore tackle whose brilliant performance against A.S.U. earned him the game's outstanding defensive player award.

"We'll try to put it all together. I think we had enough to do the job this year. I think this team is capable of playing with anybody. Five points meant the whole season. What can you say?"

The five points in question were the difference between winning and losing the fourth game of the season when Kentucky dealt the Lions their only defeat, 24-20.

Score by Periods						
Penn State	14	3	7	18	—	42
Arizona State	0	14	0	16	—	30

Of its first 44 players, Penn State will lose only 11 to graduation, including seven from the defense.

"There's a lot of anticipation about next year," acknowledged quarterback Chuck Fusina. "I don't think we'll settle for second place next year. I know I won't.

"I'm not bragging. I just know the guys are ready to sacrifice for it (to be No. 1). There hasn't been a national championship here and we want it so bad."

Fusina would have preferred a more pleasant afternoon at Sun Devil Stadium, A.S.U.'s home turf, before a record crowd of 57,727 and a national television audience.

Giving barely a glimpse of the talent that allowed him to throw for more than 2,000 yards during the regular season, the McKees Rock junior hit nine of 23 passes for 83 yards.

"I just wasn't throwing well," he said, "and I didn't read the defense well. The first couple of times I set up, I didn't feel right. But I'm still happy."

The source of Fusina's elation was the final score, achieved with a punishing ground attack in the second half after the Lions — although never trailing — had amassed a sickly 81 yards total offense through two quarters.

"We weren't that determined in the first half," Coach Joe Paterno explained. "That's why you play 60 minutes."

Center Chuck Correal agreed with his coach's assessment. Against an A.S.U. defense that bedeviled the Lions with quickness and shifting formations that led to a surprisingly heavy pass rush, the offensive line was wary.

"We were a little hesitant in carry-

Coach Joe Paterno leads his team through a Fiesta Bowl pre-game workout.

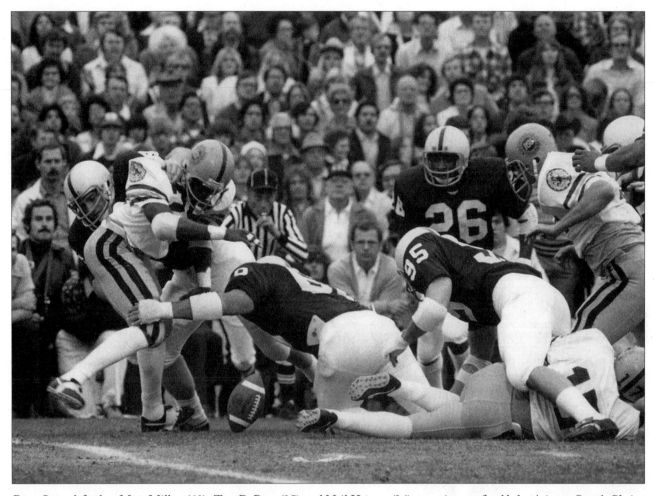

Penn State defenders Matt Millen (60), Tom DePaso (95) and Neil Hutton (26) move in on a fumble by Arizona State's Chris DeFrance. Millen earned the game's outstanding defensive player award.

ing out our assignments," Correal noted. "They just fired out and they were really quick, probably the quickest team we faced all year.

"It took a little longer for us to get used to their defense. In the second half, we just came out and laid it on 'em."

Steve Geise, the only runner who'll be leaving, and fullback Bob Torrey both registered 100-yard games. Matt Suhey, who accounted for 76 yards rushing, twice powered his way for touchdowns from inside the five during the final quarter.

"Geise had some three-yard runs that he turned into six-yard plays," Paterno marveled.

After the determined tailback softened up the Sun Devils, Torrey demolished them with his bulldozing style, breaking loose for runs of 25 and 54 yards. The carries led to one of two Matt Bahr field goals and a Suhey touchdown that put the Lions ahead, 42-28, with three minutes left.

Offensively, A.S.U. was denied what it needed most, the explosive scoring play. During the week, the Sun Devil receivers, particularly all-America John

Jefferson, spoke confidently in the papers of burning the Penn State secondary.

Dennis Sproul, who went all the way as the A.S.U. quarterback with the exception of one play, completed 23 of 47 passes, none of them longer than 36 yards. A questionable starter because of a back injury, he threw scoring passes of 11, 13 and 30 yards, finishing as the outstanding offensive player.

"We wanted to keep from getting beat deep," said safety Gary Petercuskie, who fielded one of two interceptions against Sproul. "We wanted

John Dunn (62) gives Penn State quarterback Chuck Fusina time to throw over Arizona State's Kit Lathrop (92) during the 1977 Fiesta Bowl. Fusina completed nine passes, one for a touchdown.

to make them drive with the ball."

The satisfaction rushing into his voice, Petercuskie, a 177-pound senior, added, "And we shut out Jefferson."

Controlling the A.S.U. passing game satisfied everyone among the Lions with the exception of Millen, who seemed to be everywhere but in the secondary. When Sproul resorted to dumping short passes in great haste to avoid the rush, Millen was stranded.

"I hate those passes," he said, disgustedly. "There's nothing you can do to stop them."

There was no one to stop Penn State defensive end Bill Banks in the opening quarter when he burst through to block an A.S.U. punt, Joe Lally picking up the ball and scoring from 21 yards out.

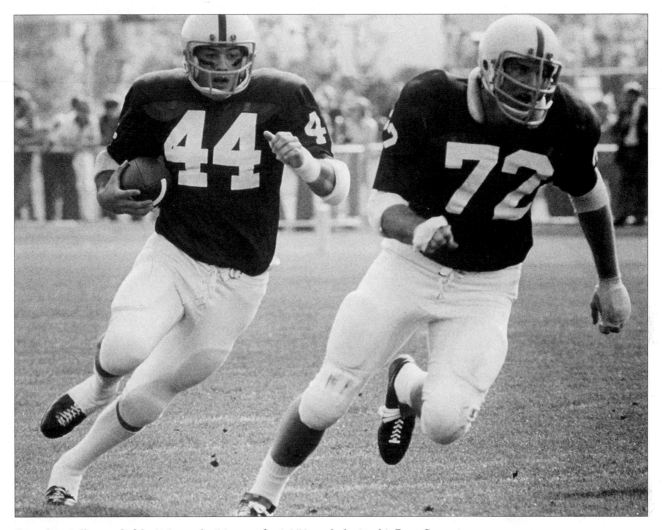

Penn State's Jimmy Cefalo (44) caught 56 passes for 1,058 yards during his Penn State career.

The play, which gave the Lions a 7-0 edge, reflected the thoroughness of Paterno and his staff. "From looking at the films, we were sure we could get to the punter," Banks said. "I went in clean. Nobody touched me."

While his returning teammates anxiously await a new season, Banks bowed out with a play he can savor for a lifetime.

"That was my first blocked punt," he said. "It feels great, too. It saved me from running all the way downfield."

Nittany Notes

Jimmy Cefalo, who led the nation in punt returns, ran back an A.S.U. kick 67 yards, setting up a field goal ... A.S.U. had been unbeaten in four previous Fiesta appearances and was bidding for a sixth straight post-season victory.

Fusina revealed that he and his mother had received mailed threats two weeks ago, the incidents similar to those which have occurred before each of Penn State's last two games against Pitt. ...

Cefalo and tight end Mickey Shuler will play in the Hula Bowl Jan. 7.

The officiating was suspect, including a pair of pass interference calls on the Sun Devils' final scoring drive. ... "Rick Donaldson was two yards in front of the receiver on one of the calls," Banks said. "I wondered how he could have rushed the receiver." ... The other call was made after Neil Hutton was sprinting upfield with an interception he delivered while alone in the flat.

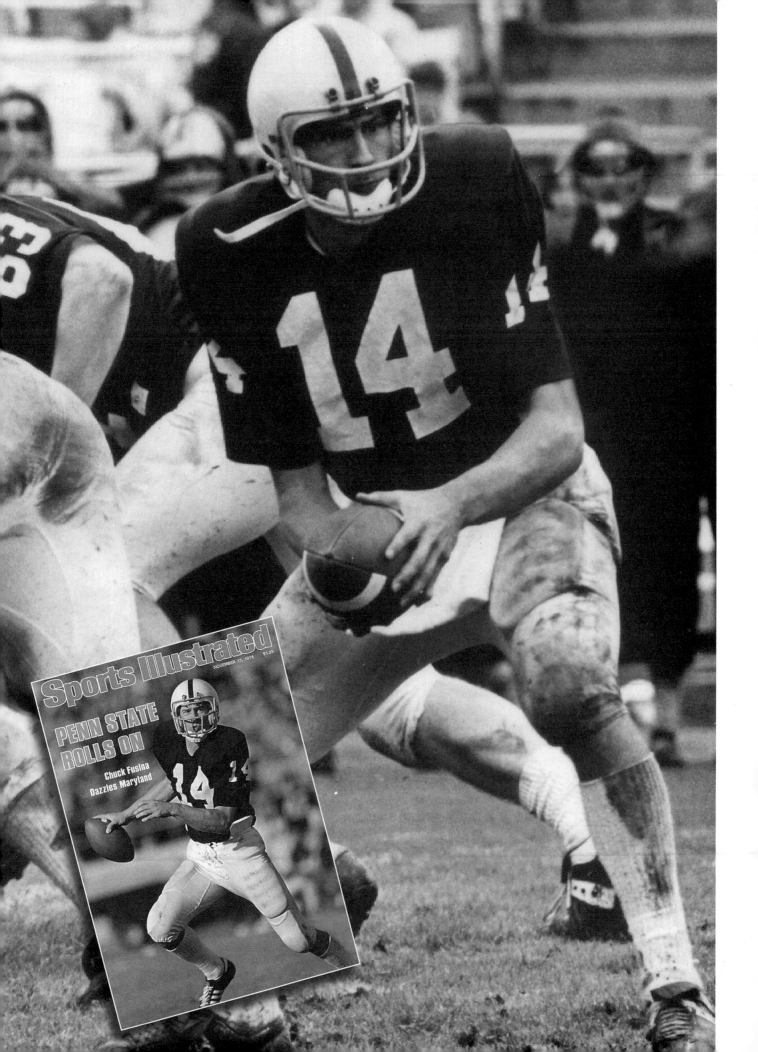

Sports Illustrated
NOVEMBER 13, 1978 $1.25

PENN STATE ROLLS ON

Chuck Fusina
Dazzles Maryland

Buckeyes' Frosh Gamble Fails; Lions Feast, 19-0

By Bill Heufelder
The Pittsburgh Press

Columbus, Ohio, Sept. 16, 1978 — Coach Woody Hayes threw a freshman quarterback to the Lions yesterday with disastrous results. Art Schlichter was intercepted five times, lost a fumble and took a pounding, as Penn State smothered Ohio State, 19-0.

The identity of the Buckeye quarterback was a mystery until Schlichter and his predecessor, Rod Gerald, who was switched to split end, came out together for the first O.S.U. series. When the Buckeyes had the ball for the last time Schlichter was pondering a collegiate debut that brought 12 completions in 25 attempts.

However, the 88,202 packed into Ohio Stadium for the third largest crowd in its history had to be impressed with the poise and courage of the youngster who was last season's Ohio high school player of the year.

His counterpart, Chuck Fusina, who suffered through five sacks and some erratic early throws, passed sparingly but effectively in the second half and commanded a rushing attack that came to life with a robust, 80-yard drive in the third quarter.

Overall, the Lions, while less than spectacular, were capable of making folks forget the two previous weeks with

Score by Periods					
Penn State	3	0	7	9	— 19
Ohio State	0	0	0	0	— 0

Matt Bahr kicked four field goals.

the exception of one striking reminder. Matt Bahr was very much in evidence again, kicking four field goals, the longest covering 41 yards. In three games, Bahr, who missed a 30-yard attempt against O.S.U., is 9-for-11.

When Penn State's reserve defense held the Buckeyes, with Greg Castignola at quarterback, on the 5-yard line in the closing seconds, they were assured of being shut out for the second time in 14 years.

The artificial surface, soaked by a morning rain, seemed to affect Fusina and definitely bothered his receivers, who often slipped while running their routes. Whatever the effect the wet field, which dried beneath an emerging sun in the second half, had upon Schlichter was not nearly as significant as the Penn State defense.

Perhaps Hayes was gambling on Schlichter's record: The 18-year-old had never started a losing game in high school. The outcome of the decision was to showcase a freshman with a brilliant passing arm, but overmatched against traditionally one of the finest college defensive units in the nation.

Afterward, the O.S.U. coach admitted the kid was given a murderous assignment. "He will be as fine a quarterback as there is in college football someday," Hayes predicted, "But I think we were asking too much of him right now. We decided to start Schlichter because Gerald had been out so much of pre-season."

On O.S.U.'s opening drive, Schlichter started well, hitting a pair of short passes in three tries before safety Pete Harris produced his first of two interceptions and returned the ball 33 yards to midfield.

Fusina, passing four times, connected only once, but it was a 27-yard strike to Mike Guman that set up a 30-yard field goal after almost 10 minutes of play.

The Lions, eighth-ranked and aspiring to be No. 1 when the season ends, protected the lead through the remainder of the half. Ohio State, which committed a total of eight turnovers, eased the task. Schlichter's 44-yard pass to Gerald at the Penn State 22 went sour when Gerald coughed up the ball, Rick Donaldson recovering for Penn State late in the first quarter.

The punting of Tom Orosz kept the Lions at bay, but didn't do anything for his club's offense. His 72-yard kick eventually gave the Buckeyes possession at their 45. They moved to the Penn State 31 before defensive end Larry Kubin rocked Schlichter and managed to gather in a loose ball while still on the ground.

After beating Temple and Rutgers by a total of 19 points — the same margin of victory in stopping No. 6 Ohio State — the Lions finally put precision in their ground game after Orosz's third-quarter punt bounded into the end zone. Behind a revamped line that placed tight end Irv Pankey at tackle to replace injured all-America Keith Dorney, fullback Matt Suhey powered 29 yards in six carries and Guman added runs of eight and four yards.

Fusina, in the face of a fierce rush, then hit Bob Bassett for 17 yards on a play that struck a nerve with the otherwise calm Hayes. The O.S.U. coach thundered onto the field protesting to the officials that the Lions were guilty of illegal motion. Hayes returned to the sideline and watched Suhey cut inside Guman's block on a three-yard scoring run, three plays later.

Down 10-0, the Buckeyes reverted to a more conservative offense without any change in the results. Early in the fourth quarter, Schlichter, who had slipped away from onrushing Bruce

Penn State defensive tackle Bruce Clark became the first junior to win the Lombardi Award when he was honored in 1979.

Clark and Kubin to fire a 15-yard pass a moment before, was victimized again. Steam evaporated from the throw thanks to Clark's crunching hit, the freshman triggered his third interception, linebacker Lance Mehl making the steal.

The Buckeyes found a way to neutralize Clark and partner Matt Millen at the tackles, but Mehl was outstanding in plugging the holes. The performance did not go unnoticed by Paterno, who said, "Mehl must have had a great game. He seemed to be everywhere out there."

Bahr turned the interception into another field goal and closed the scoring late in the game after Schlichter had delivered his final fling of the long afternoon, a steal by Harris.

In a day of surprises that included Brad Scovill, a sophomore walk-on, admirably handling Pankey's tight end job for the Lions, Woody Hayes was left to utter a shocker.

Having lived by the ground game for an eternity, the O.S.U. coach said, "What we have to do now is go back and establish a running game to go along with our passing."

Penn State's Lance Mehl closes in on Ohio State quarterback Rod Gerald (8).

Alabama Defeats Lions in Dramatic Goal-Line Stand

BY RUSS FRANKE
The Pittsburgh Press

New Orleans, Jan. 1, 1979 — For Penn State, the moment of truth was 92 years and six inches away.

That moment came deep into Alabama territory and deep into the fourth quarter of yesterday's Sugar Bowl showdown between No. 1 Penn State and No. 2 Alabama, and it went deep into the brain of the man making the most decisive defensive play of the collegiate football season — Barry Krause, an Alabama linebacker who underlined his all-America stamp by stopping Mike Guman on the six-inch line on fourth and goal.

And the Crimson Tide went on to win the game, 14-7, and very probably the national title.

"It was one of the hardest hits I ever made," said Krause, and it deprived Penn State of a prime chance to win the first national championship in 92 years of football. The hit left Krause even more stunned than the Penn State offense, and he lay flat on the ground long enough for the trainers to come onto the Superdome turf and treat him.

"I wasn't really unconscious but I was dazed," said Krause. "I busted my helmet. From watching films, we knew they scored a lot of touchdowns by diving over the top, and I knew in my heart I had to be there to stop him."

The play typified an afternoon of

Score by Periods

Penn State	0	0	7	0 —	7
Alabama	0	7	7	0 —	14

superior defense by both teams, and for once Penn State's defense, the best in the country going in, came out second best. The Nittany Lions gained a great deal of notoriety by limiting their regular-season opponents to 54 yards a game, but Alabama exceeded that by holding Penn State to 19 yards rushing, and that is another story in itself.

Krause and his coach, Bear Bryant, said that Alabama's pass rush was the big factor, something the Tide worked on especially hard in order to take away Chuck Fusina's passing game. Fusina was caught seven times for minus 64 yards, accounting for the low team rushing total.

"I don't believe I've ever been associated with a team that did so well on defense," said Bryant. "I think we could have beaten any team in America today, and today is what counted, wasn't it? We went into the game trying to play as if we were two points behind all the time."

Alabama never was behind, actually. A last minute pass just before halftime gave the Tide a touchdown lead. Penn State tied the score in the third period and Alabama got the winning touchdown four minutes later following Lou Ikner's 62-yard punt return — an event that seldom occurs against Penn State — to the 11-yard line.

Four plays later, Major Ogilvie became at least a general by taking Jeff Rutledge's cleverly delayed pitchout eight yards off the left side, and there was nothing Pete Harris or Rick Milot could do about the execution of the play, the kind of wishbone play that makes Alabama a perennial power.

There was no question that the wishbone was the toughest option offense Penn State had to battle all season, perhaps for a number of seasons. The Tide rolled for 208 yards out of it, with halfback Tony Nathan getting 127. Even so, it required supreme efforts, particularly by Lance Mehl, Bruce Clark and Matt Millen, to prevent the Tide from dominating the game.

On a Tide touchdown pass just before the halftime, the effectiveness of a well-manned wishbone asserted itself. The irony in that a guard-oriented offense lends itself to the long bomb, and that is also another story that revealed itself after the game when

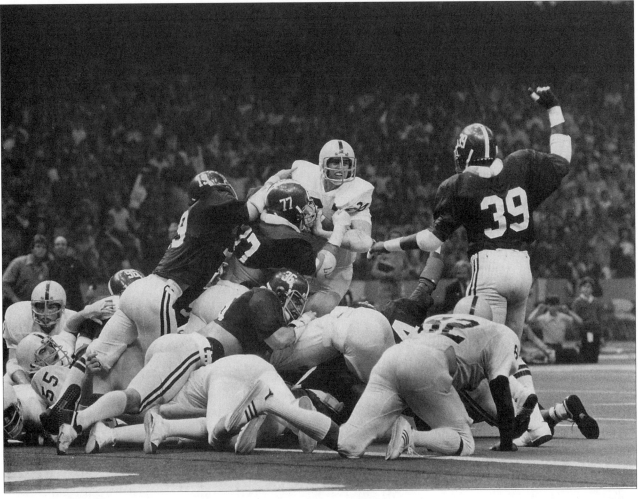

Above, Alabama's defense stops Lions halfback Mike Guman in a memorable fourth-quarter, goal-line stand. Below, Paul (Bear) Bryant and Joe Paterno visit prior to the 1979 Sugar Bowl game.

Rutledge talked to the reporters.

"That touchdown pass was a new play," said Rutledge. "The man I threw it to was actually the decoy, Bruce Bolton. He was the third man and I went to him when I realized he had his man one-on-one (sophomore Karl McCoy). They had our fullback and tight end in a crowd."

The pass was for 30 yards and it ended an 80-yard drive that started with 1:11 to go before halftime.

Until then, defense was the name of the game and even though Alabama controlled the ball and kept State out of field position with the punting of Woody Umphrey, it could be said that the Nittany Lions defense was better in the clutch simply because most of the first half was played in Lions territory.

Penn State didn't make real penetration until the TD drive that started with six minutes remaining in the third period. Harris, known as "Franco's brother," but now a celebrity in his own right as the leading interceptor in the nation, picked off a Rutledge pass at the Alabama 48.

The Lions quickly capitalized, living up to their tradition for the only time in the game. Fusina hit Guman with a 25-yard sideline pass to the Tide 19, and after Guman picked up two yards, Fusina showed the Superdome crowd of 76,824 his arm by drilling the ball deep into the end zone.

Scott Fitzkee scored Penn State's only touchdown with this end-zone catch.

Privy To Bear's Prayer

BY RUSS FRANKE
The Pittsburgh Press

What a delicious moment it was — before one of Bear Bryant's state troopers spoiled it.

Shortly after the Penn State-Alabama Sugar Bowl game was over, this reporter walked into the Alabama dressing room — by mistake, it turned out — the mistake obviously attributed to a red leisure suit that passes for crimson as in Crimson Tide, hardly noticeable in a tide of Alabama assistant coaches and players.

It was fun while it lasted, being privy to the innermost relationship between the Alabama team and the coach who is legend, until the trooper, noticing the interloper, crooked his finger and said politely, "Outside, sir, y'all can't be in here."

And outside was a hallway full of reporters, crushing one another to get closer to the door and to the interviews that would be forthcoming when Bryant and his players were ready to receive them and talk about the Tide's 14-7 win.

What went on in the Alabama quarters was a rewarding insight into the Bryant mystique. While Bryant was still out on the Superdome Turf (hugging Joe Paterno, he said, but unable to hear Paterno's compliments), the players were chanting anti-Pennsylvania slogans and pro-Alabama rhymes. It was all in good spirit, nothing malicious ("If you don't go to 'Bama, go to hell," for example.)

An assistant coach anticipating Bryant's arrival, summoned the players with, "When Coach Bryant comes in, y'all drop to ya knees, hear?"

And when Bryant finally did come in, the hush was enough to create a lump in the throat. The Bear, not at all exultant or vain, quietly went to

Alabama halfback Major Ogilvie rips through the Lions defense for 4 yards.

Scott Fitzkee also showed the crowd on the national TV audience something — a great deal of hands and feet. He made a Lynn Swann-type catch over the head of the defender and somehow kept his feet inside the end line for a TD. Matt Bahr, itching on the sidelines all afternoon, got his only chance to kick a ball through the upright and it was 7-7.

Mehl, Millen, Larry Kubin and Joe Lally pulled the wishbone apart in the next series to force a punt. But State couldn't move the sticks and when Fitzkee had to punt, Ikner took the ball down the left sidelines and made a nice cut inside his blocking for 62 yards.

Freshman Matt Bradley saved a touchdown by dragging down Ikner from behind, but it served only to delay the Tide's winning thrust on Ogilvie's eight-yard run.

the floor with his players, all heads bowed. He prayed genuinely and in a quiet voice that could not be heard distinctly in the hallway.

What a truly nice man. Small wonder that he can motivate, and small wonder that his players are so respected by their opponents. As Paterno told the media more than once during the week preceding the game, the Alabama players are select people.

Bryant put his stamp on them, and no one has been stamping players so successfully over the years than he.

When the time came for Bryant's press conference, he was amiable, fighting the strain he had experienced in beating an equally good

Penn State team. He was sweating and he had the sniffles from a cold, and he said he couldn't hear in one ear because of "too many airplane rides (recruiting)."

He did not wear his familiar houndstooth hat. It was announced that since he was a Southern gentleman and the game was being played indoors, he would go bare-headed, probably in deference to the ladies present.

"Before the game," said his quarterback, Jeff Rutledge, "Coach Bryant was singing to himself. I knew then that he was relaxed and we'd have a good chance to win.

"He was singing so low I couldn't tell what the song was, but I knew he was loose."

Bryant kept his press conference lively with some salty jibes at the Southern writers he knew, and he constantly praised Penn State. When linebacker Barry Krause was brought in to pose for the cameras as the game's most valuable player, Bryant creaked, "Congratulations — I didn't know you made MVP. Of course, I'll have to look at the films …"

When he was serious, Bryant said he didn't think he could recall a harder-hitting game both ways, that his pass rush was the best he's had in a long time, that on the big play when Krause stopped Mike Guman short of the goal line, "I expected them to use the same play they did when they beat Pitt. The play they used was halfway in between."

Alabama Defeats Penn State at Own Game

BY PAT LIVINGSTON
The Pittsburgh Press

In a sense, it was a matter of second-ranked Alabama beating top-ranked Penn State at the Lions' own game — defense.

That was the simplest way to sum up the manner in which the Crimson Tide eked out a 14-7 victory over Penn State at the jam-packed Superdome yesterday.

The Tide had it when it counted. The Lions didn't.

And when it counted most came in the fourth quarter, Penn State trailing, 14-7, with six and a half minutes to play. Alabama faced its stiffest challenge of the game. The Tide had their backs to the wall, third and goal at the one, following a fumble recovery by Penn State's Joe Lally three plays earlier at the Alabama 19. That might have been Penn State's only legitimate break at the game.

After an 11-yard run by Matt Suhey and Chuck Fusina's pass to Scott Fitzkee had moved the ball down to the one, it looked like Alabama's shaky lead was about to be overcome. Unfortunately for the Lions, it didn't work out that way, perhaps because Bear Bryant, the Alabama coach, remembered something he had seen in the Lions' victory over Pitt a month ago.

Fusina, on third down, sent Suhey hurtling into the line. After a sideline conference with his coach, Joe Paterno, the Lions quarterback came back and sent Mike Guman over the other side of center Chuck Correal. Suhey picked up all but six inches, but Guman didn't get any yardage at all.

"We expected them to dive over, or run off tackle," said Bryant after the game, "like they did against Pittsburgh."

"It was a percentage call," said Paterno, admitting that he had considered a pass play as an alternative. "I know we weren't going to go wide, the way they were ganging up against the outside. We had to go through them or we weren't going to get there at all."

While Penn State's failure to capitalize on its only break of the game might have disappointed the Lions, it didn't demoralize them at all. Four plays later, with Alabama forced to punt from inside their own ten, the Lions failed to capitalize on another break — a 9-yard punt to the 18.

But this time Penn State, ironically, had 12 men on the field.

"It was ironic, wasn't it?" shrugged Paterno. "Win a bowl game one year because they had 12 men on the field. Today, we lost because we had 12 men out there."

Paterno declined to identify which of his players had failed to come off the field.

"What good would that do?" he asked.

Actually, Paterno's bench might have tipped off the officials to the presence of the extra man on the play.

"We kept yelling at him to come out, come out," said Paterno. "If we had kept our mouths shut, the official might never have noticed we had too many men on the field."

Aside from that sequence of plays — and a couple of bang, bang plays, as Paterno described them, by Alabama — it was a brutal, nerve-wracking game. One worthy of its billing as a test of champions.

The Tide won it, not by rolling over the Lions as they had done to so many teams over the season, but by putting together the game's most impressive drive at the end of the first half, and cashing in on a 62-yard punt return by an alternate running back, 175-pound Lou Ikner, that set up the game-winning touchdown shortly before the third quarter ended.

Paterno's strategy assisted Alabama's first touchdown drive, a march that ate up 80 yards in the last minute of the half.

After the first two plays of that march, the Lions called time out, stopping the clock with Alabama inside their own 30-yard line.

"We wanted to force them to punt." said Paterno. "We figured if we could make them kick, we'd pick up a first down on a pass and then kick a 55-yard field goal."

It was a strategy which, eventually, went awry as an Alabama receiver, lean Bruce Bolton, a walk-on senior, made a diving scoop of Jeff Rutledge's 30-yard pass in the end zone. One of those bang-bang plays Paterno talked about after the game.

Even though they had lost their No. 1 ranking as well as the game, Penn State's prestige didn't suffer in the heart-breaking defeat. They were still a great team, said Bryant, the Alabama coach.

"Penn State is a great defensive team," said Bryant. "They are a great team, period. They forced us into doing things we preferred not to do."

Unfortunately, great teams don't

always win.

Why Penn State didn't win, Paterno and most of his players conceded, was because of the manner in which Alabama's linebackers, playing behind a 4-3 and 5-2 alignment, dominated the action.

"The men I was blocking against weren't too strong," said Chuck Correal, the Lions' 250-pound center, "but their linebackers, man, were they active and quick. We didn't seem to be able to handle them."

Fusina, who spent most of the day running away from linebackers and blitzing safeties, also was aware of their intimidating presence.

"Their linebackers made some excellent plays," said Fusina. "I don't think they blitzed as much against other teams as they did against us."

Paterno didn't think they did either. If there was one thing that surprised Paterno, it was the frequency with which the Alabama secondary was chasing down Fusina behind the line of scrimmage.

"It was their rush that concerned us," said Paterno. "Every time we were in a passing down, they kept coming at us with a lot of people."

Earlier in the week, Paterno had indicated privately he thought there might be some leaks in the Alabama secondary, that it might be vulnerable because the Tide had so many injuries to players in those positions. He was asked if he felt he had underestimated the Alabama's secondary.

"Maybe that's why they were doing so much blitzing," said Paterno.

Jim Bob Harris (9) steals a pass intended for Lions receiver Bob Bassett.

Penn State Grounds Buckeyes' Air Attack in Fiesta Bowl

BY BOB BLACK
The Pittsburgh Press

Tempe, Ariz., Dec. 27, 1980 — Penn State coach Joe Paterno called it "simply a matter of making a minor adjustment in the second half."

Of course, the result was very much like trading in a .22 and replacing it with a cannon. Or replacing a school of guppies in your fish tank with a school of piranha.

That's basically what happened in front of a record-breaking Fiesta Bowl crowd of 66,738 fans here yesterday at Sun Devil Stadium.

And that "minor adjustment" Paterno talked about resulted in Penn State turning around a nine-point halftime deficit which had seen Ohio State quarterback Art Schlichter passing for 244 yards into a complete shutout in the third quarter.

That's right. No yards passing. No yards running. Nothing.

And it also resulted in the Lions turning this into a 10-win season via a 31-19 victory over Ohio State which could push Penn State as high as fifth or sixth in the final ratings after all the bowl games have been played.

Todd Blackledge (14) and Joe Paterno observe the action from the sidelines.

Score by Periods					
Ohio State	6	13	0	0	— 19
Penn State	7	3	6	15	— 31

It also occurred after Penn State safety Pete Harris had been removed from the game when he suffered stretched ligaments in his leg at the end of the first half.

That resulted in replacing Harris, who is Penn State's most experienced defensive back as a fifth-year senior and who also stands 6-2, with 5-8 sophomore Dan Biondi from Penn Hills.

Considering that Biondi's only previous games with significant playing time were in easy wins over Colgate, Texas A&M and Temple, any betting man would have wagered the house, the car and most of his negotiable

paper that Schlichter would continue picking apart the Lions secondary in the second half.

It didn't work that way, however.

With Biondi subbing for Harris and the Lions defensive line taking control of Ohio State's offensive line, Penn State was able to keep the Buckeye seniors 0-for-career in four bowl appearances.

And to say that it was a significant win was like saying the Mona Lisa is a significant work of art.

"Beating a team like Ohio State on national TV helps restore our reputation," said senior defensive tackle Frank Case, who was named the defensive player of the game. "Against Pitt we thought we outplayed them, yet we lost — on national TV."

"And against Nebraska we turned the ball over seven times and lost — on national TV."

"So this time we were able to win one of those BIG football games."

And a big reason for that was the usual strong defensive performance turned in by the Lions in the second half while the offense was taking its cue from the defense and playing ball control.

"There's no question one group helps out the other," said Penn State offensive guard Sean Farrell, who along with seniors Bill Dugan and Bob Jagers was a principal reason the Lions were able to rush for 351 yards and pass for 117 more against the Buckeyes.

"We use a lot of people when we play. As a result, our starters are still fresh late in the game. It think that was a key. They (Ohio State) seemed to be tiring late in that game."

They probably were tired of chasing Curt Warner, who finished with the most productive rushing performance of his career — 155 yards on 18 carries — fullback Booker Moore and

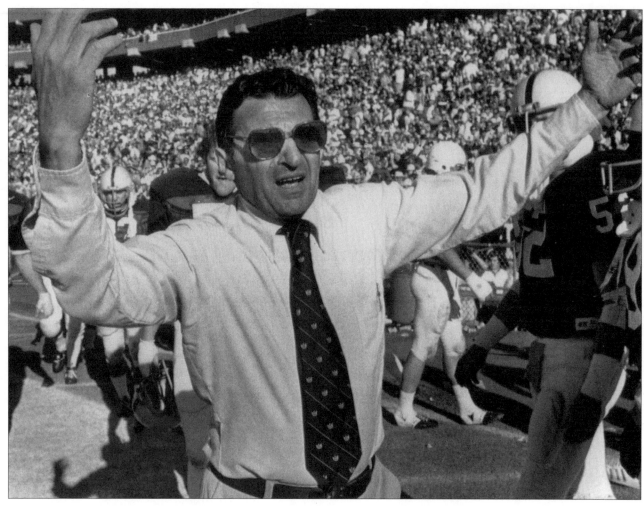

After defeating Ohio State, 31-19, coach Joe Paterno joins in the Fiesta Bowl postgame celebration.

backup tailbacks Joel Coles and Jon Williams and backup fullback Mike Meade.

"You gotta be impressed with their running game," said Penn State coach Earle Bruce. "They keep bringing in new backs. And they keep picking up yardage with them."

But in the first half, it was Ohio State with Schlichter passing to Doug Donley and Gary Williams which rolled up the impressive stats.

After Warner gave Penn State its only significant offensive play of the

first half — going 64 yards for a touchdown on the Lions' first play from scrimmage of the game — it was left to Dr. Schlichter to operate on the Penn State secondary.

First he hit Donley with a 23-yard touchdown pass to complete an 83-yard, six-play drive accomplished in less than two minutes.

When Buckeye kicker Vlade Janakievski missed his first extra point of the year after hitting 45 straight, the Lions still held a one-point margin,

But again Schlichter went to work,

this time covering 84 yards in seven plays in less than three minutes. He gave the Buckeyes the lead on a 32-yard touchdown pass to Williams.

This time Case dropped Schlichter in his own backfield on the Buckeyes' attempt at the two point conversion.

Again Schlichter chipped away at the Lions secondary and covered 77 yards in seven plays and just one minute 35 seconds, and Penn State looked like easy pickings.

But after Herb Menhardt closed out the first-half scoring with with a 38-

Curt Warner (25) outsprints Ohio State's Ray Ellis (27) and Vince Skillings (48) on a 63-yard touchdown run.

yard field goal, Penn State put on a new game face for the second half.

"Our defense was being hurt by their inside curl pattern," said Paterno. "And they were completing a lot of short passes over the middle. So we decided we'd have to adjust a few things and take those plays away from them."

One thing Paterno might not have been figuring having to adjust, however, was replacing Harris with Biondi at safety.

But Biondi, who has been primarily a special teams player this season, was ready.

"I wasn't concerned about them throwing over me," Biondi said of the prospect of Schlichter attempting to hit Donley and Williams against him.

"Their receivers aren't any bigger than ours. And I go against ours in practice. Besides that, Coach Paterno had us all ready to go this week. Because of the heat we knew a lot of people would be playing in this game."

And in the second half, those people combined to wear down an Ohio State team which never was able to regain its first-half form.

"They started stunting and playing more man-to-man coverage," Schlichter said of Penn State's second-half performance. "Our game plan was to throw on them. But we didn't have the field advantage in the second half we did in the first.

"At halftime, we thought we had them. But after they started picking up momentum in the third quarter, we weren't able to come back."

The Lions started their second-half comeback by covering 75 yards in 10 plays with quarterback Todd Blackledge bootlegging the final 4 yards for the touchdown.

Then, in the fourth quarter, the Lions took advantage of good field position set up by a 17-yard punt return by Williams.

The freshman big-play tailback, who runs behind Warner and Coles at that position, scored the go-ahead touchdown by plunging four yards for the score.

And Moore finished off the Buckeyes by scoring on a 37-yard run in the final minute of play.

"Wow, what a way to finish off your college career," Moore said. "I couldn't believe how that hole opened up for me. I guess maybe they (Ohio State) were getting a little tired at the end."

Warner Runs Wild on Nebraska Defense to Lead Nittany Lions

BY BOB BLACK
The Pittsburgh Press

Lincoln Neb., Sept. 26, 1981 — They call it "Red Power." In most cases when opponents look up into a sea of red worn by nearly 76,000 Nebraska fans, the experience is very unnerving.

Obviously, Penn State tailback Curt Warner doesn't believe in Red Power. Especially after his performance here yesterday in a 30-24 victory over the Cornhuskers.

Warner, a streak in blue and white, was preceded by the kind of blocking that left Nebraska defenders black and blue and also red-faced.

The 6-foot, 195-pound junior from Wyoming, W. Va., improved on his opening-game credentials by picking up 238 yards on 27 carries to guide the No. 3-ranked Lions to a 414-397 edge in total offense.

Much of that yardage was necessary to help offset turnover problems, which plagued both teams throughout the game.

"That was an extra-special game for all of us out there," Warner said. "We did today what we wanted to do last year. But last year we just never seemed to be in the situation where we could attack them."

Unlike last year, when Nebraska capitalized on Penn State turnovers,

Score by Periods					
Penn State	3	14	3	10 —	30
Nebraska	0	10	14	0 —	24

yesterday it reciprocated by matching the Lions turnover for turnover.

"Play was a little sloppy by both teams in that first half," said Penn State coach Joe Paterno. "But part of the reason for that was the hard hitting going on in there. That was a very physical football game."

An example of how physical it was came during Penn State's first drive for a score on what looked like a touchdown run by Warner at the 1-yard line. Warner was crunched so hard the ball popped loose back to the 11, where Joel Coles fell on it. The Lions settled

for the first of five Brian Franco field goals.

It was one of the few times Nebraska was able to contain Warner, who evenly distributed his ground gaining, with better than 100 yards in each half.

"They have an outstanding offensive line, there's no doubt about that," said Nebraska coach Tom Osbourne, whose Huskers are off to their poorest start (1-2) since 1961. "But there's no question Warner was the difference in this game. They have a good group of running backs and he's their leader."

The game was expected to be a battle between Nebraska's all-everything I-back Roger Craig and Warner, with the passing and kicking games providing the difference.

But the difference wound up being Warner's 238 yards compared to just 122 for Craig, who also carried the ball 24 times.

"I thought Craig was a good test for our defense," Paterno said. "He's a good football player, but I though out defense did an outstanding job of trying to contain him."

Without five field goals from Franco — whose performance is a Penn State record — Warner's game might have gone all for naught.

"This was my first opportunity to make this kind of contribution in four years," said Franco, who first sat behind Matt Bahr and Herb Menhardt and then had just the latter ahead of him the past two years.

"I really didn't feel any pressure kicking out there, despite the size and noise of their crowd. Once I kicked the first one, the rest of them were easier."

Included among those five field goals was a 48-yarder which narrowed an early Nebraska lead to 7-6. After Penn State opened the scoring in the first quarter with Franco's 29-yard field goal, the Huskers took advantage of a breakdown in Penn State coverage, connecting on a 55-yard pass to the Lions 16. Three plays later, Craig crashed over from the 2 and Nebraska had the lead.

Franco's second field goal trimmed the margin to one point and, when Nebraska's Mike Rozier fumbled at his own 26, the Lions recovered the ball, but settled for a 39-yard Franco field goal.

After Jon Williams fumbled late in the second quarter, Nebraska's Ric Lindquist recovered at the Husker 41 and Ed Neil kicked a 30-yard field goal for a 10-9 Nebraska lead.

Penn State came back with its most impressive passing performance of the game, a 26-yard screen to Warner, followed by a 33-yard touchdown pass to Kenny Jackson with just 30 seconds left in the half, to carry a 17-10 lead into the locker room.

"I wasn't that satisfied with my passing game," said Penn State quarterback Todd Blackledge, who missed on his first four attempts before finally completing one for minus-2 yards. "I got my confidence back on that drive and I think it helped me in the second half."

But, after finishing the half with such a flourish, the Lions proved to be their own worst enemies in the second half, when Williams fumbled a punt and the Huskers drove 20 yards in five plays to tie it up.

The Lions followed with an impressive drive of their own to the Nebraska 4, but again settled for a Franco field goal, to grab a three-point lead.

In a game of impressive drives, however, the Huskers turned around and drove 74 yards in 10 plays to go ahead again, 24-20, on a 16-yard pass from Mark Mauer to Scott Woodard.

After the Lions covered 61 yards in eight plays, capped by a 2-yard run by Coles with 11:02 remaining, their defense stiffened and Nebraska's scoring was closed down. Franco wrapped up things with a 32-yard field goal with less than five minutes remaining.

"This one helps prove that we can win the big game when we have to," said Paterno. "And I also think it proves that Curt Warner is one of the finest running backs in the country."

There aren't many people from Nebraska who would dispute that claim. For one day at least, Nebraska's Red Power was silenced by a blue and white streak.

Lion Lines

One the first play of the game, Blackledge fumbled the snap but recovered it for a three-yard loss. "It was a little noisy and I guess I got a little rattled," he said. "I'm glad we didn't lose the ball. After that fumble, I was all right." Blackledge finished with just four completions in 13 attempts for one touchdown and 87 yards.

Warner moved into eighth place in career Penn State rushing, passing Fran Rogel, with 1,673 yards. He was just 12 yards away from the single-game record of 250 yards rushing set by Eugene (Shorty) Miller. Miller rushed for those 250 yards in 1912 against Carnegie Tech.

Penn State's Ralph Giacomarro punted six times for a 39.7 average, but booted one out of bounds at the Nebraska 2 and also had a 54-yarder. … The two teams fumbled 11 times in the first half and combined for seven turnovers in the game. Penn State turned it over three times and Nebraska four.

Curt Warner had two 200-yard rushing games in the 1981 season.

No. 1 No More: Hurricanes Level Penn State, 17-14

BY BOB BLACK
Special to The Pittsburgh Press

Miami, Oct. 31, 1981 — The No. 1 jinx is alive and well, thank you. Look out Pitt, Southern Cal, Clemson or whoever. Next week, it could be your turn.

Playing completely out of character, Penn State was forced to go to the passing game when it was unable to run on Miami yesterday at the Orange Bowl in a game which alternated between rain and clear weather, depending on which team had the ball.

In the end, however, it was Penn State that got rained on. The Nittany Lions staged a late comeback that fell three points short, 17-14, a loss that assures the Lions of a tumble from their No. 1 spot in the polls.

Despite getting a school-record 358 years passing from quarterback Todd Black-ledge, the Lions were unable to overcome the strong passing game turned in by East Brady's Jim Kelly for Miami.

Although Kelly passed for only 220 yards, he did it with the precision of a surgeon as the Hurricanes were building up a big lead in the first half.

"I've said all along that Kelly was a good quarterback and would

be as good as anybody we'd face so far this season. Today I guess he proved it," said Lions coach Joe Paterno.

"The difference in this game from the last two was the fact that they had a kicker who provided them with more than a one-dimensional offense."

With Dan Miller converting field goals from 28 and 42 yards in the first quarter and Kelly finding a gaping hole in the Penn State secondary for an 80-yard touchdown pass to Larry Brodsky, Miami had 14 first-half points while Penn State was finding it impossible to do the usual job of dominating the line of scrimmage to establish a running game.

"They were a very physical team," said Penn State guard Sean Farrell, usually the main man in moving defensive linemen out of the way. "We got behind early and just got out of character. We didn't do things the way we're capable of doing them. It was just a disappointing game for us overall."

The most disappointed player for Penn State had to be kicker Brian Franco, who missed four field-goal attempts — any one of which would have lifted the Lions into a tie.

"We have a great team. I can't let them down like I did. There's no excuse for that," said Franco.

He missed three attempts in the first half alone, from 52 yards, 47 yards and finally a 22-yarder at a bad angle into the wind.

The second missed field goal, attempted while Miami held a 6-0 lead, was into the wind on the first play of the second quarter after Penn State failed to call a time out

Score by Periods

Penn State	0	0	0	14	— 14
Miami	6	8	0	3	— 17

Gregg Garrity led the 1981 Penn State squad with 23 receptions for 415 yards.

to stop the clock and give him a shot with the wind.

"There was a lot of confusion around our bench area as the quarter was running out," Paterno said. "I lost my concentration and failed to call the time out."

And after turning the ball over to Miami at the Hurricane 20, the upset proceeded. Kelly found Brodsky with the 80-yard touchdown pass and Miami was pumped up for the second half.

"This just goes to show where our football program has come," said Miami coach Howard Schnellenberger. "Every time we need a big play they rise to the occassion. The biggest asset they have is believing in themselves. That's why we were able to hold them off there at the end. I thought Penn State showed a lot of character coming back like they did."

The loss seemed especially painful to Blackledge, who had by far his best game at Penn State, and tailback Curt Warner, who sat out most of the game after reinjuring a hamstring pull in the first half.

"Yes, I'd have to say we were out of character out there," Blackledge said, "Mainly because we're used to winning. I'm sure we'll survive this, but it still hurts."

"It was frustrating not being able to help," Warner said after being held to just 27 yards on 13 running attempts — all in the first half. "There's no question they were a good football team. But I just don't think we were able to show people how good we are. We're better than we looked today."

For Penn State, which lost its two nationally televised regular-season games last season — to Nebraska and Pitt — it was a continuation of tube-itis, being unable to win on TV.

"I really don't think the No. 1 jinx or TV had anything to do with it,"

Sean Farrell and the Lions had a lot to celebrate in 1981 but not the Miami game.

Paterno said. "We just got beat by a good football team. It's unfortunate we weren't able to come back and win it after playing the way we did in that final quarter."

What Penn State did in those closing minutes was come within a fumble on a bread-and-butter play of winning No. 7 without a loss this season.

After Miami had expanded its lead to 17-0 on a 23-yard field goal, Penn State — led by Blackledge's arm — attempted its comeback.

Blackledge was forced to throw in the rain, which seemed to intensify every time Penn State had the football. But after completing passes of 16 and 21 yards to Gregg Garrity, he found tight end Mike McCloskey in the end zone for a touchdown and the

beginning of a comeback. His attempt for the two-point conversion to Kevin Baugh went awry, however, and with just 8:51 remaining it looked like the party was over for Penn State.

But after Miami's Smokey Roan fumbled and Paul Lankford picked the ball out of the air for Penn State, suddenly it was a football game again.

"We really got up at that point," Lankford said. "We had been down before (in the Nebraska game) and came back, so we felt like maybe we were going to do it again."

The recovery at the Miami 26 was followed by a two-play Penn Sate drive for the touchdown. On the first, fullback Mike Meade was stopped for no gain off-tackle and, on the second, Blackledge hit Kenny Jackson with a 26-yard touchdown pass.

After halting Miami's next drive, the Lions again were hit by rain—and a mistake. Jon Williams fumbled a quick pitch after being the receiver on a 32-yard play that moved the ball to the Hurricane 25.

"It wasn't a bad pitch," said Blackledge. "But it was a cutback. And he was getting the ball just as he cut, and he slipped."

And when he did, he fumbled. Tony Chickillo fell on the loose football for Miami.

"It wasn't a daring play," Paterno said when asked about the play's advisability in those final futile minutes.

"That's been one of our basic plays all season. But with the rain and wet field conditions it just didn't work."

With the fumble went Penn State's hopes of retaining the nation's No. 1 rating for another week.

The Lions had one last shot at catching up, but Blackledge's pass was intercepted by Miami's Fred Marion with a little more than a minute to play.

Lions Ground Marino, Pierce Pitt's No. 1 Dream

By Bob Smizik
The Pittsburgh Press

Pittsburgh, Nov. 28, 1981 — No one ever said that this was a football team that could not be beaten. But no one ever dreamt, not even Joe Paterno, that this was a football team that could be beaten so badly.

No more national championship talk, no more No. 1 rating. The talking is over, the football playing is over. Penn State is a winner. Is it ever!

Fumbles, interceptions and penalties were a part of this monumental defeat of the Pitt Panthers, but more than those critical errors it was a great football team that did them in yesterday.

Penn State spotted Pitt two early touchdowns, thus allowing the Panthers to believe they were some kind of invincible juggernaut, then went to work, putting six touchdowns and two field goals on the scoreboard while the No. 3 scoring offense in the country didn't get another point as the Lions roared to a 48-14 win before 60,260.

The No. 1-ranked and Sugar Bowl-bound Panthers (10-1) will probably fall to the bottom half of the Top 10. The ninth-ranked and Fiesta Bowl-bound Lions (9-2), who destroyed the No. 1 defense in the nation, should move up several notches.

"I never dreamt this could happen," said Pitt tight end John Brown. "When

Score by Periods

Penn State	0	14	17	17	— 48
Pitt	14	0	0	0	— 14

it rains, it pours. And it really rained on us today."

It rained in all kinds of forms on the Panthers, who had not lost at home since losing to Penn State in the final game of the 1977 season.

Much-maligned Penn State quarterback Todd Blackledge threw for 262 yards and two touchdowns. Forgotten Kenny Jackson, who had caught only 14 passes all season, made the Pitt secondary look like amateurs, grabbing five balls for 158 yards and two touchdowns. Injured Curt Warner was healthy enough to rush for 104 yards on 21 carries and became the fourth Penn State

back in history to go over 1,000 yards for the season.

From Warner, such an afternoon is not unexpected. But from Blackledge and Jackson, such games have been rare this season.

"We didn't play that well in the secondary," said Pitt coach Jackie Sherrill.

Free safety Tom Flynn was more colorful. "He (Jackson) is good, no doubt about that," said Flynn. "We didn't expect that at all. We didn't really know how good he was. He was having a bad year, but he turned around and put it in our face."

It didn't start that way, not that way at all. A Pitt Stadium crowd which was some 4,000 beyond capacity because of special bleachers in the end zone, figured it was in on a rout right from the start, but that it would be the Panthers doing the routing.

Pitt quarterback Dan Marino was positively brilliant, completing nine of 10 passes in the first quarter as the Panthers scored on their first two possessions.

But if Pitt fans and players were expecting a rout, Paterno was not. "Nobody can stay that hot all day," said Paterno.

And sure enough, Marino was intercepted in the end zone on the first play of the second quarter. It was the first in a series of interceptions (four), fumbles lost (three) and penalties (13) that, along with a fine Penn State defense, were to render the heretofore explosive Pitt offensive null and void.

But for the first 11 minutes of the game, the Panthers were near-perfect on both offense and defense. While scoring 14 points and not having to punt, the Panthers also held the Lions to minus yardage.

The Panthers moved 48 yards for their first score, with Marino passing 28 yards to Dwight Collins, who had a

Penn State quarterback Todd Blackledge (14) ties the game on an 8-yard run.

next play and the Lions were in business.

Later in the quarter, with the Lions in possession on their own 39, Jackson was in a footrace down the middle of the field with Flynn and Pappy Thomas, who were matching him stride for stride. But when Blackledge put the ball in the air, Jackson turned on the afterburners and all Flynn and Thomas could do was hope he would drop the ball.

He didn't. Flynn made the tackle on the 8. Blackledge then scored on the next play.

Pitt had a chance to recapture the momentum before the half when Pat McQuaide recovered Jackson's fumble on a punt on the Penn State 41. Marino passed 19 yards to sophomore Bill Wallace, and Bryan Thomas, who became the third Pitt runner in history to pass 1,000 yards, ran for 6 to move the ball to the 22. A Marino to Thomas pass put the ball on the 4, but the play was called back when offensive guard Rob Fada was called for a personal foul on Penn State defensive end Walker Lee Ashley.

"He was talking trash and throwing cheap shots all afternoon," said Fada. "On that play he hit me in the jaw. The ref had to see it. But they had lost control of the game. But I shouldn't have done it. I lost my cool."

And Pitt lost a probable touchdown. On the next play, Wayne DiBartola fumbled.

Pitt continued to make mistakes in the second half. On the fourth play of the half, sophomore fullback Bill Beach, playing in place of DiBartola, who had injured his ankle, fumbled after running for 13 yards to the Penn State 44. That was all Jackson and Blackledge needed.

From the Pitt 42, Blackledge hit Jackson almost perfectly a step from the sideline at the 10. But instead of going

superb day with six catches, for the touchdown.

And that was it. For a while, the Panthers continued to move the ball, but as the mistakes mounted to sap their motivation, and as Penn State started to score and score and score, Pitt became a shell of the team that had won 17 straight games.

Starting on the 20, following Roger Jackson's interception, the Lions began their incredible comeback. With Blackledge completing short passes and with Pitt defensive end Al Wenglikowski contributing a 15-yard, face-mask penalty, the Lions moved to the Pitt 30, where Flynn — on a safety blitz — was a millisecond from nailing him, Blackledge passed 28 yards to tight end Mike McCloskey. Mike Meade scored on the out of bounds, Jackson pivoted back to the middle of the field, leaving Flynn and strong safety Dan Short in the lurch as he ran for a touchdown.

A few minutes later Jackson left cornerback Tim Lewis some 15 yards behind him as he took a 45-yard pass for a touchdown.

"Poor Tim Lewis," said Pitt defensive coordinator Foge Fazio. "He guessed wrong and got burned."

And the fire was out of the Panthers.

Other than a 32-yard pass to Collins, which was followed by three plays that netted minus-6 yards, the Panthers had no more offense in the third quarter.

Penn State's Roger Jackson hammers Pitt receiver Julius Dawkins, sending the ball into the air for the Nittany Lions' Mark Robinson to grab an interception.

Blackledge Bests Marino In Battle Of QB's

BY BOB BLACK
The Pittsburgh Press

He had just finished passing for 262 yards, including two touchdown passes and just one interception in 23 attempts. Yet to Penn State quarterback Todd Blackledge, given the James Coogan Award as the outstanding player in the Pitt-Penn State game, it was not to be construed as a personal victory over the most celebrated quarterback in college football — the Panthers' Danny Marino.

It was merely a 48-14 win over the No. 1-ranked team in the country. The fact that the team happened to be Penn State's biggest rival made it just that much sweeter for the Lions.

A deeply religious player who credits his best performances to "the Lord," Blackledge also proved to be a deeply talented quarterback against Pitt. The 6-foot-3½, 225-pound sophomore from North Canton, Ohio, was every bit the equal of the guy on the other side of the field who has already been named to a number of all–America teams.

"I don't consider this to be an unusual performance for Penn State," Blackledge said of Penn State's most lopsided win over Pitt in 10 years. "People in Pittsburgh see what the Steelers and Pitt have been doing all year and maybe they came to expect the same thing from us.

"But that's not our style. We've been a big-play team when we needed it this season — and I think we proved that today. But in a number

of cases we weren't forced to play the kind of game we did today.

"On several of those pass plays we guessed right and they guessed wrong. Sometimes that's the difference between a successful passing game and an unsuccessful one."

In Blackledge's case, it was a matter of guessing right many more times than he guessed wrong.

In the first period, while Pitt was playing a game of pitch and catch that looked as easy as stealing candy from a baby, Penn State unsuccessfully tried its running game, falling behind by 14 points.

But then, looking more innovative than the Ronald Reagan-styled offense people have come to expect from Penn State, Blackledge started doing his thing.

And the more he did it, the bet-

Pitt's Michael Woods (96) applies a bear hug to Lions quarterback Todd Blackledge.

And still Penn State came. Pitt was down and the Lions wanted lots more. And they got lots more.

Brian Franco added field goals of 39 and 38 yards to start the fourth quarter and those were followed by a sustained drive which ended when all-American offensive guard Sean Farrell fell on a Warner fumble in the end zone and — the ultimate insult — a 91-yard return of a Marino interception by safety Mark Robinson.

"Give Penn State the credit," said Brown. "They outplayed us. They deserved to win. They're a great team. But we're a great team, too."

"It's football and someone has to win and someone has to lose," said

middle guard J.C. Pelusi. "We're disappointed. We were trying to nail down the national championship. They're the best team we've played. That's evident."

"Too many mistakes, too many fumbles, too many interceptions," said Marino. "You can't do that against a great team and expect to win."

As for Sherrill, who was seeking his third straight win over Penn State but got his third loss in five tries instead, he said, "When a locomotive gets out of control, there's nothing you can do to stop it."

Penn State was the train that steamrolled Pitt's national championship hopes.

---

ter Penn State played, both offensively and defensively.

First it was a 28-yard pass to tight end Mike McCloskey to the Pitt 2, which set up a 2-yard lunge by fullback Mike Meade.

Then it was a 52-yard bomb to wide receiver Kenny Jackson to the Panthers' 8, which Blackledge followed with a quarterback keeper for the tying touchdown.

And from there it just continued to get better for him.

He opened the second half with a 42-yard touchdown pass to Jackson and followed just 2½ minutes later with a 35-yard touchdown pass to the same receiver.

After that it was a 44-yard pass to McCloskey on a drive that ended in a Penn State field goal.

By the fourth period there was no question Blackledge was the man in control. When the Lions needed a first down on a third and long, he

would pass for it. When only short yardage was needed, he'd hand off to Curt Warner — whose 104 yards gave him his 11th 100-yard game — Mike Meade or Jon Williams, or he'd get whatever was necessary himself.

"Todd Blackledge has got the makings of a great quarterback," said Penn State coach Joe Paterno. "But then I've said that all year. He's got a great arm and he's a tough kid. He's had a lot of pressure on him this season. But we've played some great defensive teams.

"He also proved to a lot of people how good of a quarterback he was in the Miami game (when he passed for 358 yards, breaking a single-game Penn State passing record). When we weren't able to run on them (Pitt's defense), Todd started hitting the passing game. And that also made our running game work better in the second half."

Blackledge entered the game hav-

ing passed for 1,295 yards and 10 touchdowns while throwing 13 interceptions. Marino had completed 178 of 294 passes for 2,348 yards and 32 touchdowns, while throwing 17 interceptions.

For one period, Marino made it look easy, quickly riddling Penn State's defense for a pair of touchdown passes. But then Blackledge took over and also made it look easy.

The difference was that when Blackledge got started, Pitt quit, and the result leaves Fiesta Bowl people very happy with a matchup between two 9-2 teams in Penn State and Southern Cal.

Along with the impressive credentials of Warner and Southern Cal's Marcus Allen, they have a quarterback who, in his most important game of the year, outperformed the most impressive college quarterback in the country.

Penn State, Warner Run Over Trojans; Allen Held in Check

By Bob Black
The Pittsburgh Press

Tempe, Ariz., Jan. 1, 1982 — They had just conquered American's Bowl Team by reducing American's Heisman Trophy winner to mere mortal status. Yet there seemed to be something more important on the minds of the members of perhaps American's most unappreciated college football team.

Easily handling Southern Cal, 26-10, in front of a record Fiesta Bowl crowd of 71,053 rainsoaked fans at Sun Devil Stadium, Penn State held Marcus Allen to just 85 yards on 30 carries.

It was only the second time Allen had been held under 100 yards rushing since taking over as the Trojans' tailback two season's ago. It was also 62 yards below his previous low of the season — 147 yards against Notre Dame.

But as far as Coach Joe Paterno, linebacker Chet Parlavecchio, offensive guard Sean Farrell and a handful of other Nittany Lions were concerned, yesterday's Penn State win over a team with 19 previous bowl victories (more that any other NCAA team) provided a legitimate claim at being the No. 1 team in the country.

"When you play the kind of schedule we had this season and come out of it as well as we did, then I think you deserve to be considered the best there

Score by Periods

Penn State	7	10	9	0	—	26
U.S.C.	7	0	3	0	—	10

The 1982 victory was the third Fiesta Bowl triumph for the Nittany Lions and Coach Joe Paterno, below.

is," Paterno said. "I felt going into this game that the winner had a legitimate claim at being the best in the country."

Considering that the Lions started with Nebraska, Miami (Fla.), Alabama, Notre Dame, Pitt and finally Southern Cal to the list of this season's opponents, it might be difficult to question the validity of that statement.

That being the case, the Lions laid unofficial claim to the national title on the strength of the offensive line, which opened holes through which junior tailback Curt Warner rushed for 145 yards and two touchdowns on 26 carries. And a sophomore quarterback, Todd Blackledge, who completed 11 of 14 passes for 175 yards and one touchdown. And a defense, keyed by Parlavecchio and Leo Wisniewski, which held the Trojans to 60 yards rushing, compared to their 299 per game average.

They also did it by taking advantage of five Southern Cal turnovers, which included a pair of fumbles by Allen.

"We were plagued by mistakes all day," said Trojans coach John Robinson. "We didn't run the ball very well. We didn't block very well. And we didn't catch the ball very well, either. I guess we didn't do very many things right.

"But we were beaten by a good football team which played like it wanted to win much more than we did."

That, according to several Penn State players, may have been one of the contributing factors to the Lions' impressive win.

"No way they wanted this football game as much as we did," said Parlavecchio. "Maybe because it wasn't the Rose Bowl, it didn't mean as much to them. I don't know. I do know it meant a lot to us."

That was obvious from the opening series, when the Lions took advantage

Gregg Garrity (19) leaps into the arms of teammate Mike Meade (38) after catching a touchdown pass in the second quarter.

of U.S.C.'s first mistake of the game and turned it into a touchdown.

After Allen fumbled a pitch going around his left end, the Lions' Roger Jackson grabbed the loose football at the Trojan 17.

Two plays later, after Blackledge had missed a pass to tight end Vyto Kab in the end zone, Warner went 17 yards off left tackle for the touchdown.

"That came too easy," said Warner. "And, as a result, we really didn't get into the game until that second half. That second half showed how strong this football team can be."

A strong second half became necessary when the Lions failed to take advantage of numerous scoring opportunities in the first half.

The Trojans tied the score in the first quarter when linebacker Chip Banks picked off a Blackledge pass and went 20 yards for the touchdown.

Earlier in the quarter, Lions placekicker Brian Franco had missed a 36-

yard field goal attempt, which he followed with a miss of a 37-yarder in the second quarter.

The Lions grabbed the lead on a 52-yard pass from Blackledge to Gregg Garrity and added three more points when Franco finally hit a field goal — from 21 yards — after Penn State had been stopped at the 9 following a recovery of an Allen fumble by Wisniewski at the Trojans 24.

But, despite owning field advantage for most of the first half, the Lions missed three scoring opportunities during that period — the two missed field goals and their final possession before halftime, when Blackledge failed to plunge in from the 2.

"I was a little concerned," said Blackledge. "We weren't sure what to expect from Southern Cal in the second half. But we didn't panic. We just came out and drove on them to open the second half. That drive was the most important series of the

game for us."

The Lions took the ball and drove 80 yards in nine plays — with Blackledge throwing 14 yards to Kab, 15 to Kenny Jackson and seven to Mike McCloskey before Warner carried it in from the 21.

"It was just a quick pitch with the offensive line wiping out the defense," said Warner. "They did a good job of that all day."

But, if Penn State's offense was impressive, its defense was devastating.

"Our defensive scheme wasn't that different than it was in previous games," said Wisniewski, a former high school linebacker and fullback at Fox Chapel, who was named the most valuable defensive player in the game. "We were just more fired up than they were. Physically, we just beat Southern Cal the whole game. That's the only way you can control a team like them."

Though the Trojans added a 37-yard field goal by Steve Jordan, they never really threatened the Lions, who got their final points on a blocked punt by Dave Paffenroth, who knocked it out of the end zone for a safety.

"For some reason, we have to keep trying to prove how good a football team we have," said defensive end Rich D'Amico from Central Catholic High School, who finished with nine tackles. "You could tell by their attitude that they really didn't take us that seriously. Any time a team does that, they give us something to prove."

And what they proved was that the Lions may not finish the season ranked No. 1 in the polls, but, of their performance against Southern Cal, there may not have been a team in the country which could have stayed with them today.

Penn State runner Mike Meade bursts through the middle of the Trojans' line in the second quarter. Meade finished with 60 yards on nine carries.

Warner Wins Duel With Trojans' Allen

BY BOB BLACK
The Pittsburgh Press

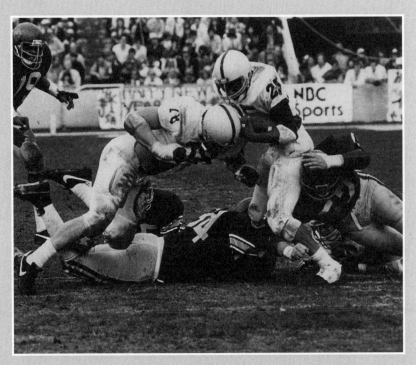

Tailback Curt Warner fights for extra yards during a second-quarter run. Warner ran for 145 yards and scored twice for the Nittany Lions.

For nearly one week, almost every phrase uttered within a 30-mile radius of this usually sun-splashed area had something to do with the merits of Heisman Trophy winner Marcus Allen.

And with good reason. Allen, the most celebrated player in college football this season, had broken or tied 13 NCAA records as a tailback at Southern Cal. The most significant of those records were 403 carries in 11 games for 2,342 yards.

In the process, another fine tailback — Curt Warner of Penn State — was virtually ignored.

While Warner had rushed for 238 yards during a win at Nebraska and a school record 256 in a win at Syracuse, a pair of pulled hamstrings had limited his play in the second half of the season, limiting him to 1,044 yards on 171 carries.

As a result, his credentials were not nearly as impressive as Allen's.

Today, here in Sun Devil Stadium in front of 71,053 fans who sat through a drizzling rain, Warner carried the ball 26 times for 145 yards and two touchdowns while Allen was picking up just 85 yards and no touchdowns on 30 carries for the Trojans.

In the process, the Lions cruised to a 26-10 victory, giving them a 10-2 record to match their 1980 effort, when they finished with a win over Ohio State in the Fiesta Bowl.

Asked if his performance meant he

was a better running back, Warner quickly sidestepped the question.

"How can I answer that?," he said. "Today I had better blocking than Marcus had. So I had a better day than he did."

But for senior offensive guard Sean Farrell, who made his final college game a most memorable one by continually opening gaping holes for Warner — the game's offensive MVP — there was no question.

"Who do you think won?," he said rhetorically. "Warner did, hands down. When he's healthy, he's as good a running back as there is in the game."

Those sentiments were echoed by Warner's coach, Joe Paterno, and Southern Cal coach John Robinson.

"People felt we went into a slump the second half of this season," said Paterno. "But the reason for that was the loss of Warner for a couple games and his limited playing time in others. Taking Warner away from Penn State is like taking Marcus Allen away from Southern Cal, and Herschel Walker away from Georgia. He's in that same class."

"Curt Warner is a great football player," said Robinson. "If he stays healthy next season, he can be one of the best in the country."

Lions Edge No. 2 Huskers on Dramatic Touchdown Pass

By DAN DONOVAN
The Pittsburgh Press

University Park, Pa., Sept. 25, 1982 — Todd Blackledge's last pass was one of his worst, but tight end Kirk Bowman clutched it to his heart one inch above the end zone grass with four seconds left to give Penn State a heart-stopping 27-24 win over No. 2 Nebraska before a record 85,304 fans at Beaver Stadium yesterday.

Quarterback Blackledge put on a spectacular performance, a Heisman Trophy-type performance before a national television audience, driving Penn State 65 yards with 1:18 left in the game.

"Todd's turning into a great leader," Bowman said. "There was a feeling of confidence on the team. We moved 65 yards in 1:18 against a very good team."

Blackledge completed 23 of 39 passes for 295 yards and three touchdowns, tying him for the school record of 15 touchdown passes in a season after only four games.

"This was a good indicator of the character on this football team," Blackledge said. "We rose to the occasion. Defensively, we rose to the occasion to stop their running game. Offensively, we rose to the occasion to establish a running game. This win gives us a lot of confidence for the Alabama game (in

Score by Periods					
Nebraska	0	7	7	10 —	24
Penn State	7	7	7	6 —	27

two weeks)."

Nebraska appeared to have the game won, driving 80 yards in 13 plays late in the fourth quarter to take a 24-21 lead, Nebraska's first lead of the game.

But a 15-yard personal foul penalty on the ensuing kickoff — an important penalty according to both coaches — gave Blackledge the ball on the 35 and he went to work, calmly leading the Lions up the field, throwing a fourth-and-11 first-down pass to Kenny Jackson and a 15-yard pass to tight end Mike McCloskey — who apparently went out of bounds without landing a foot inbounds — at the 2. With time tick-

ing away, Blackledge went back and threw to Bowman, a second tight end in short yardage situations.

Bowman, a junior, caught two touchdown passes yesterday — his first two college receptions. Bowman was a defensive end last year, an offensive guard in spring drills and a tight end when the Lions moved Ron Heller to tackle at the start of summer drills. In all, Bowman said, he's played seven positions at Penn State.

"Maybe I've found a home," he said.

Several Cornhuskers disputed the catch, but Bowman said he caught it.

"I was concerned the officials weren't going to call it," Bowman said. "I came up with the ball right away and showed it to the official — to show him that I scored."

The ending was probably the most dramatic in Beaver Stadium history and it drove the usually placid fans bananas. After freshman Massimo Manca missed the extra point and the Lions downed the kickoff to end the game, fans flooded the field and the goal post at the south end — where Bowman scored — was torn down in an instant.

"It was a great football game," Penn State coach Joe Paterno said. "It was a shame that either team had to lose it. There was enough glory in that game for both teams."

Nebraska coach Tom Osborne agreed that "obviously it was a great game for the spectators."

"We played pretty well," Osborne said. "We just couldn't stop their receivers and their quarterback. Their pass protection was good — our coverage wasn't that bad. We had to blitz about 30 percent of the time, more than we like."

The victory was a redemption of sorts for two parts of the Penn State team. The oft-criticized offensive line gave Blackledge scads of time to throw,

Nebraska's Kris Van Norman pushes Penn State's Curt Warner out of bounds at the 2-yard line, but Warner scored on a later play.

Penn State's Al Harris (88) and Walker Lee Ashley stop Nebraska's Craig Rogers.

and the Penn State defense dominated the first half, shutting Nebraska's running game down and forcing quarterback Turner Gill to throw. Gill was up to the challenge, driving the Cornhuskers 80 yards in seven passes at the end of the first half — the only real offense Nebraska generated the first half.

Led by charged up defensive tackle Greg Gattuso, the Lions held Nebraska to 61 yards on the ground in the fist half, recovering two of Nebraska's three fumbles.

If Penn State had a fault in the first half, it was not taking a bigger lead than 14-7. Twice in one drive, Blackledge had touchdown passes called back because of a motion penalty and Manca missed field goals of 50, 47 and 34 yards in the first half.

Blackledge's two first-half touchdown

drives were vastly different. One went 83 yards in six plays and moved mostly through the air, including a 13-yard pass to Gregg Garrity, a 33-yard bomb to running back Curt Warner and culminated in a 14-yard pass to Bowman. The second traveled 71 yards in six plays and went on the ground, Warner running for 15 yards, breaking a tackle and following a Jon Williams block around end for 31 yards, and scoring his first rushing touchdown of the season from the 2.

Warner gained 78 yards in 13 carries, but missed most of the second half with muscle cramps. Paterno said that Warner, Penn State's Heisman candidate before the season, may have overtrained.

"I think sometimes you can work too hard," Paterno said. "Curt may have worked too hard this summer. I think having a week off (before the Lions play Alabama at Birmingham) should help."

Nebraska played an excellent second half, mixing up the offense and gaining 180 yards rushing and 92 passing.

The teams traded long scoring drives in the third quarter, the Lions moving 83 yards in seven plays, ending in a Blackledge pass right into the gut of wide receiver Jackson. Jackson was surrounded by three defenders and a pass anywhere else might have been intercepted.

But Nebraska, which came into the game aiming for a national championship, outmuscled the Lions for the first time, running mostly behind star center Dave Rimington up the middle, going 80 yards in 15 plays to cut Penn State's lead to 21-14.

Early in the fourth quarter, Lions running back Skeeter Nichols, replac-

Penn State quarterback Todd Blackledge completed 23 of 39 passes for 295 yards and 3 touchdowns against Nebraska.

ing Warner, fumbled at the Nebraska 44 and Nebraska moved to the 20 before Kevin Seibel kicked a field goal.

Blackledge drove the Lions right back down the field, but was intercepted in the end zone.

Gill masterfully ran the Nebraska offense back up the field, driving it to the touchdown that supposedly would

win the game. Except for the spectacular arm of Todd Blackledge.

Lions Notes

Blackledge has now passed for more than 200 yards in his last five regular-season games and the 295 yards were the third highest in Penn State history.

Lions Weather Pitt, National Title Game vs. Georgia Looms

By Dan Donovan
The Pittsburgh Press

University Park, Pa., Nov. 26, 1982 — The game, literally, blew in the wind, a wind that Penn State coach and chief amateur meteorologist Joe Paterno made sure his kickers knew well.

Penn State drew a bead on Georgia, the Sugar Bowl and the national championship with a 19-10 win over Pitt that hinged on third-quarter winds that snuffed Pitt's kicking and punting games, but barely affected Penn State's.

Two well-matched and hard-hitting teams battled to a statistical draw — Penn State gained 359 yards, Pitt gained 397 — but Nick Gancitano's four field goals, Ralph Giacommaro's punting and a swirling wind sent Pitt to the Cotton Bowl 9-2 and searching for solace.

Pitt went into the third quarter leading, 7-3, but punter Tony Recchia shanked one 21-yard punt because the wind nearly carried the hike over his head, and punted twice more for 32 and 34 yards.

With the wind in its face, Pitt went into a conservative third-quarter offense, throwing only two passes — both dropped — and punting on third down from the end zone. Penn State seized the field position and turned it into 13 points. It was a tribute to the Pitt defense that the Lions didn't score more.

Score by Periods

Pitt	0	7	0	3 —	10
Penn State	3	0	10	6 —	19

"Pitt let the wind bother it a little more than it should have in the third quarter," Paterno said. "I'm not making a negative comment about them, but we are used to it. We went out Wednesday when it was really windy and cold and we kicked into the wind all day. Then we caught and threw the ball in the wind."

Compared to Wednesday, "today was a pleasure" said Gancitano, a Floridian who kicked field goals of 26, 31, 19 and 29 yards, the last two into the wind and the last in rain, too.

Early in the week, Paterno said he could feel a "typical Penn State day" coming on and was happy that Wednesday was miserable so the Lions could practice kicking and punting into the wind.

"The wind is bad a lot up here," Giacommaro said, "but I've never seen a Dr. Jekyll-Mr. Hyde day like today. It wasn't bad the first half, but the second half was tough."

Giacommaro averaged 48.3 yards on four punts, hitting a low 51-yarder into the wind in the fourth quarter.

Aside from the kicking, Pitt and Penn State were a good match.

"I hope they go on to win the national championship," said Pitt guard Ron Sams. "They are a fine bunch of guys. I enjoyed this game so much, I wished it never ended."

"Pitt didn't quit," Penn State quarterback Todd Blackledge said. "They played hard to the last play. Definitely it was intense, but it wasn't like last year where there was a lot of chit-chat across the line of scrimmage."

Penn State's Curt Warner gained 118 yards on 22 carries, making him the second Penn State runner to gain 1,000 yards two straight years, but was outgained by Pitt's Bryan Thomas, who gained 143 yards in 31 carries and caught seven passes for 46 yards.

Pitt quarterback Dan Marino completed 18 of 32 passes for 193 yards and one interception, considerably better than Blackledge's 10 of 24 for 149 yards, one touchdown and one interception.

But the No. 2 Lions are 10-1 and will play No. 1 Georgia for the national championship New Year's Day.

"We have one more big one," Blackledge said. "We've had so many big ones, it seems like it never ends, but we've got one more big one left."

Much has been made of Penn State's failure to win a national championship, but Paterno claims the Lions have won three — in 1968, 1969 and 1973, when the Lions went through the regular seasons undefeated and won their bowl games.

"Just because somebody didn't vote

Pitt runner Bryan Thomas (44) runs into a determined Walker Lee Ashley. The Nittany Lions' defense held the Panthers to one touchdown in Penn State's 19-10 victory, which set up a national-championship showdown against No. 1 Georgia.

you in, doesn't mean you didn't win it," Paterno said. "We blew our shot in 1978 (when the Lions lost to Alabama in the Sugar Bowl), so that makes us 3-1. I hope we don't make it two in a row."

Paterno praised his defense, noting it gave up lots of yardage, but only 10 points.

"They have been maligned, but they

have played against some good offensive teams," Paterno said. "We work hard for good field position and try not to give up any easy ones. We have an intelligent defense, and today they played well."

"We always bend, but we never break," said Penn State safety Mark Robinson. "we do that consistently because of the concept of our defense.

We play only two down linemen, so we know they'll make a few yards on us. But we try not to let them make any big plays on us."

The Lions gained 210 yards rushing against a Pitt defense that had been ranked third in the nation in rushing defense, giving up only 81.9 yards per game.

"Our offensive line blocked some

Nick Gancitano, center, kicked four field goals against Pitt.

pretty good defensive linemen," Paterno said. "Nobody else ran that way against Pitt."

Penn State guard Pete Speros said the aggressiveness of the Pitt defensive line, in a way, helped the Lions.

"We would just step into them and let them take us where they wanted to go," Speros said. "That opens big holes."

The Lions used the speed of Warner and Jonathan Williams to run outside, then switched and ran inside the second half.

"In the second half," Warner said, "they were slanting and taking away our outside game, and that opened up the middle. I think they were outside conscious the whole second half."

The Lions threw one interception and fumbled the ball away twice in the first half.

"We were killing ourselves in the first half," Blackledge said. "I knew sooner or later, it would turn around. This team has been through so many tough games, we have a lot of poise and a lot of confidence."

Peep Short intercepted Blackledge's slightly short bomb to Mike McCloskey in the end zone on the Lions' first possession.

On their second possession, Giacommaro outkicked his coverage and Keith Williams returned the ball 65 yards to the Penn State 20. But the official called it back because Williams gave illegal hand signals to teammate Chris Relic.

Pitt drove until Lions linebacker Dave Paffenroth tipped a Marino pass to teammate Ken Kelley.

The Lions marched to the Pitt 8, but missed three straight passes before Gancitano kicked a 26-yard field goal.

Pitt's Eric Schubert missed a 44-yard field goal, but Pitt drove 85 yards in 12 plays to take a 7-3 lead. With

Kenny Jackson scored on a 31-yard pass.

Marino on the sidelines recovering from a hard hit by Penn State defensive end Walker Ashley, Thomas

Penn State fans go after the goal posts at Beaver Stadium following the game.

absorbed a hit from Roger Jackson and got a block from backup quarterback Dan Daniels, skirting the end for a 4-yard run.

The Lions fumbled the ball the next two possessions, once each by Joel Coles and Curt Warner — and were lucky that an apparent Williams fumble at their own 20 was ruled a dead ball by the officials.

"We didn't get uptight even though we bobbled the ball the first half," Paterno said. "They showed their character in the second half when they didn't let up."

Kenny Jackson cut across the field in the third quarter, caught a pass from Blackledge and cut up field, going 31 yards for a touchdown.

"We caught them in a blitz," Blackledge said. "When I saw the linebackers coming, I knew there would be man-to-man coverage on Kenny, and he would be open."

Paterno gambled on fourth-and-1 at the Pitt 21, calling a pass to McCloskey for a first down and setting up Gancitano's 31-yard field goal.

Pitt threw up a strong goal-line stand at the end of the third quarter, stopping the Lions on a first-and-goal from the 4, forcing Gancitano to kick a 19-yard field goal.

Schubert's 17-yard field goal narrowed the Lions' lead to 16-10, but he later missed a 47-yarder.

The Lions clinched the win with a 58-yard drive on eight running plays capped by Gancitano's rainy 29-yard field goal.

"This was one of the best games we've played, especially defensively," Kelley said. "We made the big play at the right time. Pitt has a great team, but we came together as a team and rose to the occasion. We showed a lot of character."

Not to mention wind resistance.

Penn State Stakes Claim to Title of Nation's Best

By Dan Donovan
The Pittsburgh Press

New Orleans, Jan. 1, 1983 — The Ultimate Contest hasn't happened yet, but this one was pretty darn good, as Penn State survived the well-named tenacious Bulldogs of Georgia, 27-23, before a Sugar Bowl record crowd of 78,124 last night, to maybe finally reach that Holy Grail, its first undisputed national title.

The Lions led from the moment they took the opening kickoff down the field, and even built up a 20-3 lead, but that didn't tell the story of a bunch of winners, the nation's 1-A team, the Georgia Bulldogs.

The Bulldogs refused to be blown out as a normal team should.

Georgia finally fell to the high-powered, varied Penn State offense and the sure hands of a small, slightly balding walk-on from North Allegheny, wide receiver Gregg Garrity, whose spectacular diving catch on a 47-yard bomb early in the fourth quarter gave the Bulldogs too many points to overcome.

Garrity, streaking down the sideline, made the last game of his college career his best, catching four passes for 116 yards.

Named the outstanding player of the game was Penn State quarterback Todd Blackledge, who completed 13

Score by Periods					
Penn State	7	13	0	7	— 27
Georgia	3	7	7	6	— 23

of 23 passes for 228 yards, a touchdown, and, most importantly against the leading intercepting team in the nation, no interceptions.

For the second straight year, Penn State running back Curt Warner outgained the Heisman Trophy winner in a bowl game. Despite suffering cramps in his right leg, Warner gained 117 yards on 18 carries for one touchdown.

The gutsiest performance of all may have come from Georgia quarterback John Lastinger, who threw some of the worst passes ever — two were intercepted by Penn State safety Mark Robinson. Yet Lastinger also threw some timely passes, getting the Bull-

dogs back in the game just as it seemed time for them to fold.

Lastinger completed 12 of 27 passes for 166 yards and two touchdowns.

The Lions did not turn over the ball until Kevin Baugh's fumble of a punt in the fourth quarter, a fumble that set up Georgia's last touchdown. The Georgia team lived on turnovers.

Except for the fumble, Baugh had an exceptional night, returning five punts for 106 yards and three kickoffs for 26 yards.

Blackledge calmly, coolly, led the Lions to victory, even though the stunting Georgia defense sacked him five times. The most sacks against the Lions in a game all year had been three.

As the Penn State fans finally got to cheer "We're No. 1" with some conviction, Penn State coach Joe Paterno, long an advocate of a collegiate playoff championship, smiled and said, "I don't think we need a playoff this year — next year we can have a playoff.

"We should be No. 1. With the schedule we played and the people we beat, we should be No. 1. When the No. 1 and No. 2 team play each other, the winner should be No. 1."

Paterno called the Lions his best team ever, his hardest-working team ever, his closest ever. The Lions finished 11-1, losing only to Alabama, 42-21.

"This is the greatest team I've ever played on," Blackledge said. "It has so much character, poise and love for each other. After the loss to Alabama, we just wanted to go out and win every game one at a time. Praise the Lord, it's the greatest season I've ever had."

Although Georgia's secondary "played with a lot of composure," according to Blackledge, he didn't think they "realized how much speed

After coaching three unbeaten teams that did not win national titles, Penn State coach Joe Paterno won the 1982 championship with a once-beaten Nittany Lions team.

Kenny Jackson and Garrity had."

"That may have been one of the reasons we were able to get behind them. Georgia's secondary has made a lot of big plays all year. We thought they might play us tight. Our receivers ran the routes and it was up to me to throw the ball. A lot of Georgia's interceptions this year were on underthrown balls. I had to make sure I did not throw them anything short on the deep patterns."

Fans in the Superdome were treat-ed to a stormy and sensational first half in which the Lions took a 20-10 lead.

Blackledge completed his first five passes, including four for 74 yards as the Lions took the opening kickoff and drove 80 yards for a touchdown.

Blackledge had loads of time to pass, throwing a 33-yarder to tight end Mike McCloskey and a 27-yarder to Garrity. But the touchdown came on a run, as Warner faked into the mid-dle, picked up a block by Joel Coles and went outside to score from two yards out just 2:51 into the game.

Not to be outdone, the Bulldogs drove right down the field, too, though they had to settle for Kevin Butler's 27-yard field goal after a 70-yard, 16-play drive — 40 of those yards gained by Walker.

Aided by four punt returns for 106 yards by Baugh, the Lions kept the offensive pressure on the Bulldogs.

Nick Gancitano kicked a 38-yard field goal set up by a nifty 26-yard run by Warner. Warner beat one man at

Above, Penn State's Gregg Garrity cele-brates after his fourth-quarter touch-down. Right, Curt Warner gets past Georgia's Terry Hoage on a first-quar-ter run. Warner finished with 117 yards rushing and two touchdowns.

the line of scrimmage, turned up field and broke another tackle.

Gancitano just missed left on a 47-yard field goal attempt that was set up by Baugh's best punt return of the night, 65 yards through the middle of the field. It wasn't a touchdown only because punter Jim Broadway slowed him down.

Baugh returned the next Georgia punt for 24 yards and Blackledge hit Garrity going down the sideline with a 36-yard pass. Four plays later, on third and a half-yard at the 9, Warn-er stepped into the middle of the Georgia line, stopped, changed direc-tions and scored to give the Lions a 17-3 lead.

The fired-up Lions bottled up the Bulldogs at the 8 on the kickoff and quickly forced another punt, setting up a 45-yard Gancitano field goal with only 44 seconds left in the half.

But Georgia wasn't about to give up. Herschel Walker ran the kickoff back 23 yards and Lastinger threw five straight passes, completing four, the first time he passed successfully in the first half.

At the 36, Lastinger passed to wide receiver Kevin Harris who, as he was tackled by Lions cornerback Dan Biondi, lateraled to Walker, who gained 10 more yards to the 10.

On the next play, Lastinger threw high in the end zone to Herman Archie, who had dropped several pass-es early in the game.

The 6-foot-5 Archie outjumped 5-9 Biondi for the ball and the touch-down with five seconds left in the half to make it 20-10.

The Bulldogs marched down 69 yards in 11 plays on the opening dri-ve of the second half to cut the Penn State lead to 20-17.

Early in the fourth quarter, the

bomb to Garrity gave the Lions their 27-17 lead.

"That was a big factor in our regaining our momentum," Paterno said. "It was a typical Blackledge performance. He is poised, confident and can come back from adversity."

Later, Baugh, who should have played it safe and called a fair catch while fielding a punt on his own 43, fumbled the ball and Georgia recovered. Lastinger then drove the Bulldogs 43 yards in six plays, passing to tight end Clarence Kay for a touchdown. The Lions stopped Walker's attempted sweep for the two-point conversion.

With 3:53 left, the Lions took the kickoff and sat on the ball, slowly moving up the field until time ran out as a Ralph Giacomarro punt bounced into the end zone.

"Penn State played like champions," said Walker, who was held to 22 yards in the second half. "They took advantage of their opportunities and we didn't take advantage of ours."

Georgia coach Vince Dooley said that Penn State was "the best-balanced football team that I've seen since I've been coaching" — previously he thought the 1976 Panthers were the best balanced.

"I am disappointed, but I am proud of our team," Dooley said. "I thought there were a couple of times when we could have folded, but we didn't. You have to give Penn State all the credit. They've really got some big play makers. And they also have a scrappy defense."

Penn State's Mike McCloskey leaps over Georgia's Tony Flack for a reception.

National Title Sounds Sweet to Penn State

By Pat Livingston
The Pittsburgh Press

That elusive national championship, a thorn in Coach Joe Paterno's side for the last 15 years, may finally be headed to University Park this week, the result of Penn State's 27-23 victory over No. 1-ranked Georgia before a record Sugar Bowl crowd of 78,124 in the Louisiana Superdome last night.

Only a decision by a panel of football coaches and another by a group sportswriters stand in the way of a declaration that Penn State, on its fourth try, is indeed the national champion. That decision should be forthcoming this week.

The alternative is unbeaten Southern Methodist, the only unbeaten major college team in the country, whose 11-0-1 record includes an unimpressive 7-3 victory over Pitt, the Lions' arch-rivals, in the Cotton Bowl six hours earlier.

For a time last night, it appeared Paterno would have little trouble in capturing the title which had eluded him for so long as Penn State, powered by the passing of quarterback Todd Blackledge, piled up an easy 20-3 lead in the second period.

But a sudden rally by Georgia, which netted the loser two touchdowns in a five-minute stretch spanning the second and third periods, put the Bulldogs back in the game, 20-17.

And with the ever-dangerous Herschel Walker, a game-breaker if ever there was one, in the Georgia backfield, that was a perilous position for Paterno, indeed.

However, just as it appeared that the momentum, which had swung away with Georgia's rally 20 minutes earlier, was about to desert Penn State, Blackledge came up with the game's key play.

It was a 48-yard pass to his wide receiver, Gregg Garrity, who had a step on Georgia cornerback Tony Flack as he crossed the goal line. Garrity made a diving catch for a touchdown, putting Penn State in front 27-17.

There were four minutes left in the game when Georgia challenged again, getting down to the Penn State 10-yard line, largely on the passing of underrated John Lastinger, the Bulldogs' quarterback. One of Lastinger's wobbly passes, on third down, found its way into the arms of Clarence Kay, narrowing the count with 3:54 left.

Penn State stopped a two-point conversion attempt. Georgia, instead of needing a field goal to win as it would have had the conversion been successful, now needed a touchdown. Georgia trailed by four, 27-23.

The Lions were to control the ball, not giving it up until they punted into the end zone on the last play of the game.

Of course, championships have never been a thing with Paterno. Although Penn State did not win a national championship in his first 16 years as coach, he never allowed such a failing to develop into paranoia.

Throughout his coaching career,

his teams set their own standards. How they fared, not how many titles they won, was the big thing with Paterno.

"I never cared much about championships," said Paterno, "except as they affected the young men who played on those teams. I was always satisfied when we won football games, which was our purpose in the sport.

"It never bothers me that people still think we didn't win any championships. I coached three undefeated, untied teams — and one of them won 22 games in a row. There were champions as far as I was concerned. I didn't care what the rest of the country thought."

The teams Paterno referred to were the Penn State team of 1968, which won 11 straight games, the only team to do that in the country, and then whipped Kansas, the Big Eight champion, 15-14, in the Orange Bowl.

The best Paterno's team could get that year was a second-place rating by United Press International, and a third-place finish by The Associated Press.

The following year, Penn State again went 12-0-0, extending what was to become a 31-game unbeaten streak, but again the Lions were ignored in the ratings.

Paterno's third perfect season came in 1973, a year when there were seven unbeaten teams in the country at the end of the regular season. Despite the past slights, however, nobody yet was taking Penn State seriously.

Penn State's Poise Marks Championship

BY DAN DONOVAN
The Pittsburgh Press

For once, Penn State was besieged, not the one assailing the other's ramparts.

The Lions got to be 10-1 and in the Sugar Bowl by coming from behind. But Georgia, a strong come-from-behind team itself, made Penn State's 20-3 lead look less than a fortress, more like a rock garden.

When quarterback John Lastinger proved he could, indeed, throw a football, driving the football, driving the Bulldogs 66 yards in five plays and 39 seconds at the end of the first half, Coach Joe Paterno wished he weren't kicking off to start the second half. Paterno knew his squad faced a "somewhat more difficult task" than coming from behind — holding off a good, emotional team bent on coming from behind.

"I told the squad the most important part of the game would be the first minutes of the second half," Paterno said.

In the first minutes of the second half, Georgia stuffed the ball down the Lions' throats, driving 69 yards in 11 plays. The score became 20-17, and Paterno felt the game "maybe slipping away."

The Lions' offense was moribund, too.

"I was feeling their pass rush and let things get out of whack," said Penn State quarterback Todd Black-ledge.

"I thought we weren't going to

pull it off," Paterno said.

But Paterno underestimated the character and poise of this team, two attributes evident in the Lions' 27-23 victory Saturday and the prime reason UPI, AP, the Football Writers Association, the MacArthur Bowl Committee and everybody but S.M.U. considers them No. 1 in the country.

Mark Robinson intercepted a Lastinger pass late in third quarter. And early in the fourth, wide receiver Gregg Garrity blew by the Georgia defense and made a diving catch of Blackledge's 47-yard pass, cradling it in his arms in the end zone.

"A tremendous throw, a tremendous catch," Georgia coach Vince Dooley said. "That was the turning point. That and Penn State's ability to hold onto the ball late in the game. They were not rattled, able to retain possession and run the clock down. I looked at the clock and saw a big 15 minutes up there. Before I knew it, I looked up and saw five."

Even when the Lions made their first mistake, Kevin Baugh's fumble of a punt on his own 43, they remained poised. Georgia scored, the Lions stuffed Herschel Walker's two-point attempt, and Dooley decided to kick the ball off deep rather than try an onside kick.

"If I knew then what I know now," Dooley said, "I would have gone the other way. We had just scored. We had the momentum. I thought we had them rattled. I thought we could hold them and get the ball back."

But the Lions don't rattle easily. On third-and-three at the Penn State

32, Blackledge told Paterno that if the Bulldogs stayed in the same formation they'd been using, he'd call a pass. Paterno, his conservative nature violated over and over this year, said OK, as long as Blackledge was careful. Blackledge threw to Garrity 6 yards for the last first down the Lions would need.

"A great call," Dooley said, "a great play."

The Lions' poise begins with Blackledge.

"If I wanted a guy to build a team around," Paterno said, "I'd like it to be Blackledge. He showed physical as well as mental courage. Georgia hit him pretty hard and he came back."

But it is not only Blackledge.

"This team is very close," Paterno said. "They have poise and can handle adversity."

"This is a unique team," Blackledge said. "We got together early in the summer and decided it was going to be a great year. It just paid off. The closeness and friendship carried us through the tough teams this season."

Paterno said this was his best team, not his most talented team.

"We could do so many things offensively in an explosive way. We've had better defenses with maybe more dominating players. Maybe it is not the best in ability in all areas, but as for leadership and poise, this team has all that."

Two possible first-round draft choices, Blackledge and running back Curt Warner, were the stars on

On the trip back to University Park, quarterback Todd Blackledge and running back Curt Warner leave no doubt about which team is the best in the country.

offense. On defense, it was defensive end Walker Lee Ashley and safety Mark Robinson.

"Robinson was probably the difference in the game," Dooley said. "He's no safety man, he's a linebacker playing safety."

"Vince is right," Paterno said. "We relied on Robinson to make a lot of open-field tackles on Herschel Walker."

Robinson made eight unassisted tackles, one assisted tackle, knocked down three passes and intercepted two more. Paterno pulled out a sheet of paper and diagramed how Robinson's tackles were set up by Ashley, whose job it was to turn the play in and slow down Walker before he could get up a head of steam.

"If he gets headed down the field with his shoulders square," Paterno said, "no one can tackle Herschel one-on-one. But Ashley was too strong, too quick for them."

Ashley, Robinson, Warner and Blackledge are the stars who the fans will remember from this year, but in many ways Garrity characterizes the team more.

A defensive back at North Allegheny, Garrity was headed to Clarion State until his father insisted he could play at Penn State. Noting his speed, the Lions made him a wide receiver his sophomore year. He learned to catch the ball, becoming the reincarnation of Fred Biletnikoff, catching the ball no matter how big the guy hitting him.

"So he's their 'other wide receiver?'" Dooley said. "He's some 'other wide receiver.'"

The Lions are also defensive tackle Greg Gattuso, who tripped over his own feet against Rutgers, but had his best two games of the year against Nebraska and Georgia.

"Gattuso played a great game for us," Paterno said.

And they are center Mark Battaglia, a former undersized linebacker who vowed he would be better than second-round draft choice Jim Romano — and was. The Lions didn't fumble a snap all season.

The Lions are also defensive back Dan Biondi, a 5-foot-9 walk-on who made a touchdown-saving tackle on Walker. Even though the Bulldogs obviously used the difference between 6-5 Herman Archie and Biondi to score their first touchdown and were obviously throwing Biondi's way as much as possible, Paterno wouldn't take him out.

But when Biondi felt tired and afraid he might hurt the team, he took himself out. He went back in, though, and was part of the poise of a national champion.

5,000 GREET LIONS

An exuberant Gov. Dick Thornburgh led 5,000 cheering fans in a show of adoration as the Nittany Lions arrived back in Harrisburg last night in triumph, possessors at last of a college football national championship.

Lions, Alabama Battle in Thriller, Controversy Recalled

By Mike DeCourcy
The Pittsburgh Press

University Park, Oct. 8, 1983 — Many football fans, particularly those not swearing allegiance to anyone calling himself a "Cornhusker," said the 1982 Penn State-Nebraska game would never be equaled for excitement in college football. They were wrong.

Not only was it equaled Saturday, it was practically repeated.

There were only a few differences. It was Alabama playing Penn State, the disputed pass reception took a different form and the game left 4-1 Alabama in position to make a comeback run at the national championship.

But it was at Beaver Stadium, there was a beyond-capacity crowd, CBS had it on television and the game began at 3:45 under temporary lights. The most important thing that didn't change was the winning team. That was Penn State, 34-28.

Penn State (3-3) used Doug Strang's 241 passing yards and D.J. Dozier's 165 yards rushing to open a 34-7 lead after three periods, but No. 3 Alabama constructed a magnificent rally behind quarterback Walter Lewis, who led the Crimson Tide to three fourth-quarter touchdowns and passed for 336 yards.

Alabama compiled 598 total yards but could not make it 600 on the final

Score by Periods						
Alabama	7	0	0	21	—	28
Penn State	14	3	17	0	—	34

play of the game. Penn State tackle Greg Gattuso stopped freshman tailback Kerry Goode from the Nittany Lion 2 as time ran out.

"You think of ways to get back in it. You ask yourself, 'Are you going to give up or fight to win?'" said Lewis. "We put ourselves into the situation. We had to go bail ourselves out."

Lewis, the guy with the biggest bucket, helped Alabama cut the Penn State advantage to six points with 5:36 remaining when he hit flanker Jesse Bendross with an 8-yard TD pass. Alabama got the ball back with nearly three minutes left when Stan Gay

blocked Nick Gancitano's 43-yard field goal attempt and recovered it at the Alabama 49.

The situation looked familiar. Penn State had spoiled Nebraska's day by coming from behind for a 27-24 victory last fall. Alabama was set to do the same to the Nittany Lions.

"Yeah, it's funny how I was thinking this time last year that we won it in the last two seconds," said Paterno. "Were they going to do it this year with that great comeback they had?"

"Everyone was real confident in the huddle," said Crimson Tide receiver Joey Jones. "I knew we were going to score."

Alabama moved straight toward the goal line, Lewis completing four passes for 30 yards to move the Tide to the Penn State 12. On third down, freshman Kerry Goode carried for six yards and a first down.

Alabama had four plays from the six and enough time — 28 seconds — to get them all off.

First down was an incomplete pass. So was second down. Lewis scrambled for two yards on third down. Fourth down was an incomplete pass.

But not an ordinary incomplete pass. Penn State was offside on the play, which gave Alabama one more shot. Alabama's players figured they didn't need it.

Preston Gothard apparently caught Lewis' four-yard pass for the winning TD, but he juggled the ball at the top of his jump and back judge Walter Lucas ruled that Gothard didn't have possession when his body hit the end line.

"I thought I had it. The referee said I didn't have it. His judgment is what counts," Gothard said.

Gattuso's big play followed, when Alabama elected to run a "Toss-28" to Goode instead of passing, Gattuso shot

Penn State defenders Brad Harris (34) and Harry Hamilton apply pressure to Alabama quarterback Walter Lewis. The Crimson Tide suffered three fumbles and three interceptions.

the gap off right tackle and nailed Goode for no gain.

"We had not gained less than seven yards on that play all day in the same situation, against the same defense," Alabama coach Ray Perkins said. "(Their defense was) lined up like you'd like 'em to line up. We just didn't execute."

That was Alabama's problem all day.

The Crimson Tide lost three fum-

bles and three interceptions, all at the wrong time, as Penn State finally got a taste of good fortune.

In the first period, Penn State scored on an 80-yard TD pass from Doug Strang to tight end Dean DiMidio when two Alabama defenders — Freddie Robinson and David Valletto — allowed DiMidio to get behind them and misplayed Strang's floating pass.

That tied the game at 7-7, Alabama having opened the scoring with an 88-yard drive, capped by Lewis' eight-yard pass to Jones, that showed the Tide could dominate Penn State with its ground game.

They just couldn't hang onto the ball.

Penn State took Linnie Patrick's fumble and turned it into a 38-yard scoring pass from Strang to Kenny

Did he or didn't he? Alabama tight end Preston Gothard latches on to the ball and falls out of the end zone late in the fourth quarter. Officials ruled Gothard did not have possession of the ball when he went out of bounds, preserving the Lions' lead.

Controversial Call Goes In Penn State's Favor

BY MIKE DECOURCY
The Pittsburgh Press

Last year, there was bedlam. This year, there was silence. Last year, the pass was in bounds. This year, it wasn't.

Last year, the disputed call benefited Penn State. This year, the disputed call benefited Penn State.

The Nittany Lions, playing within the friendly confines of Beaver Stadium, came out on the right side of back judge Walter Lucas' decision that robbed Preston Gothard, a tight end not even listed on the Alabama depth chart, of his chance for momentary stardom, a touchdown catch that would have erased Penn State's 34-28 victory.

There were fewer than 15 seconds left in the game. Alabama had the ball on the Penn State 4. Walter Lewis was in control after driving the Crimson Tide 47 yards in 10 plays. Penn State jumped offsides, and what was to transpire when Lewis dropped back amounted to a free play. Alabama would get another chance.

But Lewis, under little pressure from the Penn State rush, found Gothard open in the back of the end zone, near

Jackson with his 27-yard run. Dozier went over the 100-yard mark for the fourth straight game with a 64-yarder that set up his own one-yard score.

A Gancintano 39-yard field goal with 6:31 left in the third quarter gave Penn State a 27-point lead and had the record crowd of 85,614 screaming.

"I thought we had it wrapped up," Paterno said. "I guess we played it too conservatively."

Alabama came back quickly and ferociously. Lewis led touchdown drives of 87, 69 and 78 yards, handed to Goode for one TD and completed two scoring passes to Bendross to get the Tide back into the game.

The comeback turned a rout into a classic.

"One of the best games I've ever been associated with?" said Perkins, tersely repeating a question. "Hell no. We lost the game."

Penn State running back D.J. Dozier rushed for 165 yards against the Crimson Tide defense.

the goalpost. Lewis fired the ball high, Gothard went up and tipped the ball. He appeared to control it on the way down, just before the upper part of his leg made contact with the end line. The Penn State crowd was stunned.

"I got up and I saw (Tide receiver) Joey Jones coming toward me. He was signaling like I scored," said Gothard. "Then he got this expression on his face, and I looked and saw the referee saying I didn't have control of the ball ...

"I thought I had it when I hit the ground."

"Our players said he had it," said Alabama coach Ray Perkins. "The referee told him he didn't have it when he came down. I'll have to take a closer look on the films."

Nebraska fans, coaches and players took a look — lots of looks — at tape and film of a play in last year's 24-21 Penn State victory over the Cornhuskers, when Penn State receiver Gregg Garrity made a catch many felt was out of bounds. It was ruled complete by officials working that game.

Penn State won on the next play, when Todd Blackledge hit Kirk Bowman with a pass in the deep end zone. People wondered whether Bowman caught that one, too.

Bowman, oddly, was also a backup tight end. People know his name since the catch. Until he challenges for the starting job at Alabama, most folks across the country will forget Preston Gothard.

"One ref said I caught it. The other said I didn't. It was a touchdown in my book."

Reserve Quarterback Makes Tide Pay on His Only Play

By Mike DeCourcy
The Pittsburgh Press

University Park, Pa., Oct. 12, 1985 — To fill the interminable moments on the sideline with more than daydreams of game-winning touchdown passes, Penn State's Matt Knizner studies defenses. He studies game plans. He studies the plays called by his coach, Joe Paterno.

Mostly, though, he studies starting quarterback John Shaffer. Knizner, the Nittany Lions' No. 2 quarterback, knows all of Shaffer's best moves, notably the one where Shaffer takes a hard hit, struggles to one knee, then recovers in time to play the next down.

"I saw that he was hurt, but John sometimes does that — gets up and plays," Knizner said. "I watch him closely, and when he gets hit, I look to see if he's all right."

Yesterday, after scrambling for 6 yards with less than 7 minutes remaining in Penn State's game against Alabama at Beaver Stadium, Shaffer was not all right. Alabama's defenders had knocked the wind out of him.

Knizner took his place, and on his only down, third-and-one from the Crimson Tide's 11, he faked a handoff to fullback Steve Smith, rolled right and completed a pass to tight end Brian Siverling, the winning touchdown in a 19-17 Penn State victory.

Score by Periods

Alabama	7	0	0	10	—	17
Penn State	3	3	3	10	—	19

It was no dream. Knizner had passed his team, No. 5 in the country, to a 5-0 record. No. 8 Alabama is 4-1.

"I was really trying to play it cool; you know, walk back to the sideline real calmly," said Knizner, a junior from Hempfield. "Then I said, 'The heck with that' and went in and jumped on the pile. It was great."

Siverling's touchdown extended Penn State's advantage to 19-10. The Nittany Lions had built the lead on the strong play of their defense — Alabama gained only 90 yards rushing — and four field goals by Massimo Manca.

"We could have knocked it in there and have been first-and-goal at the 9. I would have been happy with the field goal either way," Paterno said. "Knizner throws well on the run, and he's a good runner, so I had no qualms about him making that play."

"It does tend to surprise you when someone comes off the bench cold," Alabama coach Ray Perkins said. "I told our team to be ready for a bad snap."

It was a game filled with critical moments and crucial plays, but it was a near-perfect game. Neither team had a turnover, and only 65 yards in penalties were assessed. If there were mistakes, they came from the sidelines.

Paterno's decision to call the "157 Boot" was a shock, but how can you describe Perkins' choice of a draw play on third-and-10 at the Penn State 36 with four minutes left?

Tide tailback Bobby Humphrey was stopped after gaining 4 yards, Van Tiffin's 45-yard field goal attempt flew wide left, and Alabama was effectively through

D.J. Dozier finished his Penn State career with 3,227 yards.

A fake to Steve Smith, above, set up Matt Knizner's winning touchdown pass.

for the afternoon.

"Obviously, we've made some improvements if we can play as well as we did for 60 minutes tonight," Paterno said. "We're playing football the way I hoped we'd be playing at the end of last year."

The Crimson Tide took a 7-0 lead in the first quarter, when quarterback Mike Shula directed an 81-yard drive and ended it with a 19-yard touchdown pass to speedy flanker Al Bell.

Penn State needed three quarters to overcome that. The Lions drove patiently and set up Manca field goals of 38, 44, 50 and 20 yards at the beginning of the fourth quarter.

Alabama drove toward the lead on its next possession, moving to the Lions 17 thanks to a pair of controversial roughness penalties against Penn State.

Alabama was hit with a procedure penalty, though, and after an incomplete pass, a two-yard run and a Duffy Cobbs sack of Shula, the Crimson Tide were left with a 45-yard field goal by Tiffin and trailed, 12-10.

Penn State then put together the clinching drive, which began with a 29-yard run on a flanker reverse by Michael Timpson and ended with Knizner's pass.

"This team's had a rap of not being very consistent offensively," Paterno said. "But every time they've had to get a job done, they did it."

Shaffer played well before he was hurt, and he finished with 187 yards on 12-of-22 passing. D.J. Dozier was not at his best after missing two consecutive games with a pulled muscle, but he gained 85 yards on 27 carries.

"Did he have that many? Somebody made a mistake," Paterno said. "I got caught up in the excitement at the end of the game. He's not in condition to carry that many times."

The fourth quarter was frenzied,

Lions' Defense Paved Path to Victory

BY BOB SMIZIK
The Pittsburgh Press

For four games they had been just as their nickname suggested — a Crimson Tide. They had rolled through Georgia, Texas A&M, Cincinnati and Vanderbilt, averaging 32 points and running where they wanted when they wanted.

They ran for 1,000 yards in those four victories, gobbling up the ground at almost five yards a try. It was the run that opened up the passing game for Mike Shula, who completed 69 percent of his throws.

Then the Crimson Tide of Alabama came to Penn State. It came to the place that defense made famous. The place where Ham and Reid and Smear and a couple dozen other defensive all-Americans established Penn State as one of the reigning dynasties of college football and Joe Paterno as one of its leading geniuses.

In one of those rare football games that lived up to its notices, Penn State and Alabama went at it with a ferocity yesterday that has become common to this young but intense rivalry.

And when this classic, played before 85,444 at Beaver Stadium, was over, and Penn State was a 19-17 winner, it was clear that the Lions were worthy of their No. 5 ranking. And maybe a lot more.

Penn State has achieved this status with an offense that is adequate and can become good, and a defense

that is good and can become great.

Characteristically, Paterno refused to rate this team — "there are too many games left to play" — but the performance of the Lions spoke for the coach.

Penn State ran for 205 yards and passed for 198, but it was the defense that chiseled out this victory. Alabama did not rush for 250 yards. It rushed for 90. It did not average 5 yards a try. It averaged 2.6 yards.

The Tide scored a touchdown early and another late — when the Penn State secondary was playing soft — and didn't do much else. Shula passed for 211 yards, but 76 of those came on the closing drive.

"We were calling defenses with one eye on field position and one on the clock," Paterno said.

It did not start out that way. The Tide moved for three first downs on their first possession before punting and scored on an 81-yard drive the next time they had the ball.

"We were slow getting into the game," Penn State linebacker Rogers

Practice made perfect for Nittany Lions' Mike Zordich.

Alexander said. "I played a terrible first quarter. With me calling the defenses and everything, I needed to get into the game quicker."

It did not take Alexander and his teammates long to remedy their problems. On Alabama's next four possessions, carrying over to the fourth quarter, the Tide managed only two first downs.

Both of those came late in the second period, when Alabama advanced to the Penn State 31. But on two of the next plays, Shula was sacked — first by Pete Curkendall and then by Don Graham.

"We didn't do anything different," hero back Michael Zordich said. "We just started doing what we had been practicing for the last two weeks."

The Alabama offense was finally heard from early in the fourth quarter in a bizarre drive that produced a field goal.

After gaining 28 yards on three plays, Alabama had the ball on its 48. Its next seven plays went like this: no gain, incomplete pass, 6 yards, incomplete pass, 2 yards, loss of 8 yards.

The Tide should have been stopped twice, but two controversial penalties enabled it to get in range for Van Tiffin's 45-yard field goal.

Alexander was called for roughing the passer after Shula threw incomplete. Alexander disagreed with the call.

"The ref said I punched him. But I've been doing that for four years.

I was diving over him and I put my hands up to protect myself. If I don't do that, his helmet slams me in the chest. I can't see how he called that a penalty."

Three plays later Zordich was called for a personal foul against tight end Thornton Chandler.

The penalties might have led to a touchdown if Penn State had not responded with yet another big play. On a third and 13, Shula went back to pass — for about one second. On a corner blitz, Duffy Cobbs raced through untouched to throw the quarterback for an 8-yard loss and force the field goal try.

That particular defense, on which Cobbs has the option to blitz, had been called several times. But on each occasion, the blitz never came.

This time it was there. "I couldn't believe it," Cobbs said. "Oh my God. He's there for once."

Penn State answered the field goal that followed with a touchdown of its own, held Alabama on its next possession and then let the clock wind down to 40 seconds as the Tide scored a touchdown.

The final score bothered Alexander more than Paterno.

"The difference between this team and the 1982 national championship team is we lack a killer instinct," Alexander said. "The 1982 team had it, we don't. We've got to stop that last drive. When we can do that, we'll be like the 1982 team."

Penn State's Eric Hamilton (30) lettered for the Nittany Lions in 1985 and 1986, playing for teams that went a combined 23-1.

enough so that Paterno almost called for a two-point conversion after S+verling's touchdown. The thinking was that a 20-10 lead would keep Alabama from winning with a touchdown and field goal.

When things calmed down, the Lions realized a failed two-point try would allow the Crimson Tide to tie the game with a touchdown and two-point conversion. Manca kicked the extra point.

Alabama went on to score again, dri-ving 74 yards against a Penn State pre-vent defense, with Shula hitting Thorn-ton Chandler for a 14-yard TD. An onside kick attempt worked, but Alaba-ma was offside, and a second failed.

Knizner's TD pass stood as the win-ning points.

"I always have to be prepared. I'm always one play away from getting in," Knizner said. "When he (Shaffer) gets hurt, you get this feeling, you're going to be in next, but you never like to see anything happen."

Lions Season Goes Sour in Orange Bowl Loss to Oklahoma

By Mike DeCourcy
The Pittsburgh Press

Miami, Jan. 1, 1986 — They were never the perfect football team, but rarely were they incapable of playing perfect football. When the ball was theirs, it was theirs. Interception and fumble were words from some foreign language none of the Penn State Nittany Lions knew or cared to learn. The Lions were restricted in what they could do to beat other teams, so the trick was never to beat themselves.

It was somewhat cruel, then, that Penn State should toss the ball in Oklahoma's direction five times and have its kicker miss a chip shot during the course of last night's Orange Bowl, the bounty of mistakes precipitating a 25-10 defeat. It was a little like being shot with with your own gun.

Penn State's string of 11 consecutive victories ended in last night's game, which, at 11:25 p.m. EST, unofficially became the contest to decide college football football's national championship. Oklahoma (11-1) jumped from third to first in The Scripps-Howard poll on the basis of its victory over the No. 1 team, claiming its third national championship under Coach Barry Switzer and sixth in 99 years of playing football. Miami, which had been rated No. 2, took a 35-7 beating from underdog Ten-

Score by Periods					
Penn State	7	3	0	0 —	10
Oklahoma	0	16	3	6 —	25

nessee in last night's Sugar Bowl, removing any doubt about the validity of the Sooners' claim to the title.

"We survived the bowl day. Iowa didn't. Miami didn't. Penn State didn't," Oklahoma coach Barry Switzer said. "The easiest solution to this would have been for Penn State to win. We made it happen the hard way."

The Lions left the field with their faces encased in understandably grim, steely expressions. Center Keith Radecic and linebacker Trey Bauer rubbed the moisture from their eyes. Line-

backer Rogers Alexander, oddly, laughed and put his arm around a teammate.

"I don't like to see anyone hold his head down after giving 100 percent effort," Alexander said. "There wasn't any reason for any player on either side of the ball to hold their heads down; regardless of what mistakes were made."

Penn State turned over the ball a mere 20 times in 11 victories this season but had five turnovers last night. Massimo Manca had never missed a field goal from inside 30 yards, but was wide left on a 26-yarder with 3:15 left in the game. Penn State was trailing, 19-10, and the miss ended their hopes of victory. It was typical of Penn State's

Interceptions left John Shaffer dejected.

Oklahoma's Jamelle Holieway coughs up the ball after being hit by Lions defensive tackle Matt Johnson, right.

atypical performance.

"If we had been fourth-and-1, fourth-and-2, I was going to go for it then," Penn State coach Joe Paterno said. "But fourth-and-5, the field goal was there. Massimo will come in and make that 19 of 20 times."

Oklahoma turned two John Shaf-fer interceptions and a fumble into three Tim Lashar field goals. Shaffer completed 10 of 23 passes for 74 yards and three interceptions.

"We weren't really running smooth. We had a herky-jerky type of offense," said fullback Steve Smith, who gained 23 yards on nine carries. "The five-week layoff without a game really hurt the offense."

Turnovers were particularly impor-tant in this game, because both teams played exquisite defense. Oklahoma's irascible Brian Bosworth dashed about the field and accumulated 13 unas-sisted tackles, and Penn State displayed a "wishbone defense," its linebackers setting up a mirror image of the Oklahoma offensive formation and cracking the bone in two. Oklahoma gained 319 yards to Penn State's 267, but 132 of Oklahoma's came on two plays, and Lydell Carr's 61-yard touchdown run late in the fourth quarter had no bearing on the outcome.

Oklahoma's freshman quarterback, Jamelle Holieway, gained one yard on 12 carries, losing 28 yards and fumbling once in the first half. He

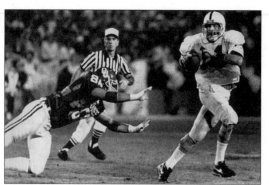

Defensive tackle Steve Bryan and the Oklahoma defense kept Nittany Lions quarterback John Shaffer on the run.

completed 3-of-6 passes for 91 yards, nearly the whole works coming courtesy of a 71-yard second-quarter scoring pass to tight end Keith Jackson.

Penn State opened the game with an impressive, 62-yard drive that ended with a 1-yard Tim Manoa touchdown run and featured a pair of magnificent catches by flanker Eric Hamilton.

Oklahoma came back, driving for a field goal to make it 7-3 and then taking a three-point lead on Holieway's pass to Jackson, which

Shaffer Feels Burden of Lions' Loss

By Gene Collier
The Pittsburgh Press

Carefully and methodically through a remarkable autumn, they fussed over the slippery and rare jewel that is an unbeaten season and polished it toward national-championship brilliance. No one said it, but often when it passed into his hands alone, they held their breath.

John Shaffer was their quarterback and his most discussed talent was jerking Nittany hearts into Nittany throats with an arm that elevated erraticism to an art form. He threw only four completions in 11 attempts against West Virginia. He was 7-for-20 at Cincinnati, 7-for-23 at Rutgers, 9-for-22 against Boston College and 15-for-36 against Temple.

But every time it looked as though Shaffer was bobbling a dream, he'd bull his neck, he'd roll, he'd throw, and he'd win. And there

he would stand, holding the jewel and smiling with mischievous intensity.

But early this morning, the jewel lay shattered in jagged little pieces all over the floor of the Orange Bowl, and Oklahoma was dancing on it and no one needed two guesses to determine who was at fault.

Even Joe Paterno, who turned a troubled 6-5 team into a brazenly efficient machine that conked out within an exit of its second national championship in four years, couldn't find an alternative culprit.

"We did not throw the ball well enough, and that's what really hurt us," Paterno said minutes after Oklahoma's title-clinching 25-10 victory in a good and noble football game. "We had some people open. We just weren't poised."

Maybe what happened to Shaffer's poise here had to do with Oklahoma's undeniable defensive excellence, maybe it had to do with the

failed inevitability of the candle that burns from both ends, and maybe it had to do with a week's worth of questions about his competence. Maybe the kind of self-doubt he could avoid between Saturdays at University Park was firmly implanted and greenhoused by the national spotlight.

"Oklahoma's defensive play was outstanding," he said in a half-teary postgame dialogue. "But it was bad throws that killed us. It's just too bad the performance of one player has to negate the kind of effort we had today.

"It's difficult to go off the field after three plays and then watch guys like (linebackers) Shane (Conlan) and Rogers (Alexander) continue to work and try to do everything themselves."

It might well be that memory will sting Shaffer most severely. Penn State's defense played heroically and Conlan turned in one of the greatest performances in the schools' line-

Joe Paterno, left, and Oklahoma coach Barry Switzer were all laughs before the game.

caught Penn State in an oddly timed blitz.

Shaffer, who was relieved in the fourth quarter by junior Matt Knizner, threw a pair of interceptions in Penn State territory in the second quarter, setting up Sooners field goals that increased their lead to 16-7.

Penn State got a break when Holieway fumbled with 10 seconds left in the half, and the Lions were able to send Manca in to kick a 27-yard field goal that made it 16-10, but that ended their scoring for the evening.

backing-built history. Assigned principally to Oklahoma quarterback Jamelle Holieway, the Sooners' primary weapon in their jet-fueled wishbone attack, Conlan was simultaneously ruthless and flawless. The net result of Holieway's first 10 carries were that Conlan chased him 28 yards backward and triggered two fumbles. When it was all over, Holieway had carried only 12 times — 42 yards forward and 41 backward, netting 1.

To Holieway's considerable credit, he stood up to flip a 71-yard pass to tight end Keith Jackson that put the Sooners ahead, 10-7, and to Shaffer's unfortunate discredit, he pretty much took it from there.

Shaffer's two interceptions in a 5-for-15 first half set up field goals that made it 16-7, and only Paterno's careful stacking of time outs in the final minute of the half bought enough time for Oklahoma's only fumble and subsequent Penn State field goal that made it 16-10.

Even at that point, Shaffer's performance was not unusually bad. It

did not become desperately bad until the first possession of the second half, which ended with a cripplingly underthrown pass to Michael Timpson that was intercepted by Oklahoma's Sonny Brown at the Sooner 1.

"We wanted him to throw because he has a tendency to look right where he's going to throw it," Brown said. "All I had to do was turn around and I knew right where it was going to be."

"The protection was good," Shaffer said. "The pattern was good. The throw was short."

Thereafter, Paterno gave Shaffer two more tries, and finally dismissed him for Matt Knizner with 6:56 remaining. Knizner threw for more yardage on 8-for-11 passing in fewer than seven minutes than Shaffer had all night.

"I thought it was a good move," Shaffer said. "Matt Knizner's always ready to play football when he gets in there."

Events get catalogued in different memories for different reasons, but

some of the witnesses beneath the Orange Bowl bleachers last night will have a difficult time remembering Shaffer's sins more easily than his bold confession.

In an era when high-profile athletes, quarterbacks in particular, exhaust every scapegoat but personal responsibility to protect their images, Shaffer took full blame and issued a full and emotional apology.

"I'm sorry I had so much to do with the outcome," he said.

From the time he was in seventh grade, John Shaffer had affected the outcomes on football games. Sometimes, they won despite him. But they always won — in 54 consecutive John Shaffer starts to be precise, until now.

"You guys always made a lot more of that streak than I ever did," Shaffer said. "I'd give all 54 back if I could have this one."

The arrangement expired at the most inopportune moment for Shaffer. He lived a nightmare last night, and he awoke grimly aware that he could no longer bargain with destiny.

Ripped Tide: No. 2 Alabama Can Muster Only One Field Goal

By Mike DeCourcy
The Pittsburgh Press

Tuscaloosa, Ala., Oct. 25, 1986 — When the Penn State Nittany Lions beat Alabama a year ago, they couldn't escape the inevitable questions about Miami. It was a lot like that today, but this time everyone was talking about the university, not the city.

Will No. 6 Penn State get an opportunity to play No. 1 Miami in some sort of national championship bowl game, as it did Oklahoma in the Orange Bowl last season? Tough question. Do they deserve the chance? Got anyone better for the Hurricanes to play?

Penn State (7-0) proved beyond a reasonable doubt there are few better teams in college football, sticking a 23-3 defeat into the craws of No. 2 Alabama and the silent majority of the 60,210 fans in Bryant-Denny Stadium. With No. 4 Nebraska also losing, Penn State figures to move up at least two, and possibly three spots in The Scripps-Howard poll.

"Someone has to play awfully well to beat us the way we're playing," Coach Joe Paterno said, adding later, "I knew we were ready. I think we were a little stronger today. It was two good teams; we just played a little better.

Penn State played about as perfectly as possible. The offensive linemen pro-

Score by Periods

Penn State	0	14	3	6	— 23
Alabama	3	0	0	0	— 3

tected quarterback John Shaffer as if he were holding their lunch money, permitting the Crimson Tide one sack, on a meaningless fourth-quarter play. All-American linebacker Cornelius Bennett made 13 tackles but never came close enough to Shaffer to read his number.

The Penn State defensive front, linebackers included, hounded Tide quarterback Mike Shula into one of his worst days, a 14-for-30, 172-yard disaster. Shula was sacked five times, twice each by Tim Johnson and Brentwood's Don Graham, and once by Freeport's Bob White.

The powerful Alabama running game was good for just 87 yards, the tailback tandem of Bobby Humphrey (27 yards)

and Gene Jelks (15) rendered ineffective. Penn State linebacker Trey Bauer had an outstanding day, making nine tackles, causing a fumble and recovering another. The Tide lost three fumbles, Penn State one.

The Lions secondary held speedy Al Bell to one catch for 4 yards. The speedier Greg Richardson got loose for four catches and 60 yards, but nothing longer than 22. Cornerback Eddie Johnson and safety Ray Isom each intercepted a pass.

There's more.

Kicker Massimo Manca, who was hitting .333 in 1986 (3-for-9), converted field goals of 37, 29 and 42 yards, the only points of the second half. He's up to .500.

Shaffer, a 40-percent passer in road games, completed 13 of 17 attempts (77 percent) for 168 yards and was not intercepted. He completed seven of eight attempts in the second half.

"We didn't get good pressure on their quarterback. If the quarterback has time to throw, I'm not surprised if he completes passes," Alabama coach Ray Perkins said. "But Shaffer's not the guy who makes their offense go. It's those backs, those Doziers and Smiths and Manoas and Clarks."

With Alabama a 6-point favorite, the game was supposed to go one way, but quickly went the other. As did Penn State's most effective offensive plays.

"We wanted to run a lot of counter plays to keep them off balance," Lions center Keith Radecic said. "They're great players, but because they're so quick, they overrun a lot of plays."

For the same reason, Penn State's running backs, including D.J. Dozier (63 yards rushing) and reserve Blair Thomas (57), were encouraged by their

Kicker Massimo Manca, center, celebrates his fourth-quarter field goal that put the Nittany Lions in front, 20-3.

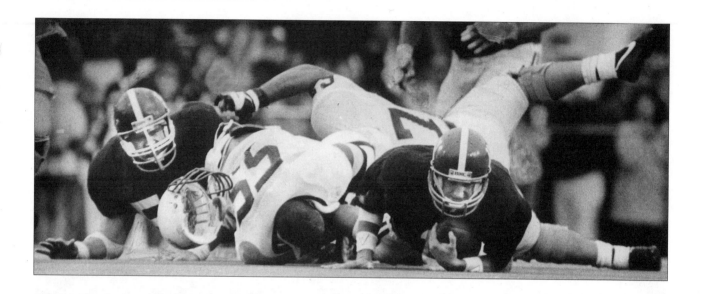

It Was Lions' Turn To 'Touch Greatness'

BY BOB SMIZIK
The Pittsburgh Press

In the glowing aftermath of victories over Florida and Tennessee, Alabama Coach Ray Perkins modestly announced that his team had "touched greatness."

Those were powerful words, words that many teams would have difficulty living up to. But the Crimson Tide touched greatness again yesterday.

You bet, the Tide touched greatness. It touched greatness all afternoon. Too often, however, that's all it did. It could touch greatness, but it could neither tackle it nor block it.

The greatness this time around, you see, was not that of the Tide. The greatness on this afternoon belonged to Penn State.

Greatness is not a word that should be used cheaply, and rarely should it be used, as Perkins did, after victories against opponents the caliber of Tennessee and Florida.

But when the opponent is Alabama, which was unbeaten, ranked second in the country by Scripps-Howard and thought to be in contention for the national championship, there is reason to consider defining the victory in terms of greatness. And when the victory is as decisive as it was yesterday, there is almost no choice but to call it greatness.

Penn State beat Alabama with the run, with the pass and with an opportunistic defense that brings to mind the great Joe Paterno teams of the past. The Lions did it at such a level of efficiency that, although they came into this game as a major question mark, they leave it as yet another Paterno team capable of winning the national championship.

The score was Penn State 23, Alabama 3, but not even those numbers tell the story of Penn State's domination of the Tide.

It was Alabama's worst loss in 31 years at Bryant-Denny Stadium, where its record is 143-13-3.

"My mother told me there would be days like this," Alabama center Wes Neighbors said, "but it's hard to take."

The victory erased all doubts about Penn State, which had won its first six games against opposition that was not universally respected. The opponents and the difficulty some of them gave Penn State made the Lions suspect throughout the land. The feeling was they had proved little in the first six games.

But it was not a feeling shared by the Penn State players.

"We know how good we are," all-American linebacker Shane Conlon said. "We don't care what people think. We're all veterans. We've been in this type of game before. It's no big deal.

coaches to cut back against the flow when the opportunity seemed ripe. They compiled 210 rushing yards against an Alabama defense that previously allowed an average of 97.9.

"Anybody we play, that's what we think: We'll run right at them, until they stop us," said Fran Ganter, Penn State's offensive coordinator. "We're a power football team, and we have to make our kids believe in that."

Alabama played that role in the first quarter, using three running plays to

Mike Shula is sacked by Tim Johnson.

reach the Penn State 49 on the opening series. One the fourth, however, fullback Bo Wright was hit by White and fumbled, and Duffy Cobbs recovered for Penn State.

Alabama got it back and mixed the same strategy with a 31-yard pass from Shula to Humphrey. That set up Van Tiffin's 41-yard field goal, the Tide's only score, to make it 3-0.

Penn State was stopped on its first two series, but the third time was a harm to the Alabama defense. Dozier gained 24 yards on a screen pass, rushed for gains of 3 and 7 yards, then broke for a 19-yard touchdown run five seconds into

the second quarter.

"I was a little nervous when they stuffed us twice at the beginning," Shaffer said. "It was just a matter of keeping our composure."

Thomas, in to give Dozier a breather, did similar damage to Alabama two series later, gaining 16 and 29 yards on draw plays and then scoring on a 3-yard reverse. Penn State led at halftime, 14-3.

"They got after us. They were the better team today," Alabama center Wes Neighbors said. "There was no doubt from the third quarter on who was going to win the game."

It's not like we were some high school team coming in here to play Alabama."

The victory had major ramifications throughout college football, especially in Miami, where the news from Tuscaloosa is bound to have a sobering effect on a team that thought it had the national championship for the taking.

The Lions are in the hunt, a legitimate challenger to the Hurricanes. Paterno is a man who knows.

"Someone has to play awfully well to beat us the way we're playing. We've played this way since the Notre Dame and Pitt games of last year. For the last 10 or 11 games we played about as well as we can play," Paterno said.

Unquestionably playing as well as he can play is quarterback John Shaffer, who runs Paterno's offense to near perfection and who himself played at such a level yesterday.

Shaffer completed 13 of 17 passes for 168 yards. He was not intercepted and thoroughly outplayed his Alabama counterpart, Mike Shula.

"This was a very big game for us in our season and in our history because

we faced one of the finest football teams I've played in my career. It's great to be able to take on a champion like Alabama and play like champions ourselves," Shaffer said.

There are no more champions to be faced. A closing schedule that looked dangerous in September has turned soft. The Lions close with West Virginia, Maryland, Notre Dame and Pitt. The first two teams are in the process of collapse, the last two do not figure to have the talent to play with the Lions.

Penn State and Miami, both independents, could not meet in any of the four major bowls, all of which have a tie-up with at least one conference. But the Sunkist Fiesta Bowl, played in Phoenix, Ariz., and the Florida Citrus Bowl, played in Orlando, might be interested in raising their guarantee to attract such a game.

ABC televises the Florida Citrus Bowl, which will be played Jan. 1 for the first time.

"To be honest, I can't see ABC coming up with the kind of money

to make the Citrus Bowl attractive enough for a game between No. 1 and No. 2," ABC spokesman Donn Bernstein said. "I would think the Fiesta Bowl might want to go for something like that."

The Fiesta Bowl, which has taken on Sunkist as its corporate sponsor, has tried hard to crack the four major bowls, but has remained only at the top of the second tier of bowl games.

If Sunkist is interested in taking that giant step this season, it might want to come up with the $2 million, which is about what it would take to put the Fiesta on a par with the Orange, Sugar and Cotton bowls in terms of payoff.

Paterno would have none of it. "I'm not going to get into those silly games," he said.

But whether he likes it or not, he is in the midst of that silly game, even as early as October, because he has an unbeaten record, a finishing schedule that should keep it that way and the most important ingredient. A great football team.

Irish Fall Short in Their Bid to Upset Undefeated Lions

BY MIKE DECOURCY
The Pittsburgh Press

South Bend, Ind., Nov. 15, 1986 — When a football team has been at this perfection thing long enough, there can come a point when that becomes decidedly more important than excellence. The team, cautious, does not play to win; it plays not to lose.

There is little question that is what Penn State was up to yesterday. By a 24-19 margin, it did not lose to Notre Dame yesterday before 59,075 at Notre Dame Stadium and a network television audience. It was the 21st consecutive time the Nittany Lions did not lose in a regular-season game.

It must have weighed two or three tons, but No. 2 Penn State (10-0) held up its end of the bargain in the negotiations for a bowl matchup against No. 1 Miami for the national championship. Notre Dame (4-5) had four shots in the last minute to ruin the plans of the Gator, Florida Citrus and Fiesta bowls but wound up 0-for-4.

"There were an awful lot of guys praying on the sideline that had never said prayers before," quarterback John Shaffer said.

There was 2:29 left in the game when Notre Dame assumed possession of the ball, 80 yards from its biggest, most important victory in five years. It took

Score by Periods

Penn State	7	3	7	7	— 24
Notre Dame	0	6	7	6	— 19

Massimo Manca's field goal gave Penn State a 10-6 lead at halftime.

slightly more than a minute for the Irish to put all but six of those yards behind them.

Notre Dame quarterback Steve Beuerlein, who humbled Penn State's defense like no quarterback since Heisman Trophy winner Doug Flutie, completed five consecutive passes for 74 yards to put Penn State's back to the goal post.

Immediately, however, the Irish began moving in reverse. On a first-and-goal option play, Lions safety Ray Isom crushed flanker Tim Brown for a three-yard loss. On second down, defensive tackle Bob White surged through the middle to sack Beuerlein 9 yards back. Third down saw Beuerlein's pass over the middle narrowly avoid the fingertips of tight end Joel Williams, his body clearly in the end zone.

Fourth down. Penn State dropped half its defense into the end zone and kept Notre Dame's receivers company. Beuerlein looked, and looked, finally spotting tailback Mark Green open at the 13. He passed, and Green caught the ball, but his knee touched the ground. The threat had ended.

"There was really no excuse for not putting the ball somewhere in the end zone," Beuerlein said. "I couldn't see anyone on our team who was open. I saw that Mark had a lot of room. If he could have just turned it up …"

Penn State probably should not have been in that situation. Its offense consistently mauled the Irish on first down, averaging 6.1 yards per play. It turned meek on third down, however, failing to convert on eight of 13 attempts.

Most of those were third-and-short situations, and on five of the first seven, Penn State called running plays. Four

Penn State all-America Shane Conlan visits with Bob Hope on the Kodak All-America TV show.

Penn State quarterback John Shaffer threw only 13 times against the Irish, but completed nine attempts for 162 yards.

of those five failed. When the Lions finally passed on third-and-2 from their 41 late in the third quarter, Shaffer found tight end Brian Siverling for a 22-yard gain that keyed Penn State's go-ahead touchdown, a 37-yard pass from Shaffer to Ray Roundtree that made it 17-13.

Penn State coach Joe Paterno told Shaffer this might have been his best game as the Lions' quarterback, and it was the quintessential Shaffer performance. He threw only 13 times, completing nine for 162 yards. And the big key: He was not intercepted, and Penn State did not fumble. Shaffer, however, was not entirely pleased.

"Short-yardage is killing us. We shouldn't have gotten into those situations, but we could easily have gotten out of them. A good team should be able to run for those 2-3 yards."

A good team can prevent it, though, and Notre Dame proved yesterday it is at least that. The Irish outgained Penn State, 418-314, and made most of the plays it needed. Notre Dame's five fumbles, two of them lost to Penn State, might have been the difference.

"We are a lot better than 4-5," said Beuerlein, who completed 24 of 39 passes for 311 yards. "You can ask Penn State about that. They knew they were in a ballgame."

Penn State led throughout the first half, with help from a Beuerlein fumble that stopped the Irish's strong drive on their opening possession at the Penn State 22. The Lions appeared set to play gambling football when Shaffer found Roundtree on second down for a 34-yard bomb. That set up Steve Smith's 1-yard run and the Lions' 7-0 lead.

Notre Dame made it 7-6 on two John Carney field goals, from 20 and 38 yards. But the first of those could have been a 97-yard kickoff return by Brown, which was called back by a

Nittany Lions' receiver Ray Roundtree made the day a miserable one for the Irish, catching three passes for 95 yards.

penalty. And Beuerlein's second fumble, the last turnover of the game, set up Penn State at the Irish 25. Massimo Manca kicked a 19-yard field goal to make it 10-6 at the half.

Beuerlein took control of the game then, completing a 50-yard pass over the middle to split end Milt Jackson and then finding Brown with a 14-yard touchdown pass to make it 13-10.

"I felt we could play with them, and we did," Notre Dame coach Lou Holtz said. "We had our chances. I thought we were going to need some turnovers, but it seemed we didn't get them."

Penn State scored twice in five minutes, the second a 1-yard sneak by Shaffer with 11:49 remaining. Both drives included long passes from Shaffer to Roundtree, who caught 3 passes for 95 yards.

"I couldn't believe how open I was

on the touchdown. All kinds of bad things go through your mind — dropping it, falling, something silly like that," Roundtree said. "They had come up on me, but I guess John did a great job with the fake, because they went for it."

Notre Dame, by rights, should have been finished when it was down, 24-13, but it wouldn't quit. Beuerlein drove 64 yards, completing things with an 8-yard touchdown pass to Brown that made it 24-19. It was Brown's turn to throw to Beuerlein on a two-point conversion attempt, but the flea-flicker pass was intercepted by Penn State's Pete Giftopolous.

"We let big plays happen. We don't think we played out best games," linebacker Shane Conlan said of the defense. "People talk about the defense all the time, but I think this is one the offense saved for us."

Perfection: Lions Seal National Title with 12-0 Record

By Mike DeCourcy
The Pittsburgh Press

Tempe, Ariz., Jan. 2, 1987 — Most of the emotion was spent on the moment, in the 90 seconds or so it took to clear the fanatics from the field at Sun Devil Stadium. Had to get those last nine seconds in. Had to be official.

So John Shaffer knelt down, cradling the football, and it was done. Penn State 14, Miami 10. The Nittany Lions had No. 1 all to themselves. It was numbing, frankly.

How does one deal with perfection? And that is what this was. Not just 12-0 and Penn State's second national championship, but the fulfillment of every goal the Lions had established within both last night's game and the entire season.

Tailback D.J. Dozier and linebacker Shane Conlan sat calmly near the rear entrance of the press tent afterward, awaiting their awards as offensive and defensive MVP's, smiling that unique smile of disbelief. They talked some about what it felt like to win what was billed as the greatest game ever played in college football and ended up, in retrospect, underplayed. The consensus: They'd have to check the films.

"We were just sitting there talking like, 'Yeah, we won.' It hasn't hit me," Conlan said. "Maybe tomorrow." Dozier's expression was blank.

Fine. The talk of this Fiesta Bowl, the most super bowl ever consummated in college football, will subside in no great hurry.

This became the Lions' second national title in five years, the first coming in 1982, and the fourth time in Coach Joe Paterno's 21 seasons they finished the season unbeaten.

A record crowd of 73,098 in the stadium and a large NBC television audience watched. The network helped move the game to prime time to showcase the showdown between No. 1 and No. 2, between Heisman Trophy winner Vinny Testaverde and his latest victims.

Testaverde fulfilled most of the requirements for victory, leading his team to 445 yards and 22 first downs and completing 26 of 50 for 285 yards. Not much in the way of points, though, and there were those interceptions. All five of them.

Particularly the last.

Blair Thomas (32) is corralled by Freddy Highsmith

Penn State linebacker Don Graham celebrates after sacking Miami quarterback Vinny Testaverde on the ground.

ning points. And then, as had happened to Notre Dame before them, the Hurricanes backward march began.

An incomplete pass first, and then Tim Johnson nearly tore off Testaverde's head with a 7-yard sack. Testaverde underthrew on third down, missing Warren Williams at the 2. On fourth down, Testaverde found Pete Giftopoulos near the goal line for the second time.

Giftopoulos plays linebacker for Penn State. His second interception clinched the victory, and the players and fans celebrated wildly on the field. When it was cleared up, the matter of the final seconds was too.

"We spent an awful lot of the football game playing pass defense inside the 30," Paterno said. "We have been awfully tough down inside the 20-yard line. And we play with confidence down there."

It was the ultimate challenge for the Penn State defense, a unit that had conquered everything but. They gave a magnificent performance under dire, but familiar circumstances. The offense was, if not dead, then sleeping soundly. It produced just eight first downs and 162 yards and ran only 59 plays to Miami's 93.

Under normal circumstances, NBC would have presented to the nation the throbbing rock beat of a "Miami Vice" rerun in this time slot. What the Fiesta Bowl almost provided was the throbbing headache of a Penn State rerun from the 1986 Orange Bowl, when the Lions lost last season's national championship to Oklahoma because the offense could not complement a superb defensive effort.

"Their rush was so good, we never had any time to get into what we wanted to do. We just couldn't double everybody up," Paterno said.

With Miami blitzing often and four

"There was just no way we could lose this game," senior linebacker Trey Bauer said. "The whole season, the way we've been getting out of situations … everybody just sucked it up. We couldn't lose."

The end couldn't have been more fitting for Penn State, nor caused more fits for Miami. It came down to the penultimate play, fourth-and-goal from the Penn State 13 with 18 seconds left, and Miami's only hope for victory was to cross the goal line.

Score by Periods					
Penn State	0	7	0	7	— 14
Miami	0	7	0	3	— 10

Falling short of a touchdown meant falling short.

Penn State had permitted the Hurricanes, trailing by four, to drive 71 yards in the final three minutes, from their 23 to within 6 yards of the win-

THE PITTSBURGH PRESS — JANUARY 3, 1987

Call It Unanimous ... Penn State Voted No. 1

There are no doubts that Penn State, which finished its season with a 12-0 record by defeating Miami, 14-10, in the Fiesta Bowl Friday night, is the nation's No. 1 college team.

In four polls announced yesterday, Penn State was named No. 1. Only in one of the polls were the Nittany Lions not a unanimous choice.

Penn State received all 31 first-place votes and 620 points in the final Scripps Howard poll, selected by sportswriters. Miami, which led virtually all year, finished second with 582 points. Orange Bowl winner Oklahoma, a loser to Miami in September, was third (564).

In the United Press International poll, Penn State swept all 49 ballots cast by the UPI Board of Coaches, receiving 735 points. Miami finished second with 673 points and third place Oklahoma got 660.

Only The Associated Press poll, selected by sportswriters, was not unanimous. Penn State was voted No. 1 with 1,137 points — three shy of unanimous — to 1,064 for Miami. Oklahoma which received the other three first-place votes, was third with 1,045.

The Football Writers Association of America awarded Penn State the Grantland Rice Trophy, symbolic of its No. 1 designation.

times sacking Shaffer, he had time on only 5 of 16 attempts, the completions covering 53 yards. D.J. Dozier gained 99 yards on 20 carries, but the rest of the Penn State running game was largely ineffective, producing 109 yards.

It did produce one solid drive, however, 74 yards in 10 plays toward a 4-yard touchdown run by Shaffer to tie the game at 7-7 with 1:49 left in the first half. Shaffer hit Eric Hamilton with a 23-yard pass over the middle on third-and-12, and Tim Manoa's 20-yard run put Shaffer in position for the touchdown.

Miami had earlier gone ahead on 1-yard run by halfback Melvin Bratton, set up by an odd fumble/interception by Shaffer plucked out of the air by defensive end Bill Hawkins.

Miami's offense never drove for a touchdown. It moved the ball, but on

Coach Joe Paterno gives some last-minute instructions from the sidelines.

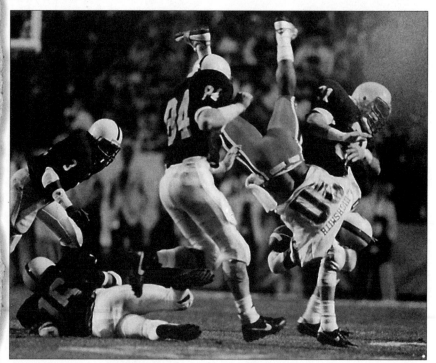

Miami tailback Alonzo Highsmith is sent airborne by Penn State's Shane Conlan (31) and Keith Karpinski (84) during the third quarter.

Greatest Moments in Penn State Football History

Penn State Awaits Validation of National Title

By Mike DeCourcy
and Curt Holbreich
The Pittsburgh Press

Penn State won the duel between college football's No. 1 and 2 teams last night at the Fiesta Bowl, but in a sense, still had to wait for the results of wire-service polls to validate its unofficial national championship.

They've been playing college football for more than 100 years, and still no one has found a better way. Or no one's listening to those who have.

Penn State coach Joe Paterno, an advocate of a Division I-A football playoff since his early days with the Nittany Lions, said the success of the Fiesta Bowl — an artistic and commercial success, as well as a 14-10 victory for Penn State against Miami at Sun Devil Stadium — should prove a tournament is necessary.

"I think it would have been a shame if we had not played this game and Miami had been rated No. 1 without us having a shot at them," Paterno said.

"I think, for that reason, we ought to have a playoff. We had one, and tonight we got more points than Miami. We're not saying we kicked their ears in, but that's the nature of competition."

'That No. 22'

Nobody knows quite where Randy Shannon came from, or who he is. He became one of the most prominent players, though, in the Fiesta Bowl.

He's "that No. 22" to members of the Penn State football team, who said

Shannon, a sophomore linebacker, sneaked up behind Lions quarterback John Shaffer and smacked Shaffer in the helmet.

It was a play Penn State tailback D.J. Dozier said, "everyone in the stadium saw," except the officials. It upset Dozier enough to send him on the field, screaming at the referees to call a penalty.

"I don't care what was said before that happened, it was not right," Dozier said, "I hope he's sorry for it. It was very unnecessary."

Otherwise, a lot of the pre-game talk that this would be a war proved folly. There was a little shoving, but not fights. Just a lot more talk.

Several Hurricanes blew through pre-game warmups — *Penn State's pre-game warmups* — talking at the Nittany Lions, warning them of impending doom.

"Before the game, they said they were the greatest ever," Trey Bauer said. "Now they've lost and they look like jerks."

Not A No-Name Punter

Punters have a hard time making a name for themselves, but not Penn State's John Bruno. Bruno, who earlier in the week helped spark the Miami "Steak Fry" walkout with jokes the Hurricanes called offensive, made things tough on them in the game as well.

Bruno, a senior from Upper St. Clair, punted nine times for an average of 43.4 yards.

"John Bruno deserves a lot of credit," Paterno said. "The cover teams

did a super job. We wanted to make sure they didn't get any easy field position."

Bruno made sure of that. Three of his first-half punts were responsible for Miami starting drives at its 2-, 9- and 11-yard lines.

Two Interceptions For Conlan

All-American linebacker Shane Conlan is the heart of the Penn State defense. So when he went down holding his left knee in the first quarter, it appeared as though the Lions might be in trouble.

"I heard a snap and it was like, 'Oh, God.' I said, 'This isn't happening.' "

Conlan returned later, injuring his right ankle. He continued to play despite the pain and fatigue, intercepting two passes, including one that set up Dozier's winning touchdown.

"I was lucky to be around," he said. "I wasn't sure I was going to last that long.

"I had a lot of problems coming off blocks. As far as running, I couldn't cut right to left.

"I was so tired I thought I wasn't going to make it. But I was going to finish. The only way they could get me out of there was to cut my leg off."

Conlan finished with eight tackles (four unassisted) and one sack.

Sophomore cornerback Eddie Johnson led Penn State with 13 tackles (nine unassisted). Senior cornerback Duffy Cobbs had 10 unassisted and two assisted tackles. He also had an interception and two pass breakups.

Bauer had nine unassisted tackles, three assisted and a pass breakup.

179

Penn State's terms. All-American wideout Michael Irvin and Brian Blades were near silent before Miami's final drive, and Brett Perriman never became a factor. Miami receivers dropped at least a half-dozen passes.

Testaverde said it might have been the change in weather or atmosphere, but finally declared, "There was no reason for it."

Really, there was. Penn State cornerbacks Duffy Cobbs and Eddie Johnson played so far off the receivers they could barely read Miami's jersey

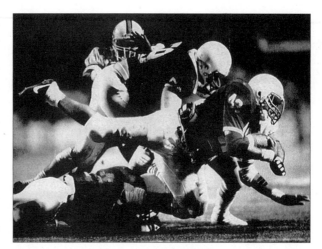

The Nittany Lions' D.J. Dozier worked hard for his 99 yards and one touchdown. Dozier also had two receptions in Penn State's Fiesta Bowl victory over Miami.

Penn State Defies Logic for Victory

By Bob Smizik
The Pittsburgh Press

As Penn State and Miami prepared to play for the national championship in the Fiesta Bowl, pre-game analysis was pretty much in agreement on these facts:

■ No way Penn State could win unless it kept Vinny Testaverde off the field.

■ No way Penn State could win unless it got something approaching a decent game from John Shaffer.

■ No way Penn State could win unless its running game dominated the Miami defense.

Uh-huh.

Testaverde, Miami's peerless quarterback, spent a lot of time standing on the grass of Sun Devil Stadium Friday night.

Shaffer, Penn State's not-so-peerless quarterback, was ineffective. He completed less than one-third of his passes (5 of 16) for 53 yards. And when was the last time a team won with a similar performance from its quarterback, let alone against the No. 1 team?

Penn State's running attack, which forged the victory, not only did not dominate Miami's defense, it was outgained by one Hurricanes running back.

So much for figuring the game.

Penn State defied armchair logic and still won, 14-10. If it were a less-than-beautiful game, it was gripping, fitting of a national-championship game.

Because the Nittany Lions did not keep Testaverde off the field, did not get anything approaching a satisfactory performance from Shaffer and did not get the dominating ground game they were supposed to need, the question is:

Why did they win?

The answer is simple.

It has to do with the guy with the thick glasses and the black hair. That crotchety old guy who is too suspicious and too idealistic. Some call him a saint, some suggest he is a scoundrel. He is neither, but closer to the former than the latter.

And he is something else, something too many of us had forgotten. He is a football genius.

We might never see another like him. Give him time and something approaching equal talent and usually he will win.

There are questions whether Paterno had anything approaching equal talent to Miami. But he had time.

There are many wondrously talented football players on the Penn State team. But Miami had more.

Miami had a quarterback thought to be the greatest to play the college game. It had swift and resourceful receivers. It had a terrific pair of running backs. It had a monster defense, led by Jerome Brown, perhaps the best lineman in the nation.

But Penn State had Paterno.

numbers, but that kept the Hurricanes from breaking big plays, and it gave the Lions running starts for some nasty, vicious hits.

"A couple of hits like that," Bauer said, "and their receivers' arms seemed to get about 8 inches shorter."

Penn State and Miami were still early in the final quarter, as both Mark Seelig of the Hurricanes (28 yards) and Massimo Manca of Penn State (49) missed field goals. Seelig connected on a 38-yarder with 11:49 remaining and gave Miami a 10-7 lead.

Penn State took the kickoff, sputtered, and gave the ball back to Miami. "I told the defense, 'Just one more time, and the offense will get you out of it,' " Paterno said. "They were tired of waiting."

On second-and-10 from his 34, Testaverde dropped back and looked toward tight end Alfredo Roberts. He passed, but toward Conlan, who made his second interception and returned it to the 5. One play later, Dozier had a touchdown run and Penn State had all the points it needed.

The loss was difficult to accept for Miami coach Jimmy Johnson, who has taken his team to within one game of the national championship the past two seasons, and can only take solace in that he's getting closer. In last year's Sugar Bowl, the Hurricanes were beaten by Tennessee, 35-7.

"Both teams gave it their all. We just had too many mistakes, too many penalties, too many turnovers," Johnson said. "Penn State did a great job. They're the best team in the country."

Paterno could not devise a game plan that would enable Shaffer to develop unerring accuracy with his passes. He could not devise a game plan that would enable his offensive line to open holes for D.J. Dozier.

But he could devise a game plan that would befuddle and frustrate Testaverde.

Only one team had stopped Testaverde since he became Miami's starting quarterback in 1985. He threw three interceptions in a 35-7 loss to Tennessee in the Sugar Bowl last year. The conventional thinking was Penn State would attempt to duplicate what Tennessee did.

Too obvious for Paterno. Wouldn't Miami be expecting such a strategy?

"We took one look at the Tennessee film and that was it," Paterno said. "We did very little what Tennessee did."

Tennessee used the blitz to rattle Testaverde. Paterno went a more conventional route. He used a standard four-man rush and went to the strength of his team — its linebacker

— to drop off in coverages Testaverde had never seen.

It came down to this: Penn State had seven men playing pass defense. Sound familiar? Does 48-14 sound familiar?

The last time Paterno went up against a quarterback who was supposed to be unstoppable was in 1981. The name was Dan Marino. Paterno didn't win a national championship that afternoon at Pitt Stadium. But he did what is almost as heroic to a Penn State fan: he took one away from Pitt.

"We changed a lot of zones and tried to disguise a lot of things and kept enough pressure on Testaverde without having to blitz," Paterno said.

"We forced him out of the pocket. He threw the ball a couple of times without seeing the linebackers. A couple of times just trying to figure out what the zone was, he just took too long, and our linebackers were there.

"I think he had a little trouble reading our zones."

Did he say a little trouble? Does five interceptions — four by linebackers — sound like a little trouble?

The biggest interception was the last one. Miami was 13 yards away from winning with 18 seconds remaining when Testaverde found Pete Giftopoulos, a Penn State linebacker, near the goal line.

"He (Giftopoulos) ran right to the curl, like he knew where I was going to throw it, exactly," Testaverde said.

Giftapoulos being in the right spot was due far more to design than accident.

"We spent hours and hours and hours trying to read some of their key routes," Paterno said.

Give him six weeks to plan and plot and you know he will come up with something that will work. He came up with a national championship this time. Typically, he directed all credit to his players.

"Our defense played as well as I've ever seen a college football team play defense."

Nittany Lions Stop Irish on Dramatic Two-Point Try

BY MIKE DECOURCY
The Pittsburgh Press

University Park, Pa., Nov. 21, 1987 — It was a moment that always will be frozen in the history of Penn State football. Or at least frozen. Goodness, it was cold. For 10 seconds, though, no one in Beaver Stadium could feel it, even those who weren't already numb.

Illuminating the scoreboard was this: Penn State 21, Notre Dame 20. It was how the game ended, but there was more drama to this than could be adequately depicted by a series of numbers.

The game had been as close as football games are permitted to be and still determine a winner and loser. The total yardage statistics for Penn State and Notre Dame wound up dead even, 312-312, and the game easily could have finished the same.

That, Notre Dame coach Lou Holtz left up to his players. They chose to try for victory, opting to attempt a two-point conversion rather than kick for a tie.

The No. 7 Irish earned the right to make this decision by driving 62 yards, scoring from 6 inches away on a dive by fullback Anthony Johnson, and consuming all but the final 31 seconds of the game. Penn State would have no reasonable chance to change the outcome.

It wasn't necessary. The few who

Score by Periods

Notre Dame	7	0	7	6	—	20
Penn State	7	7	0	7	—	21

Linebacker Keith Karpinski helped squash Notre Dame's final chance for victory.

remained of the estimated 84,000 in attendance made enough noise to confuse Notre Dame quarterback Tony Rice. Penn State switched to an unfamiliar coverage scheme, and Rice elected to run right against the Penn State defense. Instead, he ran right into it. Linebacker Keith Karpinski blocked the path to the corner and turned the play inside, and there Rice was planted at the Lions 4 by defensive tackle Pete Curkendall.

"I couldn't let him break containment," Karpinski said. "I was able to turn it in, and I looked back and it was 10 blue shirts swarming him. It looked really great."

With a temperature of 14 degrees and a 25-mph wind sweeping north-to-south across Beaver Stadium, this game couldn't have seemed further removed from Orlando's Florida Citrus Bowl, which is where the unranked Lions will take their respectable 8-3 record on Jan. 1.

"I had promised some people we weren't going to go to Florida with a 7-4 football team," Penn State coach Joe Paterno said. "I told the team that the other night: 'Don't make me look bad.' "

Notre Dame's fans threw oranges onto the field after the Irish's first touchdown, still hoping for a berth in the national championship game. Afterward, the Irish (8-2) were throwing cotton shirts and sweaters on their backs and preparing for the consolation prize of New Year's Day in Dallas.

"We thought if we defeated Penn State, the Orange Bowl would wait," said Irish receiver Tim Brown, a senior from Dallas. "I have mixed feelings about playing in the Cotton Bowl ... Right now, I'm not thinking about it much."

Neither is the Heisman Trophy a major concern at this juncture, not with

Steve Wisniewski (66), an all-America guard in 1987 and 1988.

No. 3 Miami waiting for Brown next week in the Orange Bowl (stadium) if not the Orange Bowl (game). He again got through a game without losing his grip on the award, though, catching four passes for 80 yards in absurd conditions.

There was no question, however, who was outstanding offensive player on this day. Penn State's Blair Thomas, with incredible blocking from his linemen, rushed for 214 yards on 35 carries, the first Penn State back to pass 200 yards since Curt Warner's 254 against Syracuse in 1981.

"I said before the game that Blair is the best back we've played against all year," Holtz said. "But I didn't think they would block as well as they did up front. I've never seen anyone dominate our defensive line like that."

Penn State's ease in running the ball facilitated its first two touchdown drives, but not nearly as much as Notre Dame's uncharacteristic confusion on special teams.

Early in the first quarter, Penn State found the only reasonable means of containing Brown's return ability — they put in punter Chris Clauss on third

down, before Brown could hustle onto the field.

It became an even better maneuver when safety Brandy Wells fumbled the punt, and it was recovered at ND's 19 by the Lions' Brian Chizmar. Thomas ran for nine yards and fullback John Greene the remaining 10 for a touchdown and 7-0 lead.

Notre Dame responded to that score quickly, with Brown taking a swing pass 29 yards and Rice running 32 yards on an option play for a touchdown.

It was tied, 7-7, but things turned grim for the Irish when they were forced

Notre Dame Schedule Was Just Too Difficult

By Gene Collier
The Pittsburgh Press

It took the savage cold and the stinging, horizontal snow of Centre County, and it took a courageous return to dignity by a Penn State team that whimpered in the grip of this autumn's top opposition, but Notre Dame finally, fatefully collapsed under the yoke of its awesome schedule.

Three yards short of a college football season's giddiest possibilities, Notre Dame's unlikely and yet relentless rush at a national championship dropped face-first on the frozen Beaver Stadium grass. Penn State's Pete Curkendall and Keith Karpinski rode Irish quarterback Tony Rice to the earth on an aborted two-point conversion attempt with 31 seconds left. The score was Penn State 21, Notre Dame 20.

"A lot of our hopes, a lot of our dreams, went down the drain today," said Notre Dame's Tim Brown, the dazzling pyrotechnician that Penn State and the driving wind controlled to the extent that he could be. "We thought maybe that if we beat Penn State, the Orange Bowl would wait (until Notre Dame plays Miami next week)."

Notre Dame's avenue to the virtually impossible led to a showdown with Big Eight champion Oklahoma New Year's night in Miami's Orange Bowl, but within 30 minutes of the end of yesterday's drama, the Irish were accepting an invitation to the Cotton Bowl and trying to act happy about it.

They were about as convincing as a 7-year-old forced to thank Aunt Bertha for the nice new pajamas.

"I have mixed feelings," Brown said. "I really don't want to be there. But my family is from there (Dallas).

I guess that will be nice."

It would be nice, in this, the age of disk drive, of unstoppable computerization, if the colleges could be coaxed toward something resembling scheduling equity.

No one needs to point out further that although Oklahoma and Miami, which could wrestle for the national championship Jan. 1, have dispensed with schedules that were as challenging as a 12-week ceramics course, Notre Dame has been presented Tarzan's Seven Challenges.

"It's been pretty tough trying to keep everybody up for every game," said Brown. "But Coach Holtz and his staff — even me — I've been trying to get guys up all year. Everybody plays us tough. Everybody plays their best game against Notre Dame."

You doubt that? Hey, Sal Genilla played his best game against Notre Dame.

All Notre Dame had to do to keep

to punt on their next possession. Notre Dame's Donn Grimm was flagged for a 15-yard, fair-catch interference penalty, and Penn State got the ball at ND's 33. Nine plays later, Thomas scored on a 1-yard run in the third quarter.

Notre Dame finally tied it in the third quarter, again striking quickly. Fullback Anthony Johnson broke through the line for a 31-yard run, and Rice scored four plays later on an 11-yard keeper. With Tim Gradel's extra point, hardly a given in these conditions, it was 14-14.

"The wind had a lot to do with it. It causes you to play differently," Holtz said. "I felt that we had the edge when we drove 77 yards into it to tie the game, but then Penn State drove 78 yards and ate up seven minutes."

That drive produced exactly no points. Eric Etze's 28-yard field goal attempt was wide left. But the Lions went ahead, 21-14, on a three-yard run by Greene with 7:34 left.

Penn State quarterback Matt Knizner passed for only 40 yards on 6-of-10 completions, but he hit the big passes, one in particular. With the drive stalling and no hope of a field goal into the wind, Knizner went to tight end Paul Pomfret on fourth and 4. The completion was good for six yards and set up Greene's touchdown.

Pomfret had dropped a sure touchdown in last week's 10-0 loss to Pitt, and on this play a broken pinky finger caused him to juggle Knizner's pass.

"I was excited when they called the play," said Pomfret, who didn't tell anyone his finger was in disarray. "Ever since I dropped that ball last week, I wanted to play another game to show what I could do."

late November compelling to its glory-starved following was beat Michigan, Michigan State, Southern Cal and Alabama, among others. The Irish buckled at Pitt in mid-October, but didn't fall until yesterday.

"The thing on my mind is to get over this," said Lou Holtz, who coached the spit out of a team that lost its quarterback after three games and had to start three different players at not less than five different positions. "Can we even bounce back to play Miami next week? I don't know how we're going to react. We are banged up and we don't have our dreams and goals intact."

Penn State tore open Notre Dame's defense with a suddenly ferocious offensive line. Doors flew off the Irish defense most notably on its right flank, where defensive tackle Bryan Flannery and outside linebackers Flash Gordon and Frank Stams got flipped away like inflatable practice dummies.

Penn State's Blair Thomas, who slashed for a career-high 214 yards,

established his rhythm at that point of attack and wound up stringing his virtuosity sideline to sideline.

"Penn State completely dominated our defensive line and I didn't expect that," Holtz said "I don't ever recall people blocking our defensive line the way Penn State did."

It was hard to recall Penn State blocking anyone at all. Last seen, these Lions were being stuffed in a hefty bag and stored for the winter by the brilliant Pitt defense. But any notion that Penn State had thrown in the blue-and-white towel on this Citrus Bowl season was dispelled the minute fullback John Greene ran into, onto, and over Irish safety Corny Southall for a 10-yard touchdown on Penn Sate's second possession.

And so this was a football game so closely and tersely fought that when it ended and the snow flew at dusk, Penn State's and Notre Dame's total net yards were the same figure, 312.

"I thought we got an edge when we drove into the wind (15 mph,

gusting to 25) to tie it in the third quarter," said Holtz. "But Penn State came right back and drove (76 yards) and used up more than seven minutes and took the lead."

Down to its final options, the screeching wind at its back, Notre Dame hammered it 62 yards through a flying Penn State defense to what would have been merely a tying touchdown had any time remained, had anything less than everything been at stake.

But when Anthony Johnson scored for the Irish on a 1-inch plunge with 31 seconds left, Holtz had a decision to make, and his players made the correct one for him.

Notre Dame went for two.

"He left it up to us," Brown said. "He called us over, and said, 'What do you want to do?' We couldn't win the national championship with a tie. We made the decision and now we have to live with it."

That shouldn't be so terribly difficult, at least not as difficult as this autumn was for Notre Dame.

O.J. McDuffie, an all–America end in 1992.

Defenses Dominate in Narrow Victory for Penn State

BY MIKE DECOURCY
The Pittsburgh Press

Austin, Texas, Sept. 30, 1989 — At the close of every home football game, the University of Texas permits spectators to try out their moves on its new artificial turf so they can move more quickly to the parking lots. Most of the 75,232 at the Texas-Penn State game went for the offer, and this mob scene provided about the best action on the Memorial Stadium field last night.

Penn State's offense gained only 264 yards and produced nearly as many points for the opposition as it did for the Lions. Texas tried three quarterbacks to generate some sort of offense, two of them twice.

It was probably fitting that the winning touchdown came from neither offense. It came from a second-team cornerback playing special teams, Penn State's Leonard Humphries, who picked up a punt blocked by teammate Andre Collins at the Texas 4 and ran into the end zone with 6:52 left for a 16-12 Lions' victory.

"Hey Leonard — if you'd fallen on that ball, we'd both be walking home," said Tom Bradley, the Lions' special teams coach. "We'd both be out there on I-35 with signs that say, 'Penn State or bust.'"

Penn State (3-1) nearly was a bust

Score by Periods

Penn State	6	3	0	7 —	16
Texas	7	3	2	0 —	12

in its first trip to the Longhorns' home. The Lions lost three turnovers to Texas' one, two of them coming inside the opposing 25-yard-line.

After breaking loose Blair Thomas for 54 of his 90 yards in the first quarter, the Lions' running game collapsed for lack of support from the passing attack. With quarterback Tony Sacca connecting on only 9-for-20 for 129 yards, the Texas defense was able to sit and wait for each of Thomas' rushing attempts.

"I am not happy that we lost, but we did play hard and the team did all

we asked of them," said Texas coach David McWilliams, whose team is 1-2. "They didn't move the ball much on us in the second half."

The Lions gained only 82 yards in the final 30 minutes, barely three yards per play. On their one significant drive, trailing 12-9, they moved to the Texas 21, but lost the ball on an intercepted pass from split end O.J. McDuffie. It was taken by Lance Gunn in the end zone and returned 11 yards.

Funny, but all that did was get Penn State 10 yards closer to the end zone. Texas barely moved on three plays, bringing Bobby Lilljedahl in for the punt. Oh, and Tal Elliott to snap.

Bradley had noticed that Lilljedahl was taking long strides before punting and lined up close to scrimmage. He also saw that Elliott, at 6-foot, 226 pounds, was not particularly huge and figured 230-pound Collins might overpower him with a burst of speed.

So Collins switched positions on the punt-block team with Jim Deter lining up on Elliott's nose. Collins surged through and barely had to lift his arms to crush Lilljedahl's kick. It was the fourth block of his career and second this season. Humphries chased it down and had no trouble reaching the end zone.

"I was very patient," Humphries said. "The ball bounced once, and it bounced pretty good. I was hoping it would bounce again the same way, because sometimes the ball bouces weird on artificial turf.

"I didn't even know I scored. I looked up, and the stadium was so quiet ... I thought maybe there was a penalty or something."

Penn State's real first drive was easily its best and gave an errant indication the team would escape its offensive doldrums. Aside from the game against Temple, which has been ham-

Texas was the third straight win for Joe Paterno's Lions in 1989, who opened with a loss to Virginia.

mered by each of its five opponents, the Lions have scored only two touchdowns on offense.

They moved 80 yards in only four plays, with Thomas running for 31 yards to the Texas 33 and Sacca finding David Daniels from there with a 33-yard scoring pass.

Penn State's lead remained at 6-0, however, when Ray Tarasi had his extra-point kick blocked by 6-10, 305-pound Ken Hackemack. It was the Lions' first miss since 1984, a string of 134 successful kicks that had been the best in the NCAA.

Texas had the lead back by the end of the quarter, after replacing starting quarterback Mark Murdock with redshirt freshman Peter Gardere. Three of Gardere's first four passes were complete, including a 30-yard touchdown to Johnny Walker directly in front of Penn State's Sherrod Rainge. Wayne Clements hit his extra-point try for a 7-6 lead.

Gardere completed 13 of 23 for 170 yards, but as he became erratic McWilliams called for senior Donovan Forbes. He passed only twice, completing one for 8 yards, before losing a contact lens and his spot in line to Murdock (7 of 13 for 74 yards). Gardere came back for two futile possessions.

Penn State played one more quarterback than it had in mind, subbing Matt Nardolillo for Sacca at the start of the second quarter. It was a traumatic moment for the Lions, as Sacca went down after twisting his knee. Nardolillo got the Lions a first down into the field goal range, and Sacca returned two plays later.

When he had a 21-yard completion to the Texas 2 wiped out by a holding penalty, a 45-yard field goal by Tarasi had to suffice. It was the longest of his career, his first from more than 40 yards.

*Andre Collins, an all-America
linebacker in 1989.*

Crimson Tide Block Field Goal for One-point Victory

By Mike DeCourcy
The Pittsburgh Press

University Park, Pa., Oct. 28, 1989 — Ray Tarasi heard it. Joe Markiewicz heard it. It was so quiet that the whole stadium must have heard it yesterday.

The sound was of leather hitting flesh. It was the sound of a Penn State defeat. "I looked up as soon as I heard it and knew it was over," said the Nittany Lions' Markiewicz.

"As soon as I blocked it, I knew there was no way it would get over the bar," said the Tide's Thomas Rayam.

It was Rayam, 6-foot-7, 290 pounds, who batted away an 18-yard field goal attempt by Penn State's Tarasi with two seconds left in the game, preserving a 17-16 Alabama victory and improving the No. 6 Crimson Tide's record to 7-0.

Markiewicz, the holder, handled a high snap and got the ball set, but Tarasi could not get it high enough to clear the line. There were penalty flags on the play, the last hope for those in the crowd of 85,975 who favored the Lions, but the only penalty against Alabama was for its victory celebration.

"If you are going to have an outstanding season, you must win some games like this," Alabama coach Bill

Score by Periods					
Alabama	0	3	7	7	— 17
Penn State	3	0	10	3	— 16

Curry said.

The final drive by No. 14 Penn State (5-2) had begun with 5:37 remaining after an interception by defensive tackle Rich Schonewolf — the Lions' fourth. It ended inside the Alabama 1, on the 11th consecutive carry by tailback Blair Thomas.

Penn State had eight seconds left and no time outs.

"There wasn't any other option. There wasn't anything to do but kick it," Coach Joe Paterno said. "It wasn't lost on one play … I don't want to harp on that one play."

Penn State lost for the second time at home because it was unable to control both tailback Siran Stacy (106 yards, 19 carries) and quarterback Gary Hollingsworth (26 of 43 for 244 yards).

"They passed so much in the first quarter that guys were back on their heels against the run," Lions linebacker Andre Collins said.

The Lions lost for the first time in Thomas' 12 career 100-yard games — he had a season-high 160 yards — because they were unable to score touchdowns on two possessions that crossed the Alabama 10.

One started at the 7, on Darren Perry's interception and a 33-yard return in the third quarter. The Lions moved 2 yards in three plays and settled for a 22-yard field goal by Tarasi that made it 13-10.

Five plays into the final quarter, eight plays into Alabama's next possession, Stacy blew through four Lions tacklers for a 12-yard touchdown run — the first on the ground against Penn State in 29 quarters — and a 17-13 Tide lead.

The Lions got to within a point on Tarasi's 46-yard field goal, the longest of his career, with 11:33 remaining. He also made a 26-yarder, the Lions' first points of the game.

Alabama matched everything the Lions did for the first three quarters. Philip Doyle's 32-yard field goal made it 3-3. The Lions' O.J. McDuffie scored on a 19-yard pass from Tony Sacca (9-of-21 for 91 yards), the Tide's Lamonde Russell scored on a six-yard pass from Hollingsworth.

Tony Sacca was held to 9-of-21 pass completions by the Alabama defense.

Above, Blair Thomas carried 11 straight times for Penn State during the game's final drive; Left, Rich Schonewolf intercepted a pass late in the fourth quarter to set up the Nittany Lions' final series.

State's Sacca Passes Nittany Lions Past No. 1 Notre Dame

By Mike DeCourcy
The Pittsburgh Press

Notre Dame, Ind., Nov. 17, 1990 — College football's national championship race was thrown into disarray with Penn State's 24-21 victory against top-ranked Notre Dame yesterday.

For a change "thrown" is not an inappropriate verb to use in connection with a Penn State victory.

Quarterback Tony Sacca completed 20 of 34 pass attempts for three touchdowns and a career-best 277 yards as the Lions shocked a crowd of 59,075 at Notre Dame Stadium.

"Tony grew up today," Coach Joe Paterno said.

Sacca's 14-yard touchdown pass to tight end Al Golden tied the score with 7:15 remaining, and freshman Craig Fayak of Belle Vernon then won the game with a 34-yard field goal with four seconds left.

The victory was the eighth in a row for No. 18 Penn State (8-2), which could reach the Top 10 off this upset. Notre Dame (8-2) is likely to fall from it precarious perch atop the polls, with Colorado, Miami, Brigham Young and Georgia Tech eager to replace it. A change at the No. 1 spot would be the sixth this season.

"It's hard to describe the feeling," said tailback Leroy Thompson, who

ran for 56 yards and caught seven passes for another 83. "Everybody was hugging each other, and there were guys crying ... I was crying."

Penn State had wanted to wait until after this game before making a decision on a bowl, but the rush by bowls and schools to wrap up deals last weekend left the Nittany Lions out of the New Year's Day spotlight and with a Dec. 28 game against Florida State in the Blockbuster Bowl.

Even with the Sugar Bowl possibly dumping Virginia, Athletic Director Jim Tarman said the Lions would not renege on their commitment to the Blockbuster.

"We've still got a big game against Pitt, and that's all I want to think about," Paterno said. "We've got a good matchup, one of the better matchups."

Penn State had to rally from deficits of 14-0 and 21-7, but its defense held the Irish scoreless and permitted only

Opposite, Penn State kicker Craig Fayak boots the winning kick; Below, Joe Paterno celebrates the win over the Irish.

Score by Periods

Penn State	7	0	7	10	— 24
Notre Dame	14	7	0	0	— 21

76 yards in the second half. Paterno said his secondary was giving too much room to the Notre Dame receivers in the first half and playing more aggressively was the key to turning around the game.

All-America flanker Raghib Ismail did not play for Notre Dame in the second half because of a thigh injury, after gaining 109 yards in the first 30 minutes.

Raghib Ismail did not play in second half.

Fayak Gets Lifted into Hero's Role

BY MIKE DECOURCY
The Pittsburgh Press

It is Craig Fayak who will get all the airtime, whose monumental 34-yard kick will have been replayed an estimated 21 times on CNN's "Headline News" by the time Sunday's National Football League results take over.

Were there more time, it would be correct to attribute Penn State's 24-21 upset of No. 1 Notre Dame yesterday to tight ends Rick Sayles and Al Golden, to a Nittany Lions defense that held the Irish to 76 second-half yards and to the most productive day quarterback Tony Sacca has had since Coach Joe Paterno's offense was tied to his neck.

It is more concise, without being inaccurate, to merely point out Fayak's field goal was the play that determined the outcome.

This is college football as it stands in 1990, a game in which two teams can employ 44 athletes in a glorious struggle, then brush them aside as the game is decided by someone whose primary objective is to keep his head down and follow through. Might as well be a golfer.

"As a quarterback, I was more in control of everything and had to do more," Fayak said. "But now that's my job. That's what a kicker does."

Fayak was a quarterback last year at Belle Vernon Area, good enough that no one was entirely certain after he committed to Penn State he might not be one again. When he arrived on campus this autumn, however, he found four other freshmen there to play quarterback but no one in sight with his combination of leg strength, form and accuracy.

He has been the Lions' placekicker since the season's second game and went into this game with 11 successful field goals on 16 attempts, including all the points in Penn State's 9-0 victory against Alabama.

Even though he missed a 39-yard attempt in this game, he nailed three extra points, including the one that tied the game at 21-21 with 7:15 left, then ignored his teammates and coaches and the pressure to score the winning points.

"After I tied this up with the extra point and saw how the momentum was going, I knew this would come down to me.

"Some people wanted to talk to me, but I just pushed them away. I wanted to be by myself and think about the kick. Right before the kick, I mentioned to my holder that it was just like kicking in my back yard."

He wasn't talking in a figurative sense. There really is a goalpost in the Fayak's backyard, and it was there he practiced to prepare himself for moments such as this.

There really hadn't been any other opportunities for him to win games with field goals, at least not since that midget game against Finleyville. He won that one for his Rostraver team

"No doubt we have built our offense around him," Couch Lou Holtz said, "But you have to rise to the occasion."

After Notre Dame built its lead in the first quarter on a 22-yard touchdown run by Ricky Watters and a 12-yard run by Tony Brooks, Sacca threw a 32-yard score to Terry Smith on a fake reverse play to make it 14-7.

Notre Dame took a 21-7 lead into halftime after an overpowering 92-yard drive capped by quarterback Rick Mirer's 1-yard drive.

Mirer, who finished 8 of 21 for 161 yards, threw two second-half interceptions that set up Penn State scores. The first was picked off by Mark D'Onofrio in the third quarter and returned 38 yards. Sacca followed with his 11-yard touchdown toss to tight end Rick Sayles.

Penn State drove toward a tie with two big passes, and then Sacca threw his touchdown to Golden.

With the score, 21-21, and Penn State facing fourth-and-2 at the ND 37, Paterno elected to punt with 2:35 remaining. Doug Helkowski's kick pinned the Irish at their 7.

They got one first down, but on a third-down play, Mirer overthrew split end Tony Smith and found Lions strong safety Darren Perry. Perry intercepted at the 39 and returned it to the Irish 19 to set up Fayak's kick.

---

when he was 9.

"Yep, 27 yards, left hash. Sure, I remember it."

Fayak got his chance because Penn State produced so many other heroes on this afternoon. Including the guy who goes by that name every day, hero/strong safety Darren Perry.

His interception and the 20-yard return with 59 seconds left and the game tied ended Notre Dame's last attempt to hang onto its No. 1 ranking. Equally important, though, was his role in shutting down the Irish passing game to a 21-yard completion in nine attempts after the halftime break.

"I think we had them rattled in the second half," Perry said.

Penn State's offense was at its most inventive. Sacca threw 14 times on first down, the same number of times the Lions had run on first down before their last possession, when they were merely positioning for the field goal. The Lions gained 18 first downs by passing.

Paterno brought out plays rarely before seen at Penn State, including a fake Statue-of-Liberty play on which

1990 Lions Record

S. 8	Texas	13-17
S. 15	USC	14-19
S. 22	Rutgers	28-0
O. 6	Temple	48-10
O. 13	Syracuse	27-21
O. 20	Boston Coll.	40-21
O. 27	Alabama	9-0
N. 3	West Va.	31-19
N. 10	Maryland	24-10
N. 17	Notre Dame	24-21
N. 24	Pitt	

Sacca kept the ball and threw to flanker Terry Smith for a 32-yard touchdown.

The Lions' third touchdown was on a play suggested by quarterback Tom Bill, the 80 Throwback, which calls for Sacca to roll to his right and draw the defense that way, then throw back across the field to the tight end, in this case Al Golden, who fell across the line to complete a 14-yard scoring play.

Only the call on Sayles' 11-yard touchdown reception, a timing pattern, was routine. The catch was not. He juggled the ball from the middle of the end zone all the way to the end line, where he stopped and collected the ball just before falling out of bounds.

"The guy on me jumped up and I blinked and lost the ball for a second. I didn't know for sure where I was, but you just get the feeling you're coming to the line. Plus, their crowd is so close to the end line that you can tell better."

This is the way some of college football's rulesmakers prefer a football game be decided, with catches and runs and tackles.

They took away the placement platform from kickers before last season and they are considering whether to make goalposts more narrow, as they are in pro ball, before next year.

"I have no qualms about the kicking aspect of the football game being a factor," Perry said. "Kicking wins and loses football games. That's what Joe's always preached."

Vol-Vol-Voom! Penn State Scores Five Quick TD's

BY SHELLY ANDERSON
Pittsburgh Post-Gazette

Tempe, Ariz., Jan. 1, 1992 — Trailing by 10 points with less than two quarters to play, Penn State was digging for answers.

The strategy in these situations usually is to chip away, to cut the deficit and to try to get into a position to win it.

The Nittany Lions took a few shortcuts yesterday. And long cuts. And perfect cuts.

In a span of 7 minutes 49 seconds late in the third and early in the fourth quarters, they scored five touchdowns for the final 35 points of the game to beat Tennessee, 42-17, in the Fiesta Bowl.

"If you were sitting watching at home and you went to the bathroom, you probably missed the whole game," said Penn State quarterback Tony Sacca, who threw four touchdown passes, three of them in the late burst.

Also during the surge, linebacker Reggie Givens returned a fumble 23 yards for a touchdown and his 8-yard interception return set up a 2-yard scoring run by Richie Anderson.

It was a strange game, one that left No. 10 Tennessee (9-3) dazed.

"I can't say I've seen (a game) turn around so quickly and so drastically in one quarter's time," Volunteers coach

Score By Periods						
Penn State	7	0	14	21	—	42
Tennessee	10	0	7	0	—	17

Johnny Majors said.

Tennessee clotheslined No. 6 Penn State (11-2) through most of the first 40 minutes and finished with statistics almost twice as good as the Nittany Lions' — except in points.

Only through a gift — Dale Carter's fumble to Penn State's Jeff Kerwin at the Tennessee 11 on the opening kick-off — did the Nittany Lions score in the first half. Sacca threw a 10-yard scoring pass to fullback Sam Gash on the third play from scrimmage.

Tennessee tied it, 7-7, on freshman tailback James Stewart's 1-yard dive over a crowd with 6:12 left in the first quarter, and went ahead, 10-7, on John Becksvoort's 24-yard field goal with 1:42 left in the quarter.

That's how it stood at halftime, and Penn State wasn't standing in a very good light.

Tennessee had 324 yards' total offense, Penn State 59. Tennessee had 17 first downs, Penn State five. Volunteers quarterback Andy Kelly was 16-of-26 passing for 204 yards; Sacca was 5-of-12 for 49 yards and four sacks.

"We went out the first half and we were moving the ball, but we weren't scoring," Kelly said, "and that was disappointing."

O.J. McDuffie, an all-America end in 1992.

John Sacca connected on 11 of 28 passes for 150 yards passing.

Lions Win, But Were in Trouble

BY BRUCE KEIDAN
Pittsburgh Post-Gazette

Ten minutes into the second half of the 21st Fiesta Bowl, the scoreboard insisted that Penn State trailed Tennessee by only 10 points.

Here at last was proof positive that figures do lie.

Surely Tennessee led by a hundred points. Or maybe a thousand. Or was it a hundred thousand?

Penn State was not merely losing — it was being pureed.

You watch a cat toy with a cornered mouse and it never occurs to you that the mouse is keeping the game close. You say to yourself, "If this mouse has a wife, it will soon be a widow."

And with five minutes left to play in the third quarter at Sun Devil Stadium yesterday, the question was not whether Tennessee would win but only by how large a score.

Tennessee's offensive line was pounding Penn State into a fine paste. James Stewart, the Tennessee tailback, could have been fat, 50 and hobbled by gout and still gained a lot of ground. Some of the holes that opened in front of him were wide enough to park two moving vans. End to end.

Tennessee's light but mobile defensive line, abetted by three heat-seeking missiles disguised as Vols linebackers, was dominating the line of scrimmage as well. Penn State's offensive line spreads out and dares you to dart through the gaps if you can. Tennessee's defense could and did.

Penn State had led, briefly, scoring a touchdown after Tennessee's Dale Carter fumbled the opening kickoff and the Nittany Lions recovered on the Vols' 11-yard line.

Over the course of the next 28 minutes 24 seconds that remained in the first half, the Nittany Lions managed to accumulate a total of 48 yards running and passing. Their quarterback, Tony Sacca, had completed five passes and been sacked five times. Lurching backward to pass, he looked at times like a man trying to learn the rumba by following footprints painted on the floor of a dance studio. Only less smooth.

Whatever Joe Paterno told his team at halftime, it took a long time to sink in. Penn State ran three plays and punted on its first possession of the second half. Then Tennessee rattled off a 68-yard touchdown drive on seven plays.

If someone in the crowd of 71,133 had stood up at that point and offered to wager that Penn State would eventually win by the score of 42-17, he or she would now own the state of Tennessee lock, stock and sour mash.

Even when Tennessee's Tom Hutton was thrown for a loss on an ill-advised fake punt and Penn State took over the ball at Tennessee's 42, there was no indication the tide had turned. A first-down pass went awry. A second-down run went nowhere. On third-and-10, Sacca attempted a play-action pass only to find out that no one was buying the fake. All Penn State could do was punt, and when the ball bounced into the end zone, Tennessee had the ball on its own 20-yard line and a very smug look indeed.

Then came the deluge.

Paterno had said on the eve of this game that he thought it would be decided by mistakes and by special teams. He was right on both counts.

It began with a 39-yard punt return by O.J. McDuffie. Penn State went to work at the Tennessee 35. And Tennessee made a mistake. A Tennessee lineman jumped offsides on a third-and-10 play. Given a free play, Sacca completed a 28-yard pass to McDuffie. Then a three-yard touchdown pass to Chip LaBarca on third down. Suddenly, Tennessee looked a lot less smug.

Twenty-seven seconds later, Penn State led, 21-17. Then, within 7½ minutes, it scored three more times.

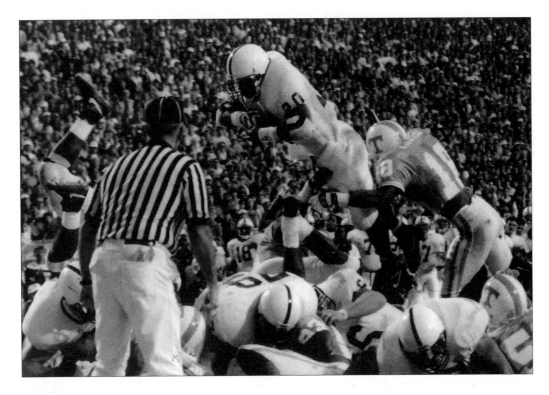

Richie Anderson takes the high road to score on a 2-yard run for Penn State in the fourth quarter of the 1992 Fiesta Bowl.

The Volunteers made it 17-7 when Kelly and split end Cory Fleming put together a 44-yard pass play for a touchdown 4:06 into the second half.

Then came the break.

Penn State's O.J. McDuffie returned a punt 39 yards to the Tennessee 35, and the drive ended with Sacca's 3-yard touchdown pass to wide-open Chip LaBarca. It was 17-14. Smelling distance.

"That ended up being the spark we needed," said McDuffie, whose role was increased because top receiver Terry Smith sat out with a pinched nerve.

On the second play of the Volunteers' subsequent possession, tackle Tyoka Jackson sacked Kelly, forcing him to fumble, and recovered on the Tennessee 13. It took Sacca one play — a 13-yard pass to tight end Kyle Brady — to give the Nittany Lions a 21-17 lead with 2:29 left in the third.

"We had struggled early. I had struggled early," Sacca said. "It took a while — it took a couple special team plays, a couple turnovers, but when it was 21-17, we said 'this game is not over.'"

The game was, however, in the middle of Penn State's rapid-fire rally.

After Givens' interception, Anderson made it 27-17 two plays into the fourth quarter.

On Tennessee's next play, cornerback Derek Bochna blind-sided Kelly. The ball popped loose and landed in Givens' hands. He ran 23 yards to the end zone. It was 35-17.

"It felt like you had a bag of money in your hand," Givens said.

And the game, by then, was in the bag. But for good measure, Sacca tossed a 37-yard touchdown to McDuffie with 10:07 left in the game.

"We were absolutely in disbelief on the sideline — probably as much as they were," said Sacca, who finished his record-setting Penn State career with the game, going 11 of 28 for 150 yards.

It made Penn State 5-0 in the Fiesta Bowl, the only team undefeated here with more than one appearance.

It was the Volunteers' first Fiesta visit, and they went away stunned, but not completely disheartened.

"Anything can happen on any given day," said defensive tackle Shazzon Bradley.

NITTANY NOTES

The crowd of 71,133 pushed the Nittany Lions' total attendance this season past 1 million for the first time, thanks to a 12-game regular season and the addition of 10,000 seats at Beaver Stadium.

'Underdog' State Turns On The Juice in Citrus Bowl Win

BY SHELLY ANDERSON
Pittsburgh Post-Gazette

Orlando, Fla., Jan. 1, 1994 — It wasn't visible to the televised audience or the Citrus Bowl record crowd of 72,456 — or to anyone not closely affiliated with the Penn State football team.

But there it was, as much a part of the Nittany Lions' cargo as any equipment bag or cooler.

The unseen cargo was a sense of urgency, grown to almost tangible proportions. Penn State felt it did not deserve to be a 9-point underdog to Tennessee and that it was time to earn a little respect.

The No. 13 Nittany Lions (10-2) did just that by spanking No. 6 Tennessee, 31-13, in the Citrus Bowl yesterday afternoon.

"We just kept our mouths shut and did the things we needed to do," said quarterback Kerry Collins, who threw for 162 yards and two touchdowns to upstage the Volunteers' renowned Heath Shuler.

"It was Heath Shuler this and Heath Shuler that, and they were going to beat us by a few touchdowns," Collins added. "I'd by lying if I said it didn't get a little personal."

Penn State receiver Bobby Engram agreed. "We knew that it would be settled on the field."

Score by Periods					
Penn State	7	10	7	7 —	31
Tennessee	10	3	0	0 —	13

Joe Paterno reacts to an official's call.

Engram, the game's Most Valuable Player, was electrifying. He had seven catches for 107 yards and a touchdown, and a 35-yard run on a reverse during a field goal drive.

This was a less dramatic replay of the 1992 Fiesta Bowl when Penn State rallied from 10 points down with five touchdowns in less than eight minutes for a 42-17 victory.

It was Coach Joe Paterno's 15th bowl win, tying the late Paul (Bear) Bryant for most in a career.

Yesterday, Tennessee (9-2-1) struck for a first-quarter lead of 10-0 on John Becksvoorts' 46-yard field goal and Shuler's 19-yard pass to Cory Fleming.

Penn State tied it on Ki-Jana Carter's 3-yard scoring run and Craig Fayak's 19-yard field goal 4:38 into the second quarter. Becksvoort's 50-yard field goal with 1:08 left in the half put the Vols back up, 13-10.

The game turned on the next score.

Penn State drove deep and, on a gutsy call to run the ball, Carter sprinted 13 yards to the end zone with three seconds left in the half for a 17-13 lead.

Paterno said he chose the play because the Nittany Lions had a time out left and could have used it to run another.

"I told Kerry, 'Let's run the counter draw,' " Paterno said. "I thought we had a chance (to score)."

The Nittany Lions built the lead to 24-13 when Collins threw a 7-yard touchdown pass to tight end Kyle Brady 5:05 into the third quarter.

It was the same play on which Brady had scored during Penn State's Fiesta comeback. Brady nonchalantly makes his way to the goal line to the right while Collins drops back and scours the left side. At the last second, Collins turns and throws to Brady, who is wide open.

Penn State quarterback Kerry Collins, who finished 15-for-24 for 162 yards and a pair of touchdowns, tries to escape from Shane Bonham (92) and the Tennessee defense.

"It seems when we really need a big play, that one's there for us," Brady said. "I kind of act like I'm not even involved in the play. Usually, one (defender) will catch it, but it's too late."

By that time yesterday, it was too late for Tennessee.

"Penn State's touchdown right before the half and the score right after the half were big factors," Vols coach Phillip Fulmer said.

Engram's 15-yard scoring pass from Collins 32 seconds into the fourth quarter sealed it.

Fulmer had a list of potential excuses for his team's loss, but would not invoke any of them. Instead, he blamed "a bunch of dropped passes" and poor play by his offensive and defensive linemen.

"Penn State did a good job of giving us enough rope to hang ourselves, and we did," he said.

The Nittany Lions, however, wanted to take a little credit for doing the hanging.

"I never said we were a great team, but that's a lot of points," Paterno said of the 9-point spread. "I think it rankled some of the kids."

"And not only were we underdogs, but a lot of people didn't give us much respect," Brady said, adding that this win might also deflect some criticism aimed at the Big Ten, which was 3-3 in bowls before Wisconsin's date in the Rose Bowl.

NITTANY NOTES

A couple of Penn State players tried to dump a water cooler on Paterno late in the game, but mostly missed … This is Penn State's 15th 10-win season, all under Paterno.

Nittany Lions Pass a Thorny Test on Way to Rose Bowl

By Marino Parascenzo
Pittsburgh Post-Gazette

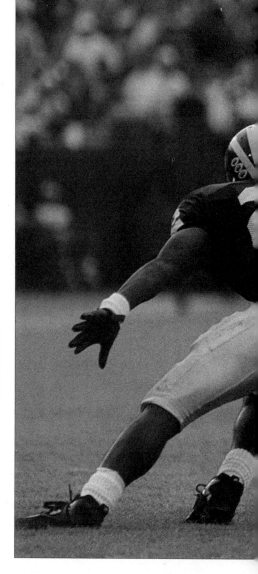

Ann Arbor, Mich., Oct. 15, 1994 — Penn Sate's unbeaten Nittany Lions blew a 16-0 lead but came up smelling like roses — possible Rose Bowl variety — with a gripping 31-24 victory over the Michigan Wolverines.

The Lions broke from a 24-24 tie with a lightning touchdown — quarterback Kerry Collins' 16-yard strike to receiver Bobby Engram with just under three minutes to play.

It was Penn State's biggest win in two years in the Big Ten, and came before 106,832, the third-largest crowd ever in Michigan Stadium and the third-largest in NCAA history.

The two had opened like a pair of old Southwest Conference gunslinger teams, then settled down into a Big Ten power bash that wasn't resolved until Lions linebacker Willie Smith set the stage for the winning drive, blitzing like a demon from the right side to nail Michigan quarterback Todd Collins on a third-and-3 at the Michigan 28.

Michigan had to punt.

And that was followed immediately by a fierce and winning Penn State drive that found the right cracks in the Michigan defense.

The drive went 55 yards in five plays, beginning with Collins hitting receiver

Score by Periods					
Penn State	10	6	8	7 —	31
Michigan	0	3	14	7 —	24

Engram for 14 yards, and ending with Engram running that devilish slant pattern from the right, coasting into wide-open country between two distant defenders, and taking Collins' 16-yard strike for the winning touchdown at 2:53.

The road to the Rose Bowl is still under construction but it looks a bit more open now.

It's heresy in the Big Ten to talk about the national championship. All eyes remain fixed on the Rose Bowl.

"But we want to go to Pasadena and win the national championship," Carter said, "And we think we can do both."

The victory keeps third-ranked Penn State unbeaten at 6-0 and drops No. 5 Michigan to 4-2. But the Big Ten records are more to the point at the moment, and Penn State is alone atop the conference with a 3-0 record. Michigan is 2-1, and Purdue, after tying Wisconsin, is 2-0-1.

"We beat a great team," Penn State coach Joe Paterno said. "They put a lot of pressure on us. I was extremely concerned about our missed chances. I knew Michigan wasn't bad, and that they'd come out hard. I was very concerned at

Penn State tailback Ki-Jana Carter ran for 165 yards against Michigan, helping Penn State to stay unbeaten for the season and take over the lead in the Big Ten title chase.

the half."

Penn State rushed for 213 yards — 165 by tailback Ki-Jana Carter, splinted right thumb and all — and Kerry Collins passed for 231 yards, piling up a 444 total against Michigan's 437.

The Lions opened not with the same

numbers but with the equivalent authority of those five blowout games against lesser opponents. That is, they scored the first three times they had the ball.

The first was a 24-yard field goal by Brett Conway on the opening possession for a 3-0 lead. Then Collins hitting tight

end Keith Olsommer on a three-yard pass for a 10-0 lead at the end of the first quarter. Then two more field goals by Conway, a 28-yarder early in the second period — set up by linebacker Jason Collins stripping the ball from tailback Tim Biakabutuka — and a 29-yarder with 5:52 left in the half.

Though considerably muted — those were not all TDs — it looked like business as usual for the club that had been outscoring opponents by a cumulative 89-12 in the first period and 87-30 in the second.

Michigan managed a field goal on the final play of the first half, Remy Hamilton's 33-yarder set up by Penn State punter Joe Jurevicius' weak 28-yard punt, and linebacker Brian Gelzheiser spearing a fallen Todd Collins, the 15-yard penalty which give Michigan a first down and new life.

The Lions were looking good, though, with a 16-3 lead at the half.

Joe Paterno consoles Michigan coach Gary Moeller after the Lions 31-24 victory in Ann Arbor.

Victory Brings Team, Season Into Focus

BY BRUCE KEIDAN
Pittsburgh Post-Gazette

"Who have they beaten?" the naysayers asked, derision taking precedence over grammar.

"Everyone we have played," Penn State said. "Everyone who was on our schedule thus far, we have lined up and whipped them."

"The lame and the halt," the skeptics said. "The bottom of the barrel. Temple and four teams that might just as well have been Temple."

"I think we're a pretty good football team," Joe Paterno said.

"Wait till you play a real team," the doomsayers said. "Wait till you play a team that doesn't roll over and die at the sight of those blue-and-white

uniforms with no numbers on the helmets. Wait till you play Michigan at Ann Arbor. Then we will find out what you are made of."

Now they know. Now the Nittany Lions do, too. They have been to the mountain. And they have scaled it.

They have looked defeat in the eye. They have asked themselves if they could live with a tie. Not just any tie, but a tie on the road against a team ranked among the nation's top five. And they have rejected the notion.

They have earned their stripes. They have stood toe-to-toe with an opponent that had both the will and the means to fight back.

They have bloodied their knuckles.

"We beat a great team," Paterno

said as darkness transformed a perfect fall afternoon into evening.

It was part accolade, part reminder.

There is nothing to quibble with now, no nits left to pick with these Nittany Lions. They have been in the Wolverines' den and emerged from it unscathed, bringing with them a 31-24 victory.

Colorado beat Michigan by a point with a prayer of a pass on the final play of the game. Colorado, like Michigan and Penn State, is one of college football's elite this year. Arguments over the relative merits of Colorado and Penn State may continue as long as this season does and beyond. Especially if both go undefeated.

If Michigan is the measuring stick, then Penn State is better. Colorado's

But you can keep lightning in the bottle for only so long, and that was the case with Michigan tailback Tyrone Wheatley.

The Lions had pretty well shut him down. He got zero yards on his first two carries in the first period, and by halftime he had accumulated the dizzying total of 11 yards on nine carries, an average of 1.2.

Then it was his turn to do the dizzying. He got one yard with the first carry, opening the third quarter, then boom.

On second down, he whipped around right end, beat Gelzheiser wide, and raced untouched 67 yards for the touchdown, cutting Michigan's deficit to 16-10.

Then Jurevisius shanked a 16-yarder on Penn State's next possession, and Michigan was in sweet position, at their own 49.

Then boom-boom-boom.

Todd Collins hit split end Amani Toomer for 30 yards, to the Lions 21, and after an incomplete pass, Wheatley took a pitchout and swept wide the rest of the way to the TD and Michigan's only lead of the game, 17-16.

The Lions retook the lead on the next possession, going 80 yards in 10 plays, with Kerry Collins throwing his third TD pass, an 8-yarder to fullback Jon Witman. Then Collins hit receiver Freddie Scott for a two-point conversion and a 24-17 lead.

The two-pointer came in handy when Michigan scored on Biakabutuka's 2-yard smash on fourth down with 11:37 left in the game. Moeller opted for the comfort of a tying extra point, and Hamilton kicked it for the 24-24 deadlock. Both teams were playing for time now.

Michigan still had some life, and nearly three minutes to enjoy it.

But they weren't done making mistakes yet. Hamilton missed a chip-shot field goal in the first quarter; Toomer dropped an easy pass back in the second quarter to be followed by Kraig Baker's feeble 23-yard punt, setting up a Lions field goal, and so forth.

This time, with 2:16 left, Toomer had beaten the defenders and was under full speed at about the Lions 3, and Todd Collins fired from the 50. But Toomer stayed to the left, and the ball was about two yards to his right.

He had made seven catches for 157 yards, but he missed the biggest catch of the day.

victory here was a fluke. Penn State's was simply a matter of nature taking its course. Penn State led by 16 points late in the opening half. When Michigan rallied and tied the score with three minutes and change elapsed in the fourth quarter, Penn State simply gathered itself and went briskly about its business.

Offense, not defense, is supposedly Penn State's long suit. But Michigan managed just one first down into the game's remaining 11-plus minutes.

So just how good is this Penn State team? Paterno continues to wave off comparisons to his 1982 national champions. "We've still got five games left," one of which does not appear on their schedule.

If all goes well, they will play their 12th game in Pasadena on New Year's Day (Once Removed), and the champions of the Pacific-10 Conference will be the opponents.

If something goes wrong, they will play in some other bowl and be swiftly forgotten. And regardless of what you may have read, there is no guarantee that won't happen. Ohio State is scheduled to visit Happy Valley a week from Saturday and Michigan State on the final Saturday in November. In between, the Nittany Lions must pay a house call on Illinois, a team which plays defense with the sort of religious zeal last seen in Champaign-Urbana when Dick Butkus was an undergraduate.

Even if these Nittany Lions conquer all five remaining conference foes and finish with a flourish in the Rose Bowl, there is no guarantee they will win the mythical, magical national championship as did their predecessors in 1982.

It may help that Florida tripped yesterday, and that none of the "Big Three" in that state is unbeaten.

It may help that Nebraska's Cornhuskers have been reduced to playing their third-string quarterback — unless Colorado beats them.

It will not hurt matters that Auburn, which conquered Florida and is 7-0, is ineligible to play in a bowl. One of the two major polls refuses to recognize Auburn's existence while that school remains on NCAA probation.

It will help that Notre Dame has been beaten so many times now that not even the subway alumni can make a case for the Irish this season.

But will all that be enough? Probably not, if Colorado runs the table. There is no team in the Pac-10 ranked sufficiently high to serve as a stepping stone to a national title.

That doesn't mean, if it wins six more games, that Penn State won't deserve one.

Lions Score at Will, Maul Ohio State in Big Ten Showdown

By Marino Parascenzo
Pittsburgh Post-Gazette

University Park, Pa., Oct. 29, 1994 — The Ohio State Buckeye's best defense yesterday was a punt late in the first half. But this was a very special punt.

The Buckeyes were fourth-and-10 at their own 40 and really hurting for points. But there was no way Coach John Cooper was going to turn the ball back over to Penn State this close, not even with a lousy 17 seconds left. You might go to halftime trailing by six touchdowns. So you punt. Better to go to halftime trailing by only five.

So the Nittany Lions finished the job in the second half, a 63-14 mauling that lifted their record to 7-0, kept them atop the Big Ten at 4-0, and possibly left them still No. 1 in the country, depending on how the pollsters assess No. 3 Nebraska's 24-7 win over No. 2 Colorado.

About rankings, Penn State coach Joe Paterno had this to say, grinning: "I don't have to talk about 'em, and I'm not gonna talk about 'em."

At any event, for a Beaver Stadium-record crowd of 97,079, the smell of the Rose Bowl got stronger. With Michigan losing to Wisconsin, Michigan, Ohio State and Illinois are all tied for a distant second in the Big Ten

with 3-2 records.

"I don't see anybody beating them," Cooper said.

Was Paterno getting even for the Buckeyes' trash-talking win of last year? Or digging Ohio State President E. Gordon Gee for saying he had been outcoached? Or trying to nail down a national ranking he insists doesn't matter at the moment?

Paterno explained 'em all.

"I'm as surprised as anybody," he said. "They didn't have a good day, and we had a great day."

And a great team, Cooper allowed. "I just hope they're as great as I think they are," he added.

At least this great:

■ Against Ohio State's fast-improving defense, No. 2 in the Big Ten, having allowed only 13.3 points per game, Penn State scored on four straight possessions in the second quarter.

■ Quarterback Kerry Collins, the nation's most efficient passer, redeemed a poor showing at Columbus last year

Score by Periods					
Ohio State	0	0	6	8	— 14
Penn State	7	28	14	14	— 63

Bobby Engram caught six passes for 102 yards against the bewildered Ohio State defense.

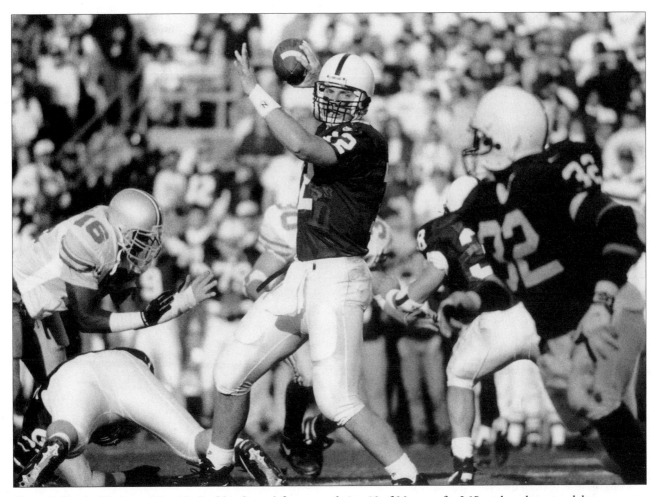

Kerry Collins had little trouble with the Ohio State defense, completing 19 of 23 passes for 265 yards and two touchdowns.

with 19 for 23 passing for 265 yards and two touchdowns before coming out late in the third quarter. He hit receiver Bobby Engram and tailback Mike Archie for TD's, both from 15 yards.

■ Engram, not even a target until early in the second period, caught six passes for 102 yards, including a diving one-hander for 12 yards that set up Ki-Jana Carter's 36-yard TD run. Engram's 15-yard TD reception also was a diving catch. All of which made him happy.

"A lot of those guys were gloating and talking down to us last year," he said. "That's not right."

Buckeyes defensive back Marlon Kerner, one of many badly burned in this game, shook his head. "I've been on teams that have won this big, but I've never lost a game like this," he said. "Not even in my wildest dreams did I think they'd scored 63 points on us."

Things got so bad for Ohio State that even Chris Maczyk scored for the Nittanies. He's a 279-pound defensive tackle, and he got his career-first TD when he intercepted quarterback Bobby Hoying's screen pass from the Ohio

State 11. Crack receiver Joey Galloway — held to three catches for 31 yards — couldn't grab the towering lob, and it dropped in Maczyk's beefy hands. He turned like a startled rhino and lumbered 10 yards for the TD and a 56-6 lead.

Hoying was intercepted two other times, both by defensive back Brian Miller and both setting up TD's.

"I don't think we can play much better than we did in the first half," Paterno said. "The defense needs to get a little sharper for us to get to the next level."

Which leaves some to wonder what level he's talking about. The Lions gained 572 yards, (286 rushing and the same passing) to 214, had 33 first downs to 12 and logged four sacks to one.

Paterno praised Collins: "If there's a quarterback playing any better, he's got to be out of this world."

And Carter: "It's hard to imagine a better tailback in the country."

The Lions "plodded" through the first half. They scored on their first possession (for the fifth time this season), going 73 yards in eight plays, with Carter darting the final 20. But it took them three minutes and 12 seconds.

In the volcanic second quarter, Carter banged a yard for one TD (a glacial 5:34 drive), Engram made his diving TD catch (2:39), Carter blasted 36 yards (1:39) and Archie took his pass (0:35).

The Buckeyes took the ensuing kickoff, made one first down, then opted for the punt with 17 seconds left in the

Penn State tailback Ki-Jana Carter (32) opens the scoring in the first quarter ...

Rout Justifies Nittany Lions' No. 1 Status

BY RON COOK
Pittsburgh Post-Gazette

Don't whine when the national polls make Nebraska the No. 1 team in America today. Nebraska, playing with its second-string quarterback beat Colorado by 17 yesterday. Penn State beat Ohio State by only 49.

Of course, Nebraska has to be No. 1.

How can the voters respect Penn State when it keeps scheduling those cupcakes on Homecoming — Brown, Temple, Ohio State ...

If Penn State is so good, shouldn't it have whacked such a weak opponent by more than seven touchdowns? The 63-14 whipping it put on Ohio State wasn't even Ohio State's worst loss. Michigan beat the Buckeyes, 58-6, in 1946 and 86-0 in 1902. Joe Paterno saw that '02 game and said Michigan had a terrific team.

Sorry, JoePa, about that cheap age shot.

And sorry about the ridiculous argument (see above) the voters will give Penn State after they jump Nebraska to No. 1.

It's probably going to happen. Nebraska, No. 2 in one poll and No. 3 in the other going into the weekend, won convincingly against Colorado, which was No. 3 and No. 2. Many voters will jump on the Nebraska bandwagon, enough, most likely, to make the Huskers No. 1.

That doesn't make it right.

"What more are we supposed to do," Penn State's big tight end Kyle Brady was asking everyone last night.

Beat Ohio State, 86-0?

That could have been the final.

"If we had been trying to run up the score," guard Marco Rivera said, "they would have really been in trouble."

"Joe was very generous to us by playing his second- and third-teamers," Ohio State coach John Cooper said. "I thanked him after the game."

The Penn State players knew Nebraska had defeated Colorado, 24-7. They knew the great Huskers' defense had made Heisman Trophy candidates Rashaan Salaam and Kordell Stewart look ordinary.

That made Penn State's task clear. It knew if it wanted to justify its No. 1 ranking, it had to rout an Ohio State team that, snide remarks aside, is solid, at least defensively.

*... Later, Carter bowls over Ohio State's Tim Patillo for some
of the Nittany Lions' 572 yards of total offense.*

half. They were already trailing, 35-0.

Cooper wasn't sure whether this was the most embarrassing loss of his career.

"But this was our first time out here," he said, "and we got embarrassed."

It could have been worse.

This was Ohio State's biggest loss since a 58-6 whipping by Michigan in 1946. But until they scored against the Penn State subs with about three minutes to play, it was looking like the worst loss since, oh, 1902 or thereabouts.

All of which created a new axiom — the longest distance between two points is the road back from State College to Columbus.

But who could have guessed it would win by seven touchdowns?

Let's put the 63 points Penn State scored into some kind of perspective. The 1973 Ohio State team gave up 64 points — all season.

The point is no longer debatable. This is Paterno's best offense in his 29 seasons at Penn State, better than his '82 offense, which produced five No. 1 draft choices in the NFL and contributed to a national championship.

"They have everything," Cooper gushed.

What Penn State has is a quarterback who now should be considered the Heisman Trophy favorite. Kerry Collins completed 19 of 23 passes against Ohio State for 265 yards and two touchdowns. He is easily America's passing-efficiency leader.

"If someone is playing better, he must be out of this world," Paterno said.

What Penn State has is a tailback who could win the Heisman if Collins doesn't. Ki-Jana Carter rushed 19 times for 139 yards and four touchdowns yesterday. He averaged 7.2 yards per carry and — get this — saw his season average drop.

What Penn State has is two terrific wide receivers. Bobby Engram made the catch of the season yesterday, a diving, one-handed number over the middle. He finished with six catches for 102 yards. Barely outdone was Freddie Scott, who had five catches for 80 yards.

What Penn State has is a tight end, Kyle Brady, who will be a high NFL pick next spring. What it has is a terrific offensive line.

One drive against Ohio State's best showed exactly what this Penn State offense is about. Late in the first half, it took possession at its 43. Collins threw passes of 11 yards to Scott and 12 and 14 yards to Engram, the last stopping the clock. After fullback Brian Milne ran for 5 yards and a Penn State time out, Collins threw a 15-yard touchdown pass to Mike Archie.

The five-play, 57-yard drive took 35 seconds and gave Penn State a 35-0 lead.

"You can't play much better than we did in the first half," Paterno said.

Still, the old coach refused to be drawn into the argument about which team should be No. 1.

"We're a really good football team that's playing really, really well. It's not necessary for me to say more now. The way I look at it, you play the season out. If we do that and win the rest of our games and I feel we're (No. 1), I'll say it then. Until then, I'll let you guys say it."

OK, we will.

Penn State is the best team in the land. No matter what the voters say.

Nittany Lions Finish Unbeaten, but Uncrowned

By Marino Paracenzo
Pittsburgh Post-Gazette

Ki-Jana Carter scores in the third quarter to break a 14-14 tie with Oregon.

Pasadena, Calif., Jan. 2, 1995 — Was this Rose Bowl the stuff of national championships?

Penn State's Nittany Lions say so, believing they staked their claim to at least a share of the national title yesterday with a 38-20 victory over the Oregon Ducks in the old bowl.

Others might argue that Penn State's victory was an exercise in crisis survival.

The win left 102,247 fans hanging on the ropes. But for much of the game, the lightly regarded Ducks — 17-point underdogs — had the Lions hanging on the ropes.

In any event, if anything would have been enough to carry the No. 2 Penn State over No. 1 Nebraska and into the national championship, this game probably wasn't it. The final vote is due out today, and if the voters follow form, Nebraska, off a come-from-behind win over Miami in the Orange Bowl Sunday night, will keep its top ranking and win the mythical title. All of which was not being swallowed here last night.

"We're going to award ourselves the national championship, no matter what the guys in their (easy) chairs say," said Penn State quarterback Kerry Collins.

Score by Periods					
Penn State	7	7	14	10	— 38
Oregon	7	0	7	6	— 20

"When a team gets inside the 20, Penn State plays really great defense," said Oregon's dynamite quarterback, Danny O'Neil, the co-Most Outstanding Player in the game. "That's why they're the national champs."

Said Oregon coach Rich Brooks, "I'm going to vote for Joe Paterno and Penn State. I voted for them coming into the game, and I didn't see anything here to change my mind."

And Penn State running back Ki-Jana Carter, the other Most Outstanding Player: "The least they could do is split it up. We worked too hard not to get it."

Carter scored three touchdowns. His first was an 83-yard bolt on Penn

Kerry Collins, an all-America quarterback in 1994.

Above, Ki-Jana Carter ran 21 times for 156 yards and scored three touchdowns for the Nittany Lions; Below, Brian Milne bangs over from the 1-yard line for a TD.

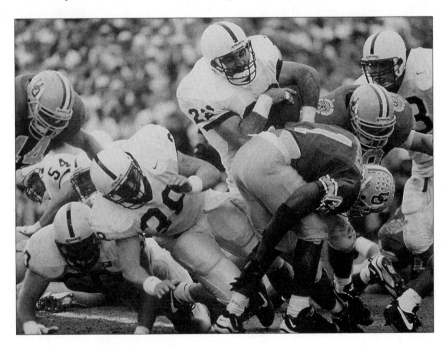

State's first play from scrimmage. He also scored from 17 and 3 yards, and had a game-high 156 yards on 21 carries.

Paterno chipped in, "We are worthy of being considered national champions like anyone else."

Passion and platitudes aside, if there is such a thing as a furious duck, that's what the Lions had to beat. The Ducks never led, but they tied the game twice. The Lions didn't begin to see daylight unitl late in the third quarter with 2:01 to play, in fact when Carter slammed in from 3 yards out for his final touchdown for a 28-14 lead.

Penn State was up by 38-14 on fullback Jon Witman's 9-yard run late in the fourth quarter. Oregon cut the score to its final margin of 18 points with Ricky Whittle's 3-yard run with 2:44 left in the game.

Penn State, the Big Ten champ, came in with an 11-0 record, ranked No. 2, and with the hottest offense in the land. Oregon, the Pacific-10 champ, was 9-3 and ranked No. 12, and was not expected to provide much more than an appetizer. The Ducks were a bone that got stuck in the Lions' throat. It was O'Neil who stuck it there.

O'Neil set Rose Bowl records with 41 completions in 61 passes for 456 yards. He also threw for two touchdowns and was intercepted twice, both times by Penn State junior free safety Chuck Penzenik, making the first start of his career.

Penzenik's second interception, late in the third quarter, set up Carter's third TD for the 28-14 lead. And when linebacker Terry Killens broke through and sacked O'Neil moments later, on the last play of the third period, the end was in sight.

The victory made Paterno the winningest bowl coach ever, with 16 victories, one more than the late Bear Bryant.

The Lions closed the season with a 12-0 record and a 17-game winning streak over two seasons. It was their first Rose Bowl win, in their second year in the Bg Ten. They lost their first Rose Bowl, in 1923.

This one started out like another ho-hummer at Happy Valley. Oregon had to punt on the opening possession.

The Lions, accustomed to

scoring in under two minutes, started at their own 17. This was over in a heartbeat. On the first play from scrimmage, Carter blasted through the right side, slammed over Herman O'Berry and raced 83 yards. This took 13 seconds. Penn

Kerry Collins passed for 200 yards against the Ducks.

State led, 7-0, with just under 11 minutes left in the first quarter.

And that's where the resemblance ended.

Now came the eerie echo from Paterno's pre-game warning, "If we're going to win this one, we're going to have to do it with good defense."

He was right, but he didn't have a good defense.

Oregon took the ensuing kickoff and O'Neil pounced on Penn State's defense like a pushy relative over the holidays. He just picked it apart like a Christmas goose. He hit tight end Josh Wilcox for 18 yards, tailback Dino Philyaw for 28,

These Nittany Lions Will Be Remembered

BY BRUCE KEIDAN
Pittsburgh Post-Gazette

In the end, it will not matter what a sportscaster in Kankakee thinks. Or a coach in Starkville.

In the long run, it won't matter if they believe Nebraska is a better football team than Penn State. Or has accomplished more. Or if Tom Osborne is their sentimental favorite. Or if some voters had an ax to grind.

In the end, history will judge this Penn State team. Not the sportswriters and sportscasters who vote in the AP poll. Not the anonymous coaches whose ballots are tabulated by the Cable News Network and USA Today. Twenty years from now, when no one remembers who won the mythical national championship of college football for the 1994 sea-

Bowl Milestones

With Penn State's 38-20 victory against Oregon in the Rose Bowl, Joe Paterno passed Alabama's Paul (Bear) Bryant with his 16th bowl victory.

Coach	Years	Wins
Joe Paterno,	1966-95	16
Bear Bryant,	1945-82	15
Bobby Bowden	1959-95	14
Lou Holtz	1969-95	10
John Vaught	1947-70	10
Don James	1971-92	10

son, no one who saw it will have forgotten this Penn State team.

Great teams come and great teams go. They leave small footprints. A

roadside sign there that reads:

Welcome to Lincoln
Home of the 1994
NCAA Football Champions
Pop. 98,601

Not this Penn State team. It was special. In a century of college football and then some, this was as close as the game ever came to producing the Irresistible Force.

Their special teams were only sporadically special. Their defense bent and occasionally broke. But nobody could stop their offense. No one they met this season. No college defense I've ever seen.

Would this team defeat Nebraska? By a field goal — if the game were played in Lincoln. By 10 points in Beaver Stadium. By a touchdown otherwise.

then Wilcox for 33 to the Lions' 1. And after a half-the-distance penalty, O'Neil finished off the dizzy Lions with a 1-yard flip to Wilcox for the TD and a 7-7 tie.

The Lions wedged ahead after Oregon kicker Matt Beldon, who blew a 23-yard field goal in the first quarter, then missed from 44 in the second.

Penn State accepted the invitation. Collins hit Bobby Engram for 18 yards, Engram again for 12, and later backup wide receiver Joe Jurevicius for 44 to the Oregon heartland. From there, Bri-

an Milne hammered over from inches out at 1:26 of the second quarter, and Penn State was taking a 14-7 lead to intermission. But

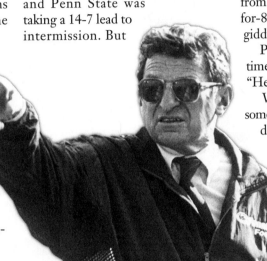

only after time ran out on Oregon. The devilish O'Neil drove the Ducks from their 18 to the Lions' 5 on an 8-for-8 passing drill that left the Lions giddy.

Paterno would need a nifty half-time talk. Something on the order of "Help!"

Whatever it was seemed to put some life and creativity into the Lions' defense for a while.

Soon, it was all over but the voting.

Joe Paterno points the way to victory.

Oregon stayed with Penn State for the better part of a half in the Rose Bowl, and no one has ever suggested that Oregon is Nebraska's peer. But Oregon features a passing offense, and pass defense is not Penn State's forte. Nebraska is a running team. Penn State would take away Nebraska's beloved option offense, putting more defenders on or near the line of scrimmage than the Cornhuskers had blockers. It would force Nebraska to throw, and Nebraska would throw some touchdown passes and some interceptions. But Penn State's offense would have its way with Nebraska, just as it did with Oregon yesterday in a 38-20 win.

Maybe that is not the issue. Maybe the pollsters differentiate between the best team and the team that accomplished most.

Nebraska wins on sheer volume, having won 13 games to 12 for Penn State. Nebraska got to be No. 1 due to the perception it had been more

impressive against elite opponents. History will question if that is so. Counting Oregon, five bowl teams fell beneath Penn State's wheels. Nebraska defeated an equal number. Were West Virginia, Texas Tech, Kansas State, Colorado and Miami superior as a group to Southern Cal, Michigan, Illinois, Ohio State and Oregon? Not by much, if at all. Were the have-nots of Penn State's dance card any less formidable than the sprinkling of tomato cans on Nebraska's schedule? They were not.

History will conclude that the greatest offensive juggernaut in the annals of college football did not win a national championship for two reasons:

1. Its coach was naive enough to believe that the margin by which he defeated a beaten Indiana team was irrelevant. Leading by three touchdowns, Joe Paterno called off the dogs. The sportscaster in Kankakee and the coach in Starkville looked at

the newspaper the following morning. They saw a final score, 35-29, and looked no deeper than that.

2. It was Tom Osborne's turn. There is nothing the pollsters like better than bestowing the title on a coach who has spent the better part of a lifetime in the futile pursuit of one. Especially if the coach happens to be a nice guy. Florida State's Bobby Bowden got his lifetime achievement award a year ago. Osborne was next in line. It makes for a heart-warming story.

Paterno does not begrudge Osborne his championship. But when Penn State fans in the crowd of 102,000-plus toasted the Nittany Lions as the best team in college football, Paterno told them, "I have to agree."

The sportscaster in Kankakee and the coach in Starkville will relegate them to runners-up. But history will have its say eventually, and history may disagree.

Auburn's Tyreece Williams (22) and Liron Thomas (38) battle with the Lions Justice Williams (27) for the ball.

State Feasts on Tigers in Rain-Soaked Outback Bowl

By Marino Parascenzo
Pittsburgh Post-Gazette

Tampa, Fla., Jan. 1, 1996 — The Outback Bowl yesterday took Terry Bowden back to his youth, when his dad, Bobby, was coach of the West Virginia Mountaineers and they were getting beat up by Joe Paterno and his big, ugly Penn State Nittany Lions year after year.

Now Terry, as coach of the Auburn Tigers, was facing them for the first time.

Same old Paterno. Same old ugly Lions.

Led by receiver Bobby Engram, Penn State bashed Auburn, 43-14.

"I haven't been beaten that badly since I was at Salem, and Delaware beat us, 56-21," Bowden said. That was 1992. He's been at Auburn for three years. He's now 28-5-1 there.

Paterno credited his defense, his offense, and two misfortunes that befell Auburn. One was a Tampa Stadium field mushy from a constant rain — it interfered with Auburn's precise passing attack — and the other was the injury that held powerful running back Stephen Davis to a limited appearance. Even so, he got 112 yards on 12 carries.

"They got a double dose of problems today," Paterno said.

Bowden also thought the field bothered his guys more than it bothered

Score by Periods:

Penn State	3	13	27	0	—	43
Auburn	0	7	0	7	—	14

Penn State, though he was at a loss to understand why.

Penn State finished at 9-3, Auburn at 8-4, and that 43-14 final included Auburn's ceremonial gift touchdown in the fourth quarter after Paterno — following a 27-point third quarter — had substituted for almost all of his offensive and defensive starters.

Off went the NFL-bound Engram, with his four catches for 113 yards and two touchdowns. Off went redshirt junior quarterback Wally Richardson, who hit on 13 of 24 passes for 217

yards and a personal high of four TD's, tying the Penn State bowl record and setting the Outback record. Out went running back Stephen Pitts and his 115 yards on 15 carries. And out went a defense that balled up Auburn quarterback Patrick Nix, a 60 percent passer averaging 234 yards a game, and stuffed him into a 5-for-25 day for 48 yards, intercepting him twice and sacking him once.

Engram packed a serious amount of damage into just four catches, and it won him the Most Valuable Player award.

He made a falling-down catch of a 37-yarder that was wasted when kicker Brett Conway missed a 29-yard field goal in the second quarter. He made an equally spectacular catch in the third, leaping high to pull in a 47-yarder that set up Richardson's 9-yard TD strike to him late in the third quarter for a 23-7 Penn State lead.

"It's just a matter of wanting them," he understated.

Later in the third, he knifed in on his celebrated slant route and took a 20-yarder for another TD and a 43-7 lead. That was his final reception and his final touchdown with Penn State. Moments later, Paterno was subbing wholesale.

It was stuff like this that moved Paterno to say Engram will be about as good as All-Pro Jerry Rice.

"I told coach to quit saying that," an embarrassed Engram said. "Jerry Rice is in a class by himself."

The Nittany Lions' performance gave Paterno his 17th bowl victory, resetting his own NCAA record. And all he had to do was sweat a little with worry before the game and then get soaked during it by a steady rain that turned Tampa Stadium into a bowl of breakfast oatmeal. "It wasn't so bad," guard Jeff Hartings said. "It was a game

Right, Penn State quarterback Wally Richardson gets off a pass despite a fierce rush from Auburn's Terry Solomon; Below, Penn State's Joe Paterno and Auburn's Terry Bowden meet at midfield following the game.

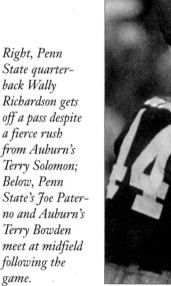

to remember — sliding around in the mud."

The Lions started off turning red in the Red Zone, as in embarrassed. They bogged down at the Auburn 1 with the opening possession and settled for the first of Conway's three field goals. Auburn went ahead, 7-3, turning an interception of Richardson's into Nix's 25-yard scoring pass to receiver Robert Baker.

The Lions crept ahead, 9-7, on two more Conway field goals, a 22-yarder after stalling out at the Auburn 5, then a 38-yarder.

Just about the time the thin, soggy crowd began to wonder whether Paterno remembered to pack his offense for the trip, it came to life.

With 1:43 to play in the first half, Nix decided to force a pass under pressure. "He should have just killed the clock," Bowden lamented.

But throw he did, and safety Kim Herring picked it off. On the first play, Richardson flicked a 43-yarder to receiver Joe Jurevicius, who dived under it at the Auburn 8. On the next play, he hit tailback Mike Archie for the TD and a 16-7 lead.

Davis returned for the third quarter, but got nothing but statistics — 11 yards on one carry in the first series, before a punt, followed by Engram's 9-yard TD catch. And in the next series he got 20 yards on another, zero on the next, and then fumbled on the third. Herring recovered, and Penn State turned that into another TD, Richardson hitting Pitts from 4 yards, for a 29-7 lead.

It was all over but the memories for Terry Bowden. Bowden said he'd called his dad for his "itinerary" for bowl games and he said it was excellent. Maybe he forgot to tell him he was playing you-know-who.

Nittany Lions Reign in Tampa's Rain

BY BRUCE KEIDAN
Pittsburgh Post-Gazette

The rain began in the hours between the time the ball fell in Times Square and the dawn of the new year's first day. Morning came and departed. Afternoon has given way now to evening. Still the rain has not stopped.

There are worse forms of winter precipitation. You don't have to shovel rain off sidewalks or driveways. It cannot be shaped into missiles and hurled at a football field from the stands. But don't try to tell Terry Bowden, the coach at Auburn, that a little rain never hurt anyone.

Perhaps on a dry, fast track, Bowden's team might have given Penn State a bit of a tussle here yesterday. But we will never know.

Late in the morning, an hour or so before the opening kickoff of the Outback Bowl, the ground crew at Tampa Stadium rolled up the tarpaulins it had used to cover the football field and removed them. Big mistake.

By game time, the rain had begun to wash the sponsor's logo from the grass at midfield.

The end zones, newly painted with the names and colors of the schools competing in the bowl game, also showed water damage. From beneath the blue of AUBURN and PENN STATE peeked "Buccaneers" in cursive, as white as the ghost of Sam Wyche.

By halftime, the field was a quagmire. By the third quarter, the game was a rout. Anyone asks you about the score of Waterworld, the answer is Penn State 43, Auburn 14.

It would have been worse, but Joe Paterno called off the barracudas after the third period, at which point his team led by 36 points. The good news from Auburn's perspective was that no one drowned.

"It seemed to affect us a lot more than it affected them" Bowden said of the weather once they managed to towel him off. "We were trying to play catch-up football in conditions that don't allow that."

OK, so it rained on both teams. And Joe Paterno, who has won more bowl games than an other mammal in the history of the planet, was quick to note: "That's the wonderful thing about football. In weather conditions like this, you cancel a baseball game. In basketball it doesn't matter, because you're playing inside. But in our game, you've got to handle the field and the weather and you've got to find some way to beat the other guy."

But the truth of the matter is, the sloppy track played right into Penn State's hands.

"I think, in fairness, that field probably hurt Auburn more than it hurt us," Paterno acknowledged. "Their (offense) is so spread out. Everything they do is so precise, and most of it is (dependent on) timing.

Penn State depends more on strength than Auburn, and less on finesse. Once the field turned into a shallow lake, Auburn's defensive linemen could not escape from Penn State's offensive linemen. And Auburn's quick little defensive backs were suddenly no quicker than Brian Milne, the 250-pound swamp buggy who plays fullback for Penn State.

The rain and Penn State's defense both played havoc with Auburn's passing game. Patrick Nix, who started at quarterback for Auburn, lived down to his reputation of being a dreadful mudder. Nix attempted 25 passes. He completed five for 48 yards. He was intercepted twice.

Auburn's only real hope on offense lay with Stephen Davis, a superior running back. He finished with 112 yards on a dozen carries. But he was injured late in the first quarter and did not play much after that. A little rain could not stop Bobby Engram. Nor can hail, nor sleet, nor gloom of night. In his final collegiate contest he made four catches — two for touchdowns — each more acrobatic than the next. Auburn defensive backs draped themselves over him. It didn't help. He was voted the game's MVP by the sportswriters in attendance. Paterno had no wish to quarrel with that vote.

"Very few athletes have been the deciding factor in more Penn State football games than Bobby Engram," Paterno said by way of farewell salute. "Someone asked me how good I though he would be (as an NFL receiver). I told them I thought he'd be as good as Jerry Rice. And I believe that."

By Steve Halvonik
Pittsburgh Post-Gazette

As an outdoorsman, Joe Paterno falls somewhere between Marlin Fitzwater and Marlin Perkins.

He isn't into mountain-climbing or bird-watching, and his idea of a fishing trip is repairing to the back porch with a dogeared copy of *The Old Man and the Sea*.

But as he enters his stretch run at Penn State, Paterno has taken up a new hobby: big-game hunting.

He's loaded for Bear.

Paterno needs only 46 more wins to break the NCAA Division I-A record of 323 victories, set by the late Paul (Bear) Bryant of Alabama.

Paterno, who begins his 31st campaign with a record of 278-72-3, could have the record in five years if he maintains his current pace of 9.3 wins a season.

Paterno, who turns 70 in December, says he would like to continue coaching five or so more years. But he denies he's gunning for Bryant.

"I'm not really interested in Bryant's record," Paterno insists. "I don't even think about it unless someone else brings it up. If it happens that I end up being here long enough to win more games than Bryant won, that would be great. But if it doesn't happen, it doesn't happen."

Paterno says his health will determine how long he remains in coaching.

terno

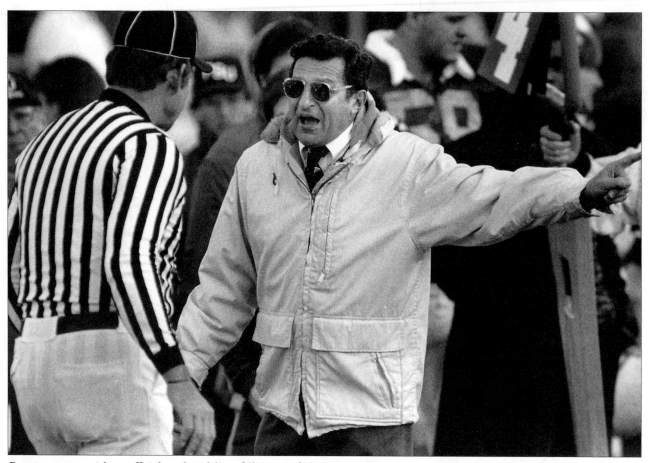

Paterno argues with an official on the sidelines following a fight between Penn State and Pitt players in 1986.

"I don't have a timetable based on how many games I have to win," he says. "I have a timetable based on how effective I am. I could wake up two, three years from now and say I'm not up to this any more and get out of it."

If health is the determinant factor, then Paterno could be around well into the next millenium. He's the Dick Clark of coaches: He seems to get younger while everyone around him gets older.

Paterno is in excellent physical condition. His hair is dark and thick, his weight is down, and his mind is sharp as a cleat.

"I just saw Joe the other night and he looks younger than ever," former Penn State athletic director Jim Tarman marvels.

Tarman, who worked closely with Paterno for 35 years as sports information director and AD before retiring in 1993, says his old friend has never come right out and openly declared his interest in surpassing Bryant.

"But deep down inside," Tarman says, "I think Joe really wants to surpass Bear Bryant's record."

"It's not the only thing that's keeping him in coaching," Tarman adds. "I think he really likes working with young people and some of the things he's doing with the university. He likes power and all that comes with it. But deep down in, he really wants to pass Bear Bryant."

Paterno's expression of disinterest would go down easier if it were any other coach. But considering Bryant's towering stature, and Paterno's coaching relationship with him, you can't help but believe he would like to finish ahead of the Bear at least once in his lifetime.

Bryant, who led the Crimson Tide from 1958 to 1982, dominated college football like few other coaches before or since. He was 232-46-9 and won six national championships in Tuscaloosa. That includes a share of the 1978 title after a 14-7 Sugar Bowl win over Penn State that denied the Nittany Lions their first national crown.

At a crucial point in the game, Paterno attempts to signal-in his instructions.

Paterno has a deep and abiding admiration for Bryant as a coach. His voice drops almost to a church whisper as he recalls his first encounter with Bryant, at the 1959 Liberty Bowl.

"He was only in his second season at Alabama," Paterno says, "but he already had the reputation of becoming one of the game's great coaches. He had a very dominant personality."

Nevertheless, as Paterno discusses Bryant, he leaves the impression that they never made a love connection. Their relationship was strictly business, nothing personal, he seems to say.

What bugs Paterno is that for all his acclaim as a big-game coach, he could never beat Bryant.

Paterno is 8-5-1 against Notre Dame, 6-4 against Miami (Fla.), 2-1 against Michigan and 3-2 against Southern Cal.

Yet is only 4-8 against Alabama, thanks to an 0-4 mark against Bryant.

Paterno readily admits that the Sugar Bowl defeat "was probably my toughest loss."

With less than two minutes remaining, Penn State failed to score on four cracks on the Alabama goal line.

"It got to me — it hammered at my ego," Paterno said of the loss in his autobiography, *Paterno: By the Book.* "When I stood toe to toe with Bear Bryant, he outcoached me."

Time has done little to relieve the pain. Paterno's face muscles still tense up as he reflects on that defeat.

"It was probably my toughest loss because I don't think I did a good job," he says. "People don't realize, but after that goal-line stand, we stopped them. They had to kick the ball and it went out of bounds. But we had 12 guys on the field and gave them a first down.

"We didn't give our kids a chance to win it. We could have won it."

Paterno also faults himself for not having himself or his team prepared for the hype and hoopla surrounding that game.

"When we got down there (to New Orleans), there were so many people, we couldn't get out of the hotel," Paterno says. "So we couldn't do the kind of job down there that we had to do to win the game, even though I thought we had the better personnel."

Even if he never breaks Bryant's record, Paterno will still be remembered as one of the game's legendary figures; the coach with the rolled-up pants and pop-bottle glasses who stood for something more than wins and losses.

Penn State's plain uniforms symbolize Paterno's philosophy of hard work, humility and personal sacrifice in the pursuit of team glory.

Paterno already ranks fourth in all-time wins, behind only Bryant, Glenn (Pop) Warner (319) and Amos Alon-

As a coach, Paterno has never been shy in expressing his views.

zo Stagg (314).

And he already holds the record for bowl victories, with 17, two more than Bryant.

His 31-year tenure at Penn State trails only Stagg's 41 at Chicago.

When he succeeded his mentor, Charles A. (Rip) Engle as head coach in 1966, after 16 years as an assistant, Penn State was little more than a run-of-the-mill, land-grant institution stuck in the middle of the Allegheny mountains. Today, it is generally recognized as one of the nation's premier public institutions.

Paterno deserves a big slice of the credit.

He owns the school's only two national championships, 17 of its 20 bowl wins, 18 of its 22 Lambert trophies (symbolic of Eastern football supremacy) and 40 percent of its 695 total victories. He's had only one losing season, has finished in the top 10 18 times, and has coached undefeated teams in the 1960's, 70's, 80's and 90's.

Under his stewardship, Beaver Stadium has nearly doubled in size to nearly 94,000 seats, making it the second largest on-campus facility in the nation.

It's estimated that Penn State football generates as much as $40 million in busines for the Centre County economy.

Paterno's impact was underscored by a preseason magazine article that rated Penn State as the fifth-best football program of the 20th century, behind only Notre Dame, Alabama, Oklahoma and Nebraska. None of these other superpowers, it should be noted, has relied so much on one coach for its reputation as Penn State has on Paterno.

"Bear was the last living legend, and there is no question that Joe is there now," says former Nittany Lion

Paterno huddles with his wife, Sue, and daughters Mary Kathryn and Diana Lynne, after being named Penn State head football coach in 1966.

Born and raised in Brooklyn, Paterno's successful coaching career and explosive personality has often been compared to another great Brooklyn native, Vince Lombardi.

Matt Millen.

Quite a tribute from a guy whom Paterno had once stripped of his captaincy.

If it's possible, Paterno has done even more for college football away from the field.

His "grand experiment," which emphasized the "student" in student-athlete, proved that universities could field successful teams without cutting academic corners or breaking NCAA rules.

"Joe's primary interest in his football players is as members of society," says Dr. Dave Joyner, an orthopedic surgeon and one of 19 first-team academic all-Americans Penn State has produced under Paterno. "He wanted you to be outstanding individuals in everything you did, not just as football players."

One reason the Big Ten Conference invited Penn State to join its league in 1989 was because of the uni-

versity's reputation for both academic and athletic excellence — an image enhanced by Paterno.

Paterno, to be sure, has his detractors. Some of his coaching peers resent his pious image, and mockingly call him "St. Joe."

Over time, however, he has earned his colleagues' grudging respect.

In a poll published by *Sports Illustrated* last fall, 30 Division I-A coaches paid Paterno the ultimate compliment by picking him as the coach they would most want their son to play for.

Paterno has long captured the imagination of Penn State fans because of his intellectual restlessness and his indefatigable desire to making University Park a better place.

He loves talking military history with Indiana basketball coach Bob Knight. He is an unapologetic Republican — not because he is against affirmative action or welfare, but because of his deep conviction that government programs are a pale substitute for civic involvement.

Most of the time, though, Paterno is more pragmatist than ideologue.

He seconded George Bush for president at the 1988 Republican Convention, but his enthusiasm waned when Bush failed to keep his promise of being the "education president."

"Joe is more than a coach," Tarman says. "He has a very complicated, complex personality. He's very bright, very articulate. He has so many interests, and they're all woven into his coaching philosophy."

Befitting his Renaissance image, Paterno has donated his time to a myriad of university projects.

He helped spearhead a fund-raising drive that raised $350 million for the university in the 1980's. He and his wife, Sue, helped raise $14 million for the library, kicking in $250,000 out of their own pockets.

Paterno also helped raise money for the $55 million Bryce Jordan Center, and he personally donated another $250,000 for the construction of a $5 million university all-sports hall of fame.

One of the reasons Paterno

Average Wins Per Year

Joe Paterno could break "Bear" Bryant's record 323 career victories by the year 2000 if he continues winning 9.26 games per season. A look at how coaches with at least 200 career wins stack up against each other in wins per season:

Coach	Years	Per Year
Tom Osborne	23*	10.04
Joe Paterno	**30***	**9.26**
Lavell Edwards	24*	8.92
Bo Schembechler	27	8.67
Bobby Bowden	30*	8.63
Bear Bryant	38	8.50
Vince Dooley	25	8.04
Lou Holtz	26*	8.00
Woody Hayes	33	7.21
Pop Warner	44	7.11
Warren Woodson	31	6.55
Hayden Fry	34*	6.26
Alonzo Stagg	57	5.51
Jess Neely	40	5.18
Eddie Anderson	39	5.15

*Current coaches.

Source: Gary E. Martzolf, Sports InfoGraphics

Paterno ponders his team's next move.

cites for sticking around another five years is his desire to help Penn State successfully complete its next fund-raising campaign, a push for $1 billion.

Only a few public institutions, like Michigan, have been able to raise that kind of money. Clearly, it's an ambitious goal. But then Paterno seldom fails.

"If we can put together a campaign to raise $800 million to $1 billion over the next five or six years, then I think that ought to put us in a position where we feel we can do some things as well as any institution in the country," he says.

Of all the things Paterno has done for the university, perhaps his most important accomplishment was getting Penn State into the Big Ten Conference. Administrators in Old Main were divided on the issue, but Paterno ultimately prevailed.

In retrospect, it's hard to understand what the fuss was all about. Big Ten membership obviously has enhanced Penn State's academic and athletic standing, and it will continue to provide benefits long after Paterno is gone.

The difference between Paterno and most other football coaches became apparent after the 1972 season, when Paterno turned down an offer from the New England Patriots that would have left him financially set for life.

Paterno broke the news to Sue one morning by joking, "You went to bed with a millionaire, but you woke up with me. I'm not going."

Paterno explained himself later that spring, in an address to Penn State's graduating seniors.

"Money alone will not make you happy," Paterno said. "Success without honor is an unsea-

Clockwise from above, Paterno and the Penn State team visit President Ronald Reagan in the White House in 1983; Paterno enjoys a joke with Vice-President George Bush; Entertains the media with Oklahoma's Barry Switzer in 1986; and attends a press conference with Darrell Royal at the 1972 Cotton Bowl.

Paterno is carried off the field after his Penn State squad defeated Georgia in the 1983 Sugar Bowl and won the National Championship.

soned dish. It will satisfy your hunger, but it won't taste good."

Paterno showed again that he was a breed apart shortly after Penn State won its first national championship, in 1982.

At a public rally on campus after the team's return from New Orleans, Paterno threw down a Bud Wilkinson-style challenge to alumni and administrators: Let's build a university the football program can be proud of.

But unlike most other coaches, Paterno backed up his words by pitching in to help. He twisted the arms of

athletic boosters, almost demanding that they give.

"A lot of people were worried that we could raise $200 million (the original goal)," Paterno says. "But we went out and raised $350 million. . . . I think we're very close (to being elite). We may not be in the top 10 or 20, but some of our departments are, and we're getting closer all the time. We need one more quantitaive leap, one more real effort, and I then I think we can brag a little bit."

Paterno doesn't behave like a football coach because he was never just a football coach. He's an English Liter-

ature major from Brown University. He came to University Park to help Engle, his old college coach, get established, and fell in love with the place.

"I didn't come here to be a coach; I came to be an educator, to be a teacher," Paterno says. "I've always been interested in education, and when I made up my mind to stay here (he turned down a lucrative offer from the New England Patriots after the 1972 season), I wanted to to do everything I could to make this as good a university as it could be."

It was at Penn State that he met Sue, who was graduated in 1962. They

Paterno and then-West Virginia Coach Bobby Bowden shake hands following a Penn State victory in Morgantown.

have four children who are Penn State graduates.

A decade or so ago, Paterno hinted that he might retire and seek a career in politics. He used to say he wanted to go out like his old friend Darrell Royal, who walked away from Texas while the Longhorns were still on top.

Nowadays, Paterno seldom talks about life after football. The game, it seems, is now his life.

Like his idol and tormentor, the Bear, Paterno would probably shrivel up and die if he retired.

"I don't see Joe Paterno ever retiring," Tarman says.

On second thought, maybe it's not the competitive instinct of a football coach that drives Paterno's pursuit of Bryant's record. Maybe it's the poet in him. More specifically, Paterno's favorite poet, Robert Browning, who once said:

"Ah, but a man's reach should exceed his grasp, or what's a heaven for?"

The Paterno Record

12-win seasons	3 times
11-win seasons	8 times
10-win seasons	5 times
9-win seasons	3 times
8-win seasons	5 times
Undefeated seasons	5 times
One-loss seasons	5 times
Two-loss seasons	7 times
Three-loss seasons	5 times
Four-loss seasons	3 times

Source: Gary E. Martzolf, Sports InfoGraphics

Penn State All-Time Lettermen

This is a listing of Penn State players who have lettered between 1887 and 1995.

A

Abbey, Don, 1967-69.
Abran, Wally, 1967.
Adams, Charlie, 1969.
Addie, Walt, 1972-74.
Adessa, Joe, 1936-37.
Adkins, Henry, 1990.
Ahrenhold, Frank, 1969-71.
Alberigi, Ray, 1955-56.
Alexander, Dave, 1959-60.
Alexander, Mike, 1987.
Alexander, Rogers, 1982-85.
Alguero, Anthony, 1978.
Alleman, Ronald, 1957-59.
Allen, Bruce, 1944.
Allen, Doug, 1970, 72-73.
Allen, George, 1968.
Allen, Robert, 1955.
Allerman, Kurt, 1974-76.
Alpert, George, 1983-84.
Alter, Spike, 1937-39.
Amprim, L.R., 1949.
Anders, Paul, 1950-51.
Anderson, Danne, 1985.
Anderson, Dick, 1961-63.
Anderson, Jeff, State College, Pa.
Anderson, Richie, 1991-92.
Anderson, Wilson, 1931-33.
Andress, John, 1975-76.
Andrews, Fritz, 1935.
Andrews, Kenn, 1971-72.
Andronici, Bob, 1964-65.
Angevine, Leon, 1966-68.
Anthony, Joseph, 1937-38.
Arbuthnot, James, 1901-03.
Archie, Mike, 1992-95.

Argenta, Ron, 1975-76.
Arnelle, Jesse, 1951-54.
Arnst, John, 1956.
Artelt, Art, 1922-24.
Ashley, Walker Lee, 1979-82.
Astle, Greg, 1991.
Atherton, Charles, 1890-94.
Atkins, Todd, 1992-95.
Atty, Ferris, 1967-68.
Aull, Charles, 1889-91.
Aumiller, Jack, 1971.
Austin, Bruce, 1977.

B

Baer, Ray, 1920-21.
Baggett, Matt, 1988-91.
Bahr, Chris, 1973-75.
Bahr, Matt, 1976-78.
Bailey, Don, 1952-54.
Baiorunos, Jack.
Baker, Ralph, 1961-63.
Ballou, Vic, 1908.
Balthaser, Don, 1952-54.
Banks, Bill, 1975-77.
Bannon, Bruce, 1970-72.
Baran, Stan, 1969.
Barninger, Michael, 1995.
Banbury, J.R., 1941-42
Barantovich, Alex, 1936-38.
Barber, Stew, 1958-60.
Barber, W.B., 1950
Barclay, Watson, 1887.
Barnett, W.D., 1908.
Barney, Don, 1950-52.
Barowski, Sean, 1987.
Barr, Adam, 1904-05.
Barr, Jim, 1949-51.
Barr, Tom, 1981-82.
Barrett, Dick, 1965.
Barrett, Fritz, 1910,.
Barron, A.M., 1910, 13-14.
Barry, P.A., 1911.
Bartek, Len, 1950-51.
Bartek, Lou, 1982.
Barth, Lou, 1934-36.
Barvinchak, Dick, 1973, 75.

Bassett, Bob, 1977-78.
Batdorf, John, 1930.
Battaglia, Mark, 1980-82.
Bauer, Trey, 1984-87.
Baugh, Kevin, 1980-83.
Beatty, Charles, 1947-49.
Bebout, James, 1911-13.
Beck, Carl, 1916, 20.
Beckish, Mike, 1984-86.
Beckwith, Dan, 1971.
Bedenk, Joe, 1921-23.
Bedick, Tom, 1962-63.
Bedoski, A.J., 1931-33.
Bell, Fred, 1945-47.
Bellamy, Herb, 1984.
Bellamy, Irv, 1987.
Bellas, Albert, 1944-45.
Bellas, Joe, 1964-65.
Benfatti, Lou, 1990-93.
Benjamin, Chuck, 1974, 76.
Bennett, Robert, 1900-01.
Benson, Brad, 1974-76.
Bentz, Newsh, 1920-22.
Berfield, Wayne, 1958.
Bergman, Bud, 1924, 26.
Bergstrom, Jeff, 1980-81.
Bernier, Kurt, 1984-87.
Berry, Parker, 1931-33.
Berryman, Punk, 1911-14.
Betts, Arthur, 1950-51.
Biesecker, Art, 1901.
Bill, Tom, 1987-90.
Biondi, Dan, 1979-82.
Black, Jim, 1917.
Blackledge, Todd, 1980-82.
Blair, R.W..
Blair, W.A., 1898, deceased.
Bland, Dave, 1971-73.
Blasentine, Joe, 1960-62.
Bleamer, Jeff, 1973-74.
Blockson, Charlie, 1953-55.
Bochna, Derek, 1990-93.
Bodle, Dave, 1977.
Bohart, Joe, 1957-58

Bohn, Wellington, 1899-1900.
Bonham, Jim, 1941.
Boone, Ed, 1983, 85.
Booth, John, 1971.
Botts, Mike, 1969, 71.
Botula, Pat, 1957-59.
Bowden, A.T., 1952.
Bower, James, 1964.
Bowes, Bill, 1962-64.
Bowman, Kirk, 1980-83.
Boyle, Rusty, 1974
Bozick, John, 1958-60.
Braddock, Edward, 1929.
Bradley, Dave, 1966-68.
Bradley, Jim, 1973-74.
Bradley, Matt, 1979-81.
Bradley, Tom, 1977-78.
Brady, Kyle, 1991-94.
Bratton, Rod, 1974.
Brennan, Thad, 1993-94.
Bresecker, A.S., 1901-03.
Brewster, Jesse, 1931-32.
Brezna, Steve, 1968.
Briggs, Bernard, 1937.
Brosky, Bernard, 1941.
Brown, Cuncho, 1995.
Brown, Conrad, 1950.
Brown, Craig, 1977.
Brown, Ed, 1895.
Brown, Gary, 1987-90.
Brown, George, 1918-20.
Brown, Ivan, 1918.
Brown, Jim, 1978-81.
Brown, Keith, 1981.
Brown, Rick, 1971-72.
Brown, Sparky, 1940, 42-43.
Brown, Sydney, 1891-92.
Brubaker, Jeff, 1988.
Bruhn, Earl, 1944.
Brunie, Jeff, 1982.
Bruno, John C., 1956.
Bruno, John, Jr., 1984-86.
Brzenchek, Dave, 1990.
Buchan, Sandy, 1962-64.
Buchman, Barry, 1985.
Buckwalter, Cliff, 1974.
Bulvin, Jerry, 1970.
Bunn, Ken, 1949-50.

Burger, Todd, 1989-92.
Burkhart, Chuck, 1968-69.
Burns, Billy, 1899.
Burns, Harry, 1906-07.
Bush, John, 1974-75.
Butterfield, Dick, 1960.
Buttle, Greg, 1973-75.
Butya, Jeff, 1981.
Buzin, Rich, 1966-67.
Bycoskie, Drew, 1984-86.

C

Calderone, Jack, 1955-56.
Caldwell, J.W., 1955
Campbell, Bob, 1966-68.
Campbell, Charles, 1905-06.
Campbell, Chris, 1994-95.
Campbell, Kevin, 1984.
Capozzoli, Tony, 1976
Cappelletti, John, 1971-73.
Cappelletti, Mike, 1976.
Caprara, Babe, 1956-57.
Capretto, Bob, 1966-67.
Caravella, Rich, 1975.
Carlson, Cory, 1994-95.
Carraher, Scott, 1983.
Carter, Gary, 1968-70.
Carter, Ki-Jana, 1992-94.
Cartwright, C.R., 1889-91.
Cartwright, Mike, 1981.
Case, Frank, 1980.
Caskey, Howard, 1944-45.
Castignola, Jack, 1943.
Caum, Don, 1961-63.
Caye, Ed, 1957-60.
Cefalo, Jim, 1974-77.
Ceh, Bob, 1990-92.
Cenci, Aldo, 1941-43.
Chamberlain, Rich, 1985.
Cherewka, Mark, 1980.
Cherundolo, Chuck,

1934-36.
Cherry, Tom, 1968.
Chizmar, Brian, 1986-89.
Christian, Greg, 1973, 75.
Chuckran, John, 1944, 48-49.
Cimino, Pete, 1959.
Cino, John, 1961.
Cirafesi, Wally, 1967, 69.
Cisar, Chris, 1988, 90, 92.
Clair, Eric, 1992-95.
Clapper, John, 1896-97.
Clark, Bruce, 1976-79.
Clark, David, 1985-86.
Clark, Harold, 1913-16.
Clark, John, 1911-13.
Clark, Richard, 1952.
Clauss, Chris, 1987.
Clayton, Stan, 1985-87.
Cleary, Anthony, 1995.
Cleaver, G.G..
Clouser, Joe, 1983.
Coates, Jim, 1985-87.
Coates, Ron, 1962-63.
Cobbs, Duffy, 1983-86.
Coccoli, Don, 1967.
Coder, Craig, 1977-78.
Coder, Ron, 1974-75.
Colbus, H.H., 1916.
Cole, Clyde, 1932-33.
Cole, Glen, 1970-71.
Coles, Joel, 1979-80, 82.
Collins, Aaron, 1994-95.
Collins, Ahmad, 1994.
Collins, Andre, 1986-89.
Collins, Chris, 1983-86.
Collins, George, 1928, 31-32.
Collins, Gerry, 1989-91.
Collins, Jason, 1994.
Collins, Kerry, 1992-94.
Collins, Phillip, 1993-94.
Colone, Joe, 1942, 46-48.
Conforto, Mike, 1978.
Conlan, Shane, 1983-86.
Conlin, Chris, 1986.
Conlin, Keith, 1992-95.
Conn, Donald, 1931.
Conover, Larry, 1916-17.
Contz, Bill, 1980-82.
Conway, Brett, 1993-95.
Cooney, Larry, 1944-45, 47-48.

Cooper, Eufard, 1985.
Cooper, Mike, 1968-70.
Cooper, William, 1933, 35.
Corbett, Wayne, 1965-66.
Corbin, Cliff, 1977
Correal, Chuck, 1977-78.
Coulson, Bob, 1906-07.
Craft, George, 1900.
Crawford, Rowan, 1943.
Cromwell, Troy, 1986.
Crosby, Ron, 1974-76.
Crowder, Randy, 1971-73.
Cripps, R.J., 1950-51.
Crummy, Bill, 1976, 78.
Cubbage, Ben, 1916, 19.
Cummings, Ralph, 1899-02.
Cunningham, Eric, 1977-78.
Cure, Dave, 1897-99.
Curkendall, Pete, 1985-87.
Curry, Jack, 1965-67.
Curry, Tom, 1930-31.
Curtin, Joe, 1895, 97-98.
Cyphers, Cy, 1906-08.
Czarnecki, Stan, 1915-17.
Czekaj, Ed, 1943, 46-47.

D

D'Amico, Rich, 1979-81.
Daily, Pat, 1983.
Daman, Bob, 1991.
Daniels, David, 1988-90.
Dangerfield, Harold, 1925-27.
Danser, Gene, 1952-54.
Darragh, Scudder, 1926-27.
Daugherty, George, 1968.
Davis, Cliff, 1961.
Davis, Jeff, 1995.
Davis, Larry, 1943.
Davis, Robert, 1941-42.
Davis, Stephen, 1985-87.
Davis, Steve, 1972.
Davis, Troy, 1987-88.
Dean, J.M., 1901.
Debes, Gary, 1971, 73.
Debler, Bill, 1941.

DeCindis, Ed, 1930.

DeCohen, Daryl, 1987.
DeFalco, Dan, 1952-54.
Deibert, John, 1963-64.
DellaPenna, Frank, 1954-55.
Delmonaco, Al, 1966.
Delp, George, 1926-28.
DeLuca, James, 1958.
DeLuca, Richard, 1954-56.
DeMarino, Danny, 1935, 37.
Demler, Fred, 1974.
DePaso, Tom, 1975-77.
DePasqua, John, 1986.
Deter, Jim, 1988-91.
Deuel, Gary, 1968-70.
Devlin, Chris, 1972-74.
Diange, Joe, 1976-77.
Diedrich, Yutz, 1928-30.
Diehl, Amby, 1897.
Dill, Richard, 1958.
DiMidio, Dean, 1983-85.
Diminick, Joe, 1976-78.
Dimmerling, Carl, 1944-45.
Dingle, Cliff, 1992-94.
D'Onofrio, Mark, 1988-91.
Dodge, Fred, 1900-02.
Donaldson, Rick, 1976-79.
Donato, Joe, 1976.
Donato, Sammy, 1936-37.
Donchez, Tom, 1971, 73-74.
Donovan, Tom, 1975-76, 78-79.
Dooley, Jim, 1951-52.
Dorney, Keith, 1975-78.
Dougherty, Owen, 1949-50.
Dowler, Henry, 1889-93.
Downing, Dwayne, 1985-87.
Dozier, D.J., 1983-86.
Drayton, Troy, 1991-92.
Drazenovich, Andy, 1978.
Drazenovich, Chuck, 1945, 47-49.
Drazenovich, Joe, 1947-49.
Dreese, Jamie, 1992.
Ducatte, Gregg, 1969-71.

Duffy, Gene, 1990.
Duffy, Pat, 1990.
Duffy, Roger, 1987-89.
Dugan, Bill, 1979-80.
Duman, Jack, 1967.
Dunn, John, 1977.
Dunn, Mother, 1903-06.
Dunsmore, J.A., 1893-96.
Dunsmore, James, 1894-95.
Dunsmore, William, 1893.
Durkota, Jeff, 1942, 46-47.
Duvall, Red, 1928-30.

E

Eachbach, Herb, 1928-29.
Eaise, Jim, 1973-74.
Eberle, Gary, 1965.
Eberly, Chris, 1995.
Ebersole, John, 1967-69.
Economos, Jack, 1935-37.
Edgerton, Robert, 1916.
Edmonds, Greg, 1968-70.
Edwards, Earle, 1928-30.
Edwards, Grover, 1977-80.
Ehinger, Chuck, 1964-65.
Elbert, J.S., 1897.
Elder, John, 1902-03.
Ellis, Buddy, 1971-73.
Ellwood, Pop, 1923.
Ellwood, W.T., 1937-38.
Emerson, Bill, 1982-83.
Enders, Paul, 1935, 37
Engle, Dad, 1910-12.
English, Rocco, 1976.
Engram, Bobby, 1991, 93-95.
Enis, Curtis, 1995.
Enyeart, Craig, 1976.
Eppensteiner, John.
Ericsson, Bill, 1970.
Etze, Eric, 1987-88.
Evans, Tommy, 1928-30.
Ewing, Mark, 1975.
Ewing, Stan, 1915-16.
Eyer, Don, 1951-53.

F

Fagan, Mike, 1993.
Farkas, Gerry, 1960-62.
Farkas, Mike, 1979.
Farley, Eugene, 1918.
Farls, Jack, 1955-57.
Farrell, Sean, 1979-81.
Fawkes, Edward, 1904.
Fay, Charles, 1891-92.
Fayak, Craig, 1990-93.
Feeney, Chris, 1995.
Felbaum, F.V., 1948-49.
Filak, John, 1924-26
Filardi, Gerald, 1994-95.
Filkovski, Greg, 1990.
Finley, John, 1945-48.
Firshing, William, 1917.
Fisher, Benjamin, 1888, 92-94.
Fitzkee, Scott, 1976-78.
Flanagan, Mike, 1987, 90.
Fletcher, Ambrose, 1994-95.
Flock, Freddy, 1922.
Flood, Robert, 1933.
Flythe, Mark, 1990-91.
Forbes, Marlon, 1992-94.
Forkum, Carl, 1902-04.
Fornadel, Matt, 1995.
Foster, Phillip, 1888-90.
Franco, Brian, 1979-81.
Frank, Calvin, 1922-23.
Franzetta, Chuck, 1968.
Freeman, Tim, 1987-89.
French, Coop, 1928-30.
Frerotte, Mitch, 1985.
Fruehan, Mark, 1982-83.
Fry, Arthur, 1934-35.
Frye, Mel, 1967.
Fugate, Thomas.
Fuhs, Bill, 1906.
Funk, Jim, 1981.
Fusetti, Greg, 1990.
Fusina, Chuck, 1976-78.

G

Gabel, Paul, 1972-73.
Gabriel, Ed, 1967.
Gabriel, Robert, 1949-50.
Gaertner, Brennan, 1987.
Gajecki, Leon, 1938-40.

Galardi, Joe, 1961-62.
Gallagher, Mac, 1991.
Gancitano, Nick, 1982-83.
Ganter, Fran, 1968-70.
Garban, Steve, 1956-58.
Garbinski, Mike, 1939-40, 45.
Garrett, Mike, 1982.
Garrity, Gregg, 1980-82.
Garrity, Jim, 1952-54.
Garthwaite, Bob, 1969.
Gash, Sam, 1988, 90-91.
Gattuso, Greg, 1981-83.
Gearhart, Tim, 1987-88.
Geise, Steve, 1975-77.
Gelzheiser, Brian, 1991-94.
Gentilman, Victor, 1936-38.
Gerak, John, 1989, 91-92.
Gernard, Robert, 1945.
Gersh, Don, 1971.
Gethers, Ivory, 1989-92.
Getty, Charlie, 1971-73.
Giacomarro, Ralph, 1979-82.
Giannantonria, A.J., 1937-38.
Giannetti, Frank, 1988-90.
Giftopoulos, Pete, 1985-87.
Gigliotti, Jason, 1992.
Giles, Darrell, 1983, 85-86.
Gillard, Chuck, 1930.
Gilmore, Bruce.
Gilmore, Deryk, 1988.
Gilmour, Robert, 1958.
Gilsenan, Mike, 1978.
Gingrich, Dick, 1963-65.
Ginnetti, Don, 1983-85.
Giotto, Tom, 1974-75.
Girton, B.J., 1934
Givens, Reggie, 1989-92.
Gladys, Gene, 1977-80.
Glassmire, H.M., 1896.
Glennon, Bill, 1977.
Glocker, Rudy, 1991-92.
Glunz, Steve, 1976.
Gob, Scott, 1986-89.
Godlasky, Charles, 1949-50.
Goedecke, Albert, 1911.
Goganious, Keith, 1988-91.

Golden, Al, 1989-91.
Gordon, Tony, 1977.
Gorinski, Clarence, 1947.
Graf, Dave, 1972-73.
Graham, A., 1889.
Graham, Don, 1983-86.
Graham, James, 1943.
Graham, Jim, 1959.
Graham, Mark, 1990-92.
Gratson, Joe, 1950-52.
Gray, Alex, 1907-10.
Gray, Bas, 1923-25.
Gray, Carl, 1995.
Gray, Gary, 1969-71.
Greeley, Bucky, 1991-94.
Green, G.R., 1925-26.
Green, Sam, 1952-53.
Green, Jason, 1994.
Greene, John, 1986-88.
Greenshields, Donn, 1926-28.
Grier, Roosevelt, 1951-54.
Griffiths, Red, 1917, 20.
Griffiths, Steve, 1979-80.
Grimes, Roger, 1966-67.
Grimshaw, John, 1930-32.
Groben, Dick, 1962.
Gross, Red, 1917.
Grube, Ryan, 1990-93.
Gudger, Eric, 1989.
Guman, Mike, 1976-79.
Gurski, John, 1983.
Gursky, Al, 1960-62.
Guthrie, Ed, 1977.

H

Haden, Nick, 1982-83.
Hager, Gary, 1971-73.
Haines, Hinkey, 1919-20.
Halderman, O.G., 1952.
Haley, Ed, 1891-93.
Hall, Galen, 1959-61.
Hall, Tracy, 1979.
Halpin, R.D., 1941.
Ham, Jack, 1968-70.
Hamas, Steve, 1926-28.
Hamilton, Darren, 1985.
Hamilton, Eric, 1985-86.
Hamilton, Harry, 1980-83.
Hamilton, Lance, 1983-85.

Hamilton, Neil, 1988-89.
Hamilton, William, 1922.
Hammonds, Shelly, 1990-93.
Hand, Brian, 1979.
Hanley, Dean, 1936-38.
Hansen, Albert, 1911-12.
Hapanowicz, Ted, 1943.
Harding, Jim, 1955.
Harlow, Dick, 1910-11.
Harper, Thomas, 1932.
Harrington, Bernard, 1927.
Harris, Al, 1981-82.
Harris, Charles, 1899.
Harris, Franco, 1969-71.
Harris, Giuseppe, 1979-81.
Harris, Pete, 1977-78, 80.
Harrison, Harry, 1936-38.
Hart, Bob, 1960-62.
Hart, Kevin, 1976.
Hart, Rob, 1991.
Hartenstine, Mike, 1972-74.
Hartenstine, Warren, 1967.
Hartings, Jeff, 1992-95.
Harvan, George, 1951.
Harvey, Dale, 1993.
Hastings, Hal, 1925-27.
Hayes, C.E., 1918.
Hayes, Dave, 1960-62.
Hayes, Lalon, 1897-98.
Hayman, Gary, 1972-73.
Heckel, Fred, 1896-98.
Hedderick, Ray, 1948-49.
Heist, M.L., 1932.
Helbig, Bill, 1925.
Helkowski, Doug, 1988-91.
Heller, Jim, 1970-72.
Heller, Mike, 1991-92.
Heller, Ron, 1981-83.
Henderson, Hernon, 1987, 89-90.
Henderson, Jason, 1994.
Henderson, Marques, 1985-87.
Henry, H., 1905-06.
Henry, Lee, 1948.
Henry, Red, 1918-19.
Heppenstall, Charles, 1892.

Heppenstall, G., 1889.
Herd, Chuck, 1971-73.
Hermann, Burke, 1911.
Herring, Kim, 1993-95.
Herron, Ross, 1945
Hershey, Frank, 1962-64.
Hershman, Charles, 1906-09.
Hesch, Matty, 1932.
Hess, Harold, 1916, 19.
Hettinger, Scott, 1977-79.
Hewitt, Earl, 1898-1901.
Hewitt, Earl, 1927.
Hicks, Robert, 1944, 47-49.
Higgins, Bob, 1914-17, 19.
Hildebrand, Charles, 1887-91.
Hile, Charles, 1888-91.
Hill, Chappie, 1956.
Hills, Lee, 1921.
Hines, Joe, 1981-83.
Hite, Jeff, 1973-75.
Hladun, Bob, 1980.
Hoak, Dick, 1958-60.
Hochberg, Jeff, 1983.
Hochberg, Jim, 1955.
Hockersmith, William, 1951.
Hodne, Todd, 1978
Hoffman, Robert, 1954-55.
Hoggard, Dennie, 1947-48.
Holes, Clint, 1994-95.
Holloway, Alfred, 1901.
Holmberg, Rob, 1993.
Holmes, Wayne, 1994.
Holuba, Bob, 1968-70.
Hondru, Bryan, 1965-66.
Hoover, Edward, 1950-51.
Horn, Keith, 1953-54.
Hornfeck, Dave, 1973-74.
Hornyak, John, 1986.
Horst, Tim, 1966, 68.
Hoskins, George, 1892-94.
Hostetler, Doug, 1976-78.
Hostetler, Jeff, 1980.
Hostetler, Ron, 1975-77.
House, William, 1924-25.
Huber, Bill, 1963-65.

Huffman, Jay, 1959-61.
Hufford, Squeak, 1920-22.
Hufnagel, John, 1970-72.
Hull, Gary, 1968-70.
Hull, John, 1970-71.
Hull, Tom, 1971-73.
Hummel, Alkey, 1975.
Hummel, Clarence, 1947.
Humphries, Leonard, 1989-91.
Huntington, Greg, 1990-92.
Hutton, Neil, 1974, 76-77.

I

Iagrossi, Mike, 1989.
Ickes, Lloyd, 1937-39.
Irwin, Mike, 1964-66.
Isom, Ray, 1984-86.

J

Jacks, Al, 1956-57.
Jackson, Joe, 1973-74.
Jackson, John, 1887.
Jackson, Kenny, 1980-83.
Jackson, Roger, 1981-82.
Jackson, Tom, 1967-69.
Jackson, Tyoka, 1990-93.
Jacob, George, 1950.
Jaffurs, Johnny, 1941-43.
Jagers, Bob, 1979-80.
Jakob, David, 1987-89.
James, Don, 1914
Janerrette, Charlie, 1958-59.
Japchen, Geoff, 1988-89.
Jeram, Jerry, 1974.
Joachim, Steve, 1971.
Joe, Larry, 1942, 47-48.
Johns, Gregg, 1985, 87.
Johnson, Andre, 1993-95.
Johnson, Barry, 1971.
Johnson, Bill, 1973.
Johnson, Brad, 1995.
Johnson, Chan, 1949-51.
Johnson, Eddie, 1985-88.
Johnson, Fred, 1909-10.
Johnson, G.R., 1888.
Johnson, Howard, 1899.

Penn State All-Time Lettermen

Riggle, Bob, 1964-65.
Rinkus, Gene, 1962.
Rishell, Bill, 1979-81.
Ritchey, Jesse, 1907.
Ritner, Thomas, 1921.
Rivera, Marco, 1992-95.
Robb, Harry, 1916-19.
Robb, Ray, 1943, retired.
Robinson, Bernard, 1975-76.
Robinson, Dave, 1960-62.
Robinson, F.A., 1894.
Robinson, Mark, 1980-83.
Robinson, Tim, 1983.
Rocco, Dan, 1979-80.
Rocco, Frank, 1980-81.
Rodham, Hugh, 1934.
Roepke, Johnny, 1925-27.
Rogel, Fran, 1947-49.
Rohland, Bob, 1954.
Rollins, Steve, 1938-39.
Romango, Kevin, 1980.
Romano, Jim, 1977-79, 81.
Rosa, Rich, 1991.
Rosdahl, Harrison, 1961-62.
Rose, James, 1887.
Rosecrans, Jim, 1973-75.
Rosenberg, Harold, 1931, 33.
Ross, Dan, 1943.
Ross, Robert, 1947-48.
Rothrock, W.R., 1888, 91.
Roundtree, Ray, 1985-87.
Rowe, Dave, 1965-66.
Rowe, Ricky, 1992.
Rowell, Lester, 1951-54.
Rubin, Lee, 1990-93.
Ruble, C.W., 1901.
Ruble, Joseph, 1896-97, 99-
   1900.
Rucci, Todd, 1990-92.
Runnells, John, 1964-66.
Ruslavage, Charles, 1956-58.
Russell, Samuel, 1901.
Russo, Mike, 1983-86.
Rutkowski, Bob, 1944-46.

S

Saar, Brad, 1982.
Sabatino, Noel, 1964.
Sabol, Bernie, 1961-62.
Sabol, Joe, 1955-57.
Sacca, John, 1992.
Sacca, Tony, 1988-91.
Sain, John, 1966.
Samuels, Bobby, 1989, 91.
Sandusky, E.J., 1991-92.
Sandusky, Jerry, 1963-66.
San Fillipo, George, 1970.

Santangelo, Mario, 1950
Sarabok, Joseph, 1946.
Saul, Bill, 1961.
Saunders, Joseph, 1904.
Sava, John, 1959.
Sayles, Rick, 1990-91.
Sayre, Ralph, 1913.
Schaeffer, Dennis, 1960.
Schaukowitch, Carl, 1970-72.
Scheetz, Stew, 1950-52, Fla.
Scherer, Rip, 1948.
Schiazza, Guido, 1961.
Schleicher, Maury, 1956-58.
Schoderbek, Pete, 1951-53.
Scholl, Henny, 1896-1901.
Schonewolf, Rich, 1986-89.
Schoonover, Ken, 1941-42.
Schreckengaust, Steve, 1964-65.
Schroyer, John, 1942.
Schuster, Dick, 1920, 23.
Schuyler, Roy, 1934, 36.
Schwab, Jim, 1961.
Scioli, Brad, 1994-95.
Scott, Charles, 1894-95.
Scott, Freddie, 1993-95.
Scott, Jim, 1971-73.
Scovill, Brad, 1978-80.
Scrabis, Bob, 1958.
Sebastianelli, Ted, 1968.
Sefter, Steve, 1981-83.
Seitz, Ellery, 1963-65.
Shaffer, John, 1984-86.
Shainer, David, 1941.
Shalvey, Bernie, 1978.
Shank, Don, 1951-52.
Shattuck, Ted, 1950-51.
Shattuck, Paul, 1953.
Shawley, Cal, 1928-30.
Shephard, Len, 1949-51.
Sherman, Tom, 1965-67.
Sherry, Jack, 1952-54.
Shields, R.K., 1931
Shoemaker, Tom, 1971-72.
Shopa, Peter, 1951-52.
Short, Stan, 1982-83.
Shukri, Dave, 1975-76.
Shukri, Rob, 1977.
Shuler, Mickey, 1975-77.
Shumaker, Earl, 1953-55.
Shuman, Tom, 1973-74.
Shumock, Joseph, 1950-51.
Sickler, Mark, 1985-87.
Sidler, Randy, 1974-77.
Sieminski, Charlie, 1960-62.
Sierocinski, Marty, 1977.
Siever, Paul, 1990-91.
Sigel, Harry, 1932-34.
Sills, Frank, 1937.
Silock, Andrew, 1950-51.
Silvano, Thomas, 1934-35.

Simko, John, 1962-64.
Simon, David, 1951-52.
Simon, John, 1944-45, 47-48.
Sincek, Frank, 1962.
Sink, Robert, 1964
Sisler, Cass, 1943.
Siverling, Brian, 1985-86.
Skarzynski, Scott, 1970-72.
Skemp, Leo, 1932.
Skorupan, John, 1970-72.
Skrip, Dan, 1991.
Sladki, John, 1965-66.
Slafkowsky, Joe, 1967.
Slamp, Ken, 1925.
Sload, Jason, 1995.
Slobodnjak, Mike, 1943.
Slusser, Tom, 1931-33.
Smalls, Irv, 1994.
Smaltz, Bill, 1939-41.
Smear, Steve, 1967-69.
Smidansky, John, 1948-50.
Smith, Andy, 1901.
Smith, Charles, 1904.
Smith, Franklin, 1934-36.
Smith, James, 1960-61.
Smith, Mike, 1968-70.
Smith, Neal, 1967-69.
Smith, R.M., 1907-09.
Smith, Rob, 1984-85.
Smith, Robert, 1951-52.
Smith, Steve, 1984-86.
Smith, Terry, 1988-91.
Smith, Thomas, 1948.
Smith, Willie, 1992-94.
Smith, Wilson, 1955, 57-58.
Smozinsky, E., 1921
Smyth, Bill, 1943.
Snell, George, 1919-21
Snyder, Chris, 1994-95.
Snyder, Robert, 1930-31.
Sobczak, Sam, 1958-60.
Sowers, Charles, 1954.
Spaziani, Frank, 1966-68.
Speers, Fred, 1971.
Spencer, Larry, 1944
Speros, Pete, 1980-82.
Spires, Mike, 1972.
Spoor, Bill, 1991.
St. Clair, Cliff, 1942.
Stahley, Skip, 1928-29.
Steinbacher, Don, 1965.
Stellatella, Sam, 1957-59.
Stellfox, Skip, 1957.
Stempeck, Stan, 1930-31.
Stephenson, Bob, 1995.
Stewart, Ed, 1963-65.
Stewart, Vin, 1992-94.
Stilley, Steve, 1971-72.
Stillman, Mike, 1982-84.
Stofko, Ed, 1967-68.

Stoken, John, 1944.
Storer, Jack, 1950.
Strang, Doug, 1982-83.
Straub, Bill, 1953-55.
Stravinski, Carl, 1938-40.
Struchor, J.J., 1950.
Strycharz, Joe, 1988.
Stuart, Tom, 1966.
Stuart, W.A., 1893.
Stuckrath, Ed, 1962-64.
Stump, Terry, 1968-70.
Stupar, Steve, 1979.
Sturges, Carl, 1948.
Stutts, Dave, 1975.
Stynchula, Andy, 1957-59.
Suhey, Larry, 1975-76.
Suhey, Matt, 1976-79.
Suhey, Paul, 1975-77.
Suhey, Steve, 1942, 46-47.
Sunday, LeRoy, 1936.
Surma, Vic, 1968-70.
Susko, John, 1972.
Suter, H.M., 1894.
Suter, Mike, 1982-83.
Swain, Ward, 1916.
Sweeney, Tim, 1987-88.
Sweet, Lynn, 1901.
Sydnor, Chris, 1982-83.
Szajna, Robert, 1951-52
Szott, Dave, 1987-89.

T

Tamburo, Sam, 1945-48.
Tarasi, Ray, 1987-89.
Tate, Dayle, 1979.
Tate, Mark, 1993-95.
Tavener, Otho, 1917.
Taylor, C.F., 1899.
Taylor, Duane, 1974-75, 77.
Taylor, H.S., 1891-92.
Tepsic, Joseph, 1945.
Tesner, Buddy, 1972-74.
Thomas, Blair, 1985-87, 89.
Thomas, Charlie, 1895.
Thomas, David, 1993-94.
Thomas, Kenneth, 1930.
Thomas, Mark, 1973-75.
Thomas, Tisen, 1990, 92-93.
Thomas, Willie, 1987-90.
Thompson, Irving, 1902.
Thompson, Leroy, 1987-90.
Thorpe, Chris, 1988.
Tielsch, Barry, 1993-95.
Tietjens, Ron, 1961-62.
Timpson, Michael, 1985, 87-88.
Tobin, Yegg, 1912-14.
Tomlinson, Ken, 1951.
Toretti, Sever, 1936-38.

Photo Credits

Allsport USA: 186, 188, 208, 214, 215-top.

AP/Wide World Photo: Front Cover-lower middle, 47, 56-top, 71, 73, 92-bottom, 94-bottom, 109-bottom, 111, 112, 118-top, 123, 127, 137, 138, 139, 141-top, 152, 158-both, 166, 167, 169, 176, 177, 179-bottom, 194, 195, 196, 202, 203, 206, 212-213, 215-bottom, 218, 220-both, 224, 228, 229-upper left, upper right and middle right.

UPI/Corbis-Bettmann Archives: 86-87, 89-top, 96-top, 97-top, 103, 105-top, 110, 116-bottom, 119-bottom, 126, 136, 141-bottom, 143, 149, 150, 150-151, 155, 159, 226-bottom.

Cotton Bowl: 88, 102, 105-bottom.

College Football Hall of Fame: 16, 28.

The Detroit News: 45, 204-205.

Orange Bowl: 91, 93-top.

Patee Library Archives, Penn State University: Front Cover-top middle, 20, 23, 31, 35, 39-top, 43-both, 46, 48, 49, 50, 54, 56-bottom, 57-both, 63, 65-left, 66-67, 70, 72, 74, 75-both, 76, 77, 79-both, 80-both, 81-both, 83, 84, 85, 89-bottom, 94-95, 96-bottom, 104, 113, 142, 157, 222-223, 225, 229-bottom, 230, 231.

Penn State University Sports Information: Front Cover-top right, lower left, 10, 11, 12, 14-15, 17, 18-19, 21, 24, 25, 27, 32, 34, 36, 37-both, 38, 39-bottom, 40, 41, 52, 53, 58, 59, 64, 65-right, 68, 69, 78, 92-top, 97-bottom, 98-all, 100, 101, 107, 114-main, 115, 116-top, 117, 124, 129, 130, 131, 147-top, 160, 162, 163, 172, 173, 174, 175, 182, 183, 189, 192, 193, 198, 199, 201, 209, 232.

Pittsburgh Post-Gazette: Front Cover-top left, lower right, 44, 99, 109-top, 120, 121, 132, 134-both, 135, 145, 146, 147-bottom, 161, 164, 165, 170, 178-top, 180, 191, 210, 211, 226-top, 227.

Time Inc.: 114-inset.